History in the Digital Age

The digital age is affecting all aspects of historical study, but much of the existing literature about history in the digital age can be alienating to the traditional historian who does not necessarily value or wish to embrace digital resources. *History in the Digital Age* takes a more conceptual look at how the digital age is affecting the field of history for both scholars and students. The printed copy, the traditional archive, and analogue research remain key constitute parts for most historians and for many will remain precious and esteemed over digital copies, but there is a real need for historians and students of history to seriously consider some of the conceptual and methodological challenges facing the field of historical enquiry as we enter the twenty-first century.

Including international contributors from a variety of disciplines – History, English, Information Studies and Archivists – this book does not seek either to applaud or condemn digital technologies, but takes a more conceptual view of how the field of history is being changed by the digital age. Essential reading for all historians.

Toni Weller is a Visiting Research Fellow, formerly Senior Lecturer, at De Montfort University, UK, and editor of the international journal, *Library & Information History*. Her publications include *Information History in the Modern World: Histories of the Information Age* (2010), *The Victorians and Information: A Social and Cultural History* (2009) and *Information History – An Introduction: Exploring an Emergent Field* (2008).

History in the Digital Age

Edited by Toni Weller

Routledge
Taylor & Francis Group

LONDON AND NEW YORK

First published 2013
by Routledge
2 Park Square, Milton Park, Abingdon, Oxon OX14 4RN

Simultaneously published in the USA and Canada
by Routledge
711 Third Avenue, New York, NY 10017

Routledge is an imprint of the Taylor & Francis Group, an informa business

British Library Cataloguing in Publication Data
A catalogue record for this book is available from the British Library

Library of Congress Cataloging in Publication Data
History in the digital age / edited by Toni Weller.
p. cm.
"Simultaneously published in the USA and Canada"–T.p. verso.
Includes bibliographical references.
1. History–Philosophy. 2. Technological innovations 3. Social change.
4. Historiography. 5. History–Study and teaching. 6. Electronic records.
7. Digital media. I. Weller, Toni.
D16.9.H565 2012
901–dc23
2012013453

ISBN: 978-0-415-66696-1 (hbk)
ISBN: 978-0-415-66697-8 (pbk)
ISBN: 978-0-203-09344-3 (ebk)

Typeset in Sabon
by Taylor & Francis Books

Printed and bound in the United States of America
By Edwards Brothers Malloy on sustainably sourced paper.

For Ed and Natasha, again, always
For Jordan, with love

Contents

Contributors

David J. Bodenhamer is Executive Director of the Polis Center, Professor of History, and Adjunct Professor of Informatics at Indiana University-Purdue University, Indianapolis, USA. He also co-directs the Virtual Center for Spatial Humanities, is general editor of the Indiana University Press Series on the Spatial Humanities, and is co-editor of the *International Journal of Humanities and Arts Computing*. He has written or edited ten books, including *The Spatial Humanities: GIS and the Revolution of Humanities Scholarship* (2010, with John Corrigan and Trevor Harris), and over 40 journal articles and book chapters.

Rosalind Crone is Lecturer in History at the Open University, UK. Between 2006 and 2011 she was Research Fellow and co-investigator on the *Reading Experience Database* project. She has published on popular culture, crime and literacy in nineteenth-century Britain and is author of *Violent Victorians: Popular Entertainment in Nineteenth-Century London* (2012).

Katie Halsey is Lecturer in Eighteenth-Century Literature at the University of Stirling, Scotland. Her most recent publications include *Jane Austen and her Readers, 1786–1945* (2012), *The History of Reading* (2011), edited with Shafquat Towheed and Rosalind Crone, and *The History of Reading*, vol. 2, *Evidence from the British Isles c.1750–1945* (2011), edited with W.R. Owens.

Valerie Johnson is Head of Research at The National Archives, a post she has held for nearly four years. Prior to that she worked as Research Officer on a history project based at the University of Cambridge History Faculty. She holds an MA with Distinction in Archive Administration, and was awarded the Alexander R. Myers Memorial Prize for Archive Administration. She also has a PhD in History for her thesis, *British Multinationals, Culture and Empire in the Early Twentieth Century* (2007), for which she won the 2008 Coleman Prize. She has worked as an archivist and a historian in the academic, corporate and public sectors.

Kevin Kee is the Canada Research Chair in Digital Humanities, and an Associate Professor at Brock University, where he teaches in the Centre for Digital Humanities and the Department of History. He runs the Simulating

History and Pastplay projects, as well as the Ontario Augmented Reality Network. He also leads a company that develops interactive media for learning and entertainment. His research lies at the intersection of history, education, computing, and game studies, and he has published on the use of computer simulations and serious games for history and history education, and on Canadian cultural history.

Brian Maidment is Professor of English at Liverpool John Moores University, UK. He also holds Visiting Professorships at the Lewis Walpole Library at Yale University and the Centre for the Study of Text and Print Culture at the University of Ghent. His main academic interests focus on Regency and Victorian mass circulation print culture, especially periodicals and the history of illustration. He is author of *The Poorhouse Fugitives* (1987), *Reading Popular Prints* (1996) and *Dusty Bob – A Cultural History of Dustmen 1780–1870* (2007). His new book *Comedy, Caricature and the Social Order 1820–1850* will be published shortly by Manchester University Press.

Jim Mussell is Lecturer in English at the University of Birmingham, UK. He is the author of *Science, Time and Space in the Late Nineteenth-Century Periodical Press* (2007) and *The Nineteenth-Century Press in the Digital Age* (2012). He was one of the editors of the *Nineteenth-Century Serials Edition* (2008) [www.ncse.ac.uk] and currently edits the Digital Forum in the *Journal of Victorian Culture*.

Charlotte Lydia Riley is completing her PhD at University College, London, UK. Her thesis focuses on colonial development under the Attlee government and the relationship between the British Empire, the Marshall Plan and Anglo-American relations in this period. She teaches British foreign and imperial history in the nineteenth and twentieth centuries. In addition, she is committed to widening participation and extending access to education, working on a number of projects in university outreach and educational liaison.

Spencer Roberts is a Research Assistant in the Simulating History Lab at Brock University in St. Catharines, Ontario. He has helped organize conferences such as 'Playing with Technology in History' (2010) and 'Interacting with Immersive Worlds' (2011), and has contributed to projects hosted by Niagara Interactive Media Generator (nGen) and Ontario Augmented Reality Network (OARN). His current research interests include adapting mobile technologies as teaching and learning tools, exploring and refining digital methods of historical research, and creating an interactive, mobile history of the War of 1812.

Mark Sandle is Professor of History at The King's University College, Edmonton, Alberta, Canada. Up until 2009 he worked at De Montfort University, Leicester in the UK. His main field of interest lies in Russian and Soviet history in the twentieth century. He has recently authored two books: *Gorbachev: Man of the Twentieth Century?* (2008) and *Communism: Seminar Studies in History* (2011).

He is currently working on a monograph on the history of post-war Soviet Moldavia 1944–56.

David Thomas is Director of Technology at the National Archives, London, a post he has held since 2005. Prior to that he held a variety of posts at the National Archives and has led their IT operations since 1995. He is currently working on the development of new systems to capture, preserve and make available digital and digitized records. He holds a PhD in History for his thesis on the crown lands under Elizabeth I. Until recently he served on the Council of the Royal Historical Society.

Luke Tredinnick is a Senior Lecturer and course leader for the BA Social Media at London Metropolitan University, UK. He specializes in digital culture, digital technologies, and the social and cultural contexts of information technology. He has published three books, including *Digital Information Culture* (2008), and *Digital Information Contexts* (2006), as well as numerous articles and book chapters.

William J. Turkel is an Associate Professor of History at Western University in London, Ontario, Canada, and Director of Digital Infrastructure for NiCHE: Network in Canadian History & Environment. He is author of *The Archive of Place* (2007). His current research interests include computational history, Big History, STS, physical computing, desktop fabrication and electronics. He blogs at http://williamjturkel.net

Toni Weller is a Visiting Research Fellow, formerly Senior Lecturer, at De Montfort University, UK, and editor of the international journal, *Library & Information History*. Her research focuses on information history during the long nineteenth century and on the origins of the information age, topics on which she has lectured and published internationally. Recent publications include *Information History: An Introduction* (2008), *The Victorians and Information: A Social and Cultural History* (2009), *Information History in the Modern World: Histories of the Information Age* (2010) and 'The information state: a historical perspective on surveillance', in *Routledge International Handbook of Surveillance Studies* (2012).

Introduction

History in the digital age

Toni Weller

History, as a field of enquiry, is standing on the edge of a conceptual precipice.

Since the popular advent of the World Wide Web in the mid-1990s, scholars have been drawing attention to the potentials and pitfalls of electronic resources in historical study. Seamus Ross has recognized that 'the growing dependence of society upon digital information will change the fabric of source material available to historians'.[1] For Terry Kuny, 'we are moving into an era where much of what we know today, much of what is coded and written electronically, will be lost forever. We are, to my mind, living in the midst of digital Dark Ages'.[2] William J. Turkel has argued that 'the use of digital sources ... completely changes the landscape of information and transaction costs that historians have traditionally faced'.[3] And yet others still have suggested that historians are facing a fundamental 'paradigm shift' in our understanding and practice of traditional history.[4] This book argues that whilst the digital age is affecting all who practice and study history professionally, historians do not need to learn new technologies or computer codes; they do not need to become computer scientists. Indeed, I would argue that part of the problem thus far has been too much emphasis on historians becoming something they are not; to the detriment of the fundamental skills and expertise that is the craft of the historian. This misplaced emphasis has had the consequence that the majority of historians, whilst aware of some of the challenges the digital age is creating, are not actively engaging with these very fundamental issues. Instead the challenge of the digital age is 'relegated to more marginal professional spaces – to casual lunchtime conversations or brief articles in association newsletters' in the words of Roy Rosenzweig.[5]

For the most part this discourse has been disparate, and between information professionals, archivists or 'digital historians', those historians directly interested in technological innovation and practice in their scholarship, rather than the vast majority of traditional historians. Students studying history at university are now themselves digital born, and take for granted that resources and communication not only are, but should be, available online. There is, to a certain degree, a generational divide between students and teachers, although this is not as simplistic as it sounds since established scholars have a much deeper tradition of historical rigour from which to draw. We find ourselves then in an odd paradox: for the most part, current historical scholars do not really engage with the conceptual impact of the digital age despite using digital resources in their work, and consequently current students of history are often not taught to think about these conceptual issues or to apply traditional historical methodologies to their everyday digital and online experiences.

This book attempts to fill the gap between those historians who are actively engaging with the issues of history in the digital age – or, digital historians – and the majority of traditional historians and students of history. It is an attempt to throw a conceptual spotlight on some of these issues which have remained for too long on the corner of mainstream historical discourse. Much of my own research and teaching has been on the origins of the information age and links between the nineteenth century and the modern information society. In the course of discussions with colleagues, students and interested amateurs alike, it became increasingly clear that there was a strong distinction between those historians who were professionally engaged in digital tools and technologies in their work, self-styled 'digital historians', and those who really did not consider the subject within their remit at all, despite regularly using email, distribution lists, digitized newspapers or images and many other online resources. It was also evident that students, particularly undergraduate students, do not think of Wikipedia or a source found on Google or via a database in the same way they think of a hard copy paper source. Digital material is not enough removed from their own everyday experiences to seem to warrant different consideration. More to the point, whether you are a historian of the late twenty-first century or of the Middle Ages, there is now source material available digitally but few history departments at universities are teaching information provenance in the digital age as part of historiography. Conversely, in my experience of also teaching and researching in information departments, information provenance forms a central role in any course. Historians themselves are not teaching digital provenance because they, too, tend to overlook it; living in the digital age means we take it for granted.

With these experiences in mind, it also became clear that there was no existing book, aimed at traditional historians, rather than digital historians *per se*, which tried to grapple with some of the more conceptual questions and issues that were impacting upon historical study caused by the digital age itself. This, then, is the concern of this volume, both in terms of reconsidering the way in which we use and apply original material that has been digitized, but also reconsidering the way in which future historians will have to engage with the contemporary historical record.

Ways of studying and researching history have changed exponentially in the last two decades but these changes need to be more fully considered and absorbed into the mainstream of historical discourse. The chapters in this book are grounded in the practice and experience of pedagogic practice and historical research of the authors since 'it is through practice that history ... is constructed, mediated, communicated and responded to'.[6] However, while there is discussion of technological developments and digital projects, the heart of each chapter, and the book as a whole, is rather more holistic. Much of what follows in this collection is unchartered territory in mainstream historical discourse, although to a digital historian this may be familiar ground, albeit a good introduction for students. The chapters almost inevitably raise more questions than they answer but this is an essential starting point in order to reconsider our relationship with the historical record in the digital age.

Digital history

It is worth making a clear distinction at this point between digital history (or digital historians), and historians more generally in the digital age (the remit of this book). Most historians are not digital Luddites. Scholars now use at least some form of digital resources, from email and the internet to scholarly databases or discussion lists, alongside more traditional sources and methodologies. But for most historians, the challenges of the digital age are not ones that are seen to directly concern their research or teaching. Andersen's suggestion that 'learning to use a database, scan materials, and query that database all consume time that could be used to write' is probably a reasonably accurate reflection of the way the majority of historians perceive digital scholarship.[7] To some extent this is a rather naive and blinkered attitude. *History in the Digital Age* aims to engage traditional historians with some of the issues that are irrevocably changing the ways in which we do (and will) interact with the past. However, there is a school of historical thought which has embraced the digital age wholeheartedly and, whilst not the main audience of this book, must be acknowledged for their significant contribution to developing our understanding of history in the digital age.

What has come to be termed 'digital history' is a recognized sub-field of the discipline which has gained increasing validity over recent years. In an online 'interchange' discussion hosted by the *Journal of American History*, William G. Thomas III posed the following definition of digital history:

> Digital history is an approach to examining and representing the past that works with the new communication technologies of the computer, the Internet network, and software systems. On one level, digital history is an open arena of scholarly production and communication, encompassing the development of new course materials and scholarly data collections. On another, it is a methodological approach framed by the hypertextual power of these technologies to make, define, query, and annotate associations in the human record of the past. To do digital history, then, is to create a framework, an ontology, through the technology for people to experience, read, and follow an argument about a historical problem.[8]

In other words, digital history is directly engaged with the role new digital technologies can play in presenting and representing the past, both in terms of the utilization of such technologies in scholarship and teaching, but also in considering new methodologies resulting from them. Implicit in this definition is that digital history can frame new types of research question thanks to the unprecedented connectivity and interactivity of the digital age. This is a stimulating prospect and one with which several of the chapters of this volume engage.

Dan Cohen has contended that 'it is now quite clear that historians will have to grapple with abundance, not scarcity' in terms of the digital historical record.[9] There are indeed millions upon millions of digital pages available to view – digitized historical documents and images as well as newly created web pages and databases, not to mention personal emails, texts and digital photographs. Such saturation can have the effect of slowing down research, requiring time and energy to sift through the superficial to find something pertinent. In some ways one could argue that the historian has always had to sift through material to find the relevant sources but the explosion of digital, and public, publication has certainly exacerbated this issue. There is also no getting around the fact that much of this digital born material is lost, deleted or on outdated media before it is preserved for future use, and that even if it is currently used by historians or students of history, the same rigorous historical methodologies are not always applied to digital and online material as they are to more traditional analogue sources. There remains a degree of condescension and suspicion towards digital resources from many mainstream historians, which can be counterproductive.

Whilst digital history is an exciting and forward-thinking field of enquiry, its very concentration on technology and digital tools means that it can be alienating to more traditional historians. The vast majority of historians have not yet begun to confront such changes, nor, for the most part, have they begun to really engage with what the digital age might mean in terms of the future of the historical record. This book does not aim to pose itself as a digital history textbook, nor is it necessarily for self-proclaimed digital historians; it does not wish to preach to the converted. Rather it offers an accessible overview of some of the key issues for traditional historians, and for students of history, who engage with online and digital resources in their research and teaching but whose primary concern is not technological development in the field. Its focus is not technological but conceptual, whilst recognizing that digital history and history in the digital age are not mutually exclusive concepts.

There is of course an irony that any printed book or article discussing such dynamic concepts as this one runs the risk of dating before it even makes it to print. As many others have noted, the traditional forms of publication in history are not suited to the fast-changing discourses of the digital age – demonstrated by the fact that most pure digital history texts tend to be in the form of websites, blogs and online articles and journals rather than the traditional historical outlet of the monograph.[10] This is particularly evident in the publications that first responded to the internet and the digital age back in the 1990s and early 2000s where the focus was largely on new forms of technology and how to apply it to historical research. These volumes suffered both from the technology they described becoming dated within just a few years and also, and significantly for the historian, an over-emphasis on technical description and explanation which alienated those without an understanding of computing, and used language that was lacklustre and dry to scholars more comfortable with prose.

I am not unaware therefore of the irony and potential pitfalls of a published hard copy book discussing history in the digital age. However, it has been a conscious choice to produce a hard copy book rather than online tools and there are three main reasons behind this choice. First, in terms of dynamic contemporary responses to the digital age, digital historians are doing it better and faster online. This book does not aim to compete with them in this respect. Second, this book's audience is the more traditional historian or student of history who is less familiar with the key issues than the specialist digital historian. Traditional historians, by and large, remain more comfortable with the printed book. Third, the central remit of this book is not to describe new technologies or prescribe how to 'do' research online with new tools. Such approaches do date quickly. Its concern is to explore and introduce some of the more conceptual issues that are changing history as a discipline, both now, and for the historian of the future. Such conceptual issues date much less quickly than technological overviews, and since most traditional historians are not as familiar with them as digital historians, there is room for discussion and consideration. This book is, fundamentally, an introduction to the other much more dynamic and reactive debate that is out there, but produced in such a way that is accessible rather than alienating to the majority of historians and students of history.

History in the digital age

Since digital technologies abound, surrounding us in every aspect of life, it can be easy and obvious to focus on these new technologies themselves rather than the bigger questions they pose for historical thought. Much digital history discusses, quite rightly, the profound implications of preservation and access but there are also some fundamental issues which are often overlooked with regard to the interaction between historians and the historical record itself. As Rosenzweig has argued in a highly succinct and articulate summary of the issues, 'the problems are much more than technical and involve difficult social, political, and organizational questions of authenticity, ownership, and responsibility',[11] but, as this book argues, they are also about interpretation, analysis and engagement – those fundamental tools of the historian.

New technologies have long suggested new and different ways of exploring the past. The print revolution of the nineteenth century saw newly affordable publications claiming they would preserve 'the life of the times' where its contents would serve the future scholar in order to 'teach him the truth about those that have gone before him'.[12] In the 1880s, the railways, telegraph and telephone had introduced such revolutionary changes to the speed in which communication took place that 'relations of time and distance' had been so affected as to predict 'a degree of ambiguity which ... will lead to complications in social and commercial affairs, to errors in chronology ... and prove an increasing hindrance to human intercourse'.[13] Even the Wellsian 'World Brain' of the 1930s suggested profound implications for the way people of the future might communicate and record knowledge for posterity.[14] This collection of essays does not suggest a

Whiggish progression or uniqueness to the digital age. However, there are some unique challenges faced by historians of today and tomorrow. Historians 'need to be thinking simultaneously about how to research, write, and teach in a world of unheard-of historical abundance and how to avoid a future of record scarcity'.[15] Such a paradox creates conceptual challenges that were unthought-of only a few decades ago.

For clarity, let us list some of these challenges (and the following two lists are by no means exhaustive):

- The preservation of original hard copy material by digitizing it (scanning, microfilm, photograph, etc., and storing in a database or other digital format).
- The preservation of digital born material (capturing a webpage with all its hyperlinks and interactions, a text message, an email, a photograph, a word-processed document or database, the interactions on a social networking website).
- Issues of migration to new formats, including the rapid obsoletion of hardware and software.
- The costs of access and dissemination, and migration and preservation – can individual scholars afford to do this (can they afford not to?), should universities be paying for access, how much should be government funded? Are such projects sustainable long term?
- Stability of technologies (on a very basic level, it is all very well digitizing your notes or using an electronic referencing tool, but what use is it if it becomes outdated or obsolete within a few years?).

- How to preserve the original experience when a source is digitized or preserved in a different format? Does the historical interpretation change when the original is altered?
- The potential transience of the contemporary historical record.
- Public history and public involvement (will the future role of the professional historian be increasingly public as well as scholarly? Do wikis and blogs and YouTube forms of dissemination help or hinder historical understanding?).
- Divisions between archives and material in public repositories and those in privately funded hands with commercial interests.
- Issues of ownership and copyright (if something is available digitally, is it protected? Can it be copied and pasted? Is it still being referenced properly, and how can we accurately reference when digital links and hyperlinks regularly change or break?).
- Information provenance (where has this source originally come from? Why and when was it digitized? What was *not* digitized?, i.e. digital collections are not necessarily the complete collections).
- What constitutes an original document when digital material can be edited so easily and so invisibly?
- The intangibility of digital material (historians of the future will increasingly be unable to physically touch a handwritten diary or letter since many will

be preserved digitally or have been originally created in a word processor, email package or mobile phone application).

- Teaching history students about engaging with all of these digital experiences (this requires a degree of application from historians themselves to value teaching such issues and, in some cases, retraining an older generation of historians and educating them about the issues).

The first list is of more practical concern and whilst historians should be involved in such debates and decisions, the majority would probably not engage with such topics in their own research. The second list though is the one which has profound conceptual and methodological implications for every historian, and for the way in which we understand and study history. Arguably, 'professional historians need to shift at least some of their attention from the past to the present and future and reclaim the broad professional vision that was more prevalent a century ago'.[16] This means engaging more directly with some of these issues, and ensuring that our students are doing so as well.

The changing historical record

Preservation of an item – whether digitally born or digitized hard copies – presents many challenges, but for the historian there is another issue to consider: preserving the original experience. In 1964, Marshall McLuhan argued that 'the medium is the message'.[17] By this he suggested that the medium and the information content within it had a symbiotic relationship, that the medium influences how the message is perceived. The classic example used by McLuhan is that of a lightbulb – although a lightbulb does not have information content *per se*, it is a medium that manifests social affect by creating light where there was dark. For him, 'a light bulb creates an environment by its mere presence'.[18] In terms of a television news report, it may be less about the content of the news story and more about what is deemed socially acceptable to broadcast into one's home. For the historian then, this can be taken one step further: the medium does not only change the message but it can also change the interpretation. In the digital age when information content and source material is regularly moved from one type of medium to another – paper to digitized form, upgraded from a cassette disk to a USB device, or even printed from screen to paper – historians must remember to note the original experience, the original medium, as much as note the actual content of the source itself.

Whilst searching for news articles on a particular subject in a digital database is undoubtedly quick and easy, it is completely removed from the original reader experience of physically holding and searching the original tangible object. As any historian knows, context is everything – where a particular article is situated on a page or within an issue gives us clues about the value and importance placed upon it by the editor, helps us understand how a contemporary reader would have first seen the item, and can give us intangible but very significant contextual information which may be lost in a digitized collection. Even the scent of a letter can give us clues about the paper on which it was written. One such example from a Portuguese archive is worth noting. One historian using the archive 'read barely a word, instead, he picked out bundles of letters and ... ran each letter beneath his nose and took a deep breath ... '. When asked what he was doing it was discovered that he was a medical historian documenting outbreaks of cholera:

> When that disease occurred in a town in the eighteenth century, all letters from that town were disinfected with vinegar to prevent the disease from spreading. By sniffing the faint traces of vinegar that survived 250 years and noting the date and source of the letters, he was able to chart the progress of the cholera outbreak.[19]

Whilst the text of the letters could have been reproduced digitally, the scent of the paper would have been lost. Potentially such details could have been included as metadata, but that would necessitate an appreciation that it was important enough to note, and the research interests, needs and methods of the future are never predictable. As William J. Turkel has highlighted, technology is changing fast enough that it is now possible to capture original smells through chemical markers,[20] but realistically not many historians would have the inclination or resources to use such technology.

Similar points may be made about the way in which digital born material may be used as part of the historical record in the future. A digitally created document may not be embedded with the scent of vinegar but each one will be time and date stamped allowing a new form of temporaneous comparison and analysis. Web pages might be preserved or emails saved or printed out for posterity, but as soon as the format is altered, the original experience is changed. Preserving a web page might allow a historian to see the content and imagery originally present, but would it also archive the pop-out ads or tailored links to the individual user which form such a large part of the digital ephemera? These may not be deemed worthwhile sources now, but they are part of social history in the twenty-first century.

In his essay on museums and public history Graham Black argued that

> In selecting what to collect, they [museums] define what is or is not history. In preserving their collections in perpetuity, they act as a permanent memory store. In the way they display and interpret that material evidence, they construct and transmit meanings.[21]

Georg Hegel and Quatremere de Quincy, the first critics of museums, complained during the early years of the nineteenth century that the museum would end up destroying history rather than preserving it because it would take objects out of their historical context.[22] Similar fears have been voiced over digital collections:

> Unlike conservation practices where an item can often be treated, stored and essentially forgotten for some period of time, digital objects will require

frequent refreshing and recopying to new storage media. Keeping the 'original' digital artifact [*sic*] is not important. Further, refreshing or 'copying' of digital information will not be confined to merely moving from one storage medium to another but will also entail translation into new formats or structures.[23]

The very act of choosing material to include is a subjective and selective act. Likewise, in digital terms, 'scholars who structure historical documents with markup languages such as XML make choices – often quite good choices, but choices none the less – about which elements of a document are most important. But future readers of those documents may have other interests or concerns, or may have other ways of scanning them'.[24] This applies equally to any archive of hard copy documents which has to be periodically 'weeded' for its perceived value to researchers or society, most usually due to restrictions of physical space or resources. The same issue is evident in the selection of what contemporary digital born material to preserve. It is not possible to preserve every single website, blog, email or text ever sent. Likewise, not every single letter, diary, photograph or newspaper in printed form has been preserved (as historians know only too well); there will inevitably be gaps in the historical record. The question is how much digital born material we should be making a conscious effort to preserve and who is the arbiter of such decisions. The potential black hole of source material for the future historian is every bit as compelling as the traditional discourses of the lost voices in history – the illiterate, women, the poor or other minority groups. As Rosenzweig, among others, has shown:

> the absolute nature of digital corrosion is sobering. Print books and records decline slowly and unevenly – faded ink or a broken-off corner of a page. But digital records fail completely – a single damaged bit can render an entire document unreadable. Here is the key difference from the paper era: we need to take action now because digital items very quickly become unreadable, or recoverable only at great expense.[25]

Traditionally, preservation of records has been the remit of archivists or curators rather than historians. Thus far, information professionals, librarians and archivists, rather than historians, have had more sustained engagement with the issue of preservation of the historic record in an age of transience,[26] but the digital age is altering the way in which we interact with the historical record. At the very least, historians need to be thinking about their methodologies, and those that they are teaching their students, to ensure they remain valid. Alexander Maxwell makes the very valid argument that historians, more than any other field of scholars, use highly eclectic source material, where 'anything can be a source of historical insight: even old phone books have their uses'.[27] Maxwell's article, while focusing on the practical requirements of digital material, also forcefully demonstrates the attitude of historians that the original printed material is paramount. This is undoubtedly true when you are studying something from decades or centuries ago, but becomes a blurrier issue altogether when you start to think about preserving the current historical record.

Preserving the current historical record has its own complications. Traditionally historical collections have been largely the preserve of public or state institutions – libraries, museums and archives. Indeed, most traditional funding for such institutions has come directly from the state or public donation. The digital age is changing this balance. Resources such as The Internet Archive, a semi-private organization that began archiving the web in 1996, are very valuable entities, but are considerably fragile and dependent upon one or two individuals for content and funding. The Internet Archive also has a commercial side since the actual technical 'crawling' of the web is done by the company Alexa Internet and used to monitor patterns of behaviour online. Alexa Internet was bought by Amazon in 1999 for $300 million, a sum of money of which most national libraries can only dream of attracting. It also does not get around the issue of preserving the originality of experience, although this may be almost impossible to do for the internet since preserving one page requires every page connected to it by hyperlinks to be preserved also, potentially *ad infinitum*. While the internet might be free to search (once you have internet access), private companies are fast realizing that there is money to be made in online collections. Traditional scholarly journals now have to offer online archives of articles as well as (or in some cases, instead of) print copy. Scholars and students expect online access to at the very least the catalogues of large collections. Digitization and preservation is not a cheap business to be in, so some private investment will be increasingly necessary, but this creates other questions for the historian.

Most significantly, it begs the question again of who is responsible for preserving the historical record in the digital age. Should it be the remit of private organizations? Do organizations, public and private, have their own agendas in terms of what they choose to preserve? Indeed, such questions are not new ones – what has been preserved as part of the historical record has always been the consequence of what was deemed fashionable, influential or political of the day. However, are traditional historians applying such basic historical methodology to digital resources or practice? Are we teaching it in our schools and universities? There seems to be a sense of pervading blinkeredness; because digital experiences and sources abound in our everyday lives, they are not deemed to require such fundamental historical questioning. In 2009 I gave a paper at a JISC (Joint Information Systems Committee) sponsored conference panel in Ireland in which I explored the mutability of the past and present in the digital age.[28] My two panel members gave fascinating accounts of their usage of digital newspaper databases in order to facilitate their research but both admitted that it had never occurred to them that they were searching for articles out of context and that they had not considered the role of original experience in the way in which they were using the results. Undoubtedly, they had been able to use the databases to facilitate their research in new ways, but they had forgotten to apply basic historical methodology whilst doing so. I would venture that there are traditional historians guilty of doing the same thing when using digital resources, and that students of history are particularly guilty of doing so, in part, no doubt, because digital information provenance does not tend to feature in historiography discussions.

There are two issues here then. One is of current scholars using digitization to explore, access, preserve and disseminate materials where the original may be decades or centuries old. The other is the question of historians of the future who wish to study the period from the mid-1990s onwards where much 'original' material was digital born. The potential transience of digital born resources is a pertinent one for the historian. The delete key has a dangerous potency when it comes to historical evidence. This is true not just of web pages and URLs (Uniform Resource Locators) but also emails, text messages, voicemails – all types of evidence which for previous generations would have been committed to paper, possibly in multiple hard copies. The 'fragility of evidence in the digital era' is significant.[29] At the same time, historians of the future may suffer from there being too much material of which to make sense. The Clinton Administration produced close to 40 million emails during their eight years in office (1993–2001), a figure which no single historian would ever be able to access and consider in their lifetime.[30] Turning it on its head, one does not really know how many of those automatically archived email messages are directly related to presidential business and how many were discussing office gossip or arranging personal social affairs. Of course, to the historian, the latter can be just as valuable when considering social history of the period, where 'anything can be a source of historical insight'.[31] And arguably of course, the historian has always grappled with the reality that they may never be able to examine every single relevant source for their topic; the digital age has just introduced this on a whole new scale. Even if one subscribes to this latter thought, it still has profound implications for the ways in which historians of the future will be able to conduct their research and what questions they choose to ask of the historical record.

The Arts and Humanities Data Service (AHDS) in the UK had the aim, in part at least, of preserving the original technology (rather than the information content, *per se*) in order that the original experience can be maintained when software and hardware became obsolete. As well as just migrating information content from floppy disk, to CD, to USB, to whatever comes next, the original experience is as preserved as possible by being able to view material on the original hardware. This is a good aim in theory but since all hardware breaks or wears down eventually, making it increasingly difficult to fix or replace, this strategy is what Rosenzweig has termed 'backward-looking'.[32] In addition, as digital technologies become more advanced, preserving the original experience becomes increasingly difficult since the content and the hardware become increasingly removed from one another: you can now check your email or browse the web on any computer screen in the world that has an internet connection as well as on your mobile phone handset. Viewing on a small touch screen is a different, more intimate experience than viewing on a computer screen at a desk. We cannot possibly preserve all original experience but we should, as historians, be aware of the implications such differences make. A response to an email via your mobile phone while you are out shopping will most likely be shorter and less considered than a response to the same email made at your desk from the leisure of your own home. As historians we are taught from first principles to ask the basic questions 'who, what, when, where and why?' of any source, but are we really applying the same rigour to digital sources that form part of our everyday experiences? More to the point, are we teaching such things to students of history who will be the historians of the future? In my experience the answer to both seems to be largely 'no'.

Despite efforts by The Internet Archive and other national institutions to build up a picture of web content, some websites, famous on their inception, but now defunct, have been permanently lost.[33] Although most historians would not use the content of Wikipedia for research purposes, it is one of the few websites which maintains a complete log of all changes and edits. However, this is not the same as seeing the older page in its original form. The architecture of the internet means that 'at any moment in time you can only get to the current representation of a resource ... The old representations – the one from yesterday, the day before, from a year ago – they are gone forever.'[34] This means that historians of the future wanting to utilize digital born content will have to develop new research and provenance skills.

Historians of the future may also find themselves in a challenging position over their very role. The digital age has allowed the interested amateur or independent scholar to express themselves alongside professional historians through the mediums of personal websites or, increasingly, blogs.[35] This can be hugely democratizing in terms of putting people (and their knowledge and resources) in touch with one another but also needs to be treated with some caution. One does not know for sure the authority or provenance of something found on the internet and blogs should be investigated the same way as any other source. Recognition from academic institutions certainly helps to sort the wheat from the chaff. The Cliopatria Awards, for example, based at the History News Network at George Mason University in America, have been running since 2005 and recognize the best history blogs. Wikipedia, although generally not recognized as a scholarly work, is a good example of the democratization of history created by the digital age. In the words of Roswenzweig, 'a historical work without owners and with multiple, anonymous authors is thus almost unimaginable in our professional culture', and yet, he concludes, the types of buried historical metadata on such open source websites as Wikipedia offer significant and insightful contextual details that affect interpretation. For example, the 'History' page on each Wikipedia entry records the IP addresses of anyone who made an edit on that entry, when they did it and exactly what they did there. Such details provide clues as to how popular a particular topic is over another one, whether it is largely the work of a small few or many hundreds, how topical it is, the quality of the entry, and so forth.[36] It is the digital equivalent of marginalia. Even more significantly, Roswenzweig argues, historians should take note of websites such as Wikipedia, blogs and suchlike, because our students do. We must give consideration to sources used by the next generation of historians, discuss the advantages and limitations of all sources, and essentially not forget to teach basic historical methodology and critical analysis in digital research.

At the George Mason University in Virginia, USA, a pioneer in digital history, there have been some innovative examples of how to teach students about the provenance of the digital materials they use everyday, whilst also getting them to think about traditional historical methodologies. In 2008, a course entitled 'Lying About History' set up a hoax Wikipedia entry for a turn-of-the-century pirate, Edward Owens. In addition, YouTube clips, blogs and genuine historiographical research into the period and context added authenticity to the Owens character.[37] Arguably, the project also demonstrated the potential ease with which people could debunk inaccuracy in the digital era (as T. Mills Kelly, the historian behind the idea, suggested, it was much harder for anyone to check the validity of the Victorian Fiji Mermaid).[38] Yet, I have certainly had experiences with students in my classes who assume Wikipedia is absolute truth (or simply do not check), or that an image they have found via Google is authentic and unedited. What was most interesting were the issues the hoax seemed to raise about historical ethics. One commentator argued that in deliberately planting a hoax in Wikipedia, the historian in question had also deliberately introduced a credibility question mark over Wikipedia as a whole: if one article is fake then how many others may be fake?[39]

Text is not the only thing that can be manipulated or faked – images can also be misused or altered, something long recognized by scholars.[40] When the periodical press first began introducing illustrations and engravings during the mid-nineteenth century in Britain, many of the images were drawn by artists who were not even present at the events on which they were supposedly reporting first hand.[41] Even the co-creator of the *Illustrated London News* (*ILN*), Henry Vizetelly, acknowledged the misleading nature of published images, observing that as far as the *ILN* went, there was 'not even a single authentic engraving in the opening number derived from an authentic source!'[42] Roger Fenton's powerful photographs of the Crimean War are still debated as to whether or not they were deliberately staged for dramatic effect.[43] The Cottingley Fairy Photographs from 1917 were convincing enough to fool Arthur Conan Doyle as well as stimulate great public debate about their authenticity.[44] In one undergraduate seminar class I ran on Fascism, I asked students to watch several propaganda clips supposedly from the 1940s that were freely available via YouTube and then to discuss them in class. I deliberately gave the students no other information about them. One of these clips was of an animated black and white Winnie-the-Pooh cartoon which had been dubbed with rousing German music and German subtitles redolent of Nazi propaganda. Not one student queried whether it might have been a fake; it was assumed that the Nazis had chosen an English cartoon (produced by an American company) deliberately for maximum effect. It was only after some directed class discussion that the issue of authenticity, provenance and basic chronology arose, as well as querying who might have uploaded it in the first place and why.[45] The seminar was vital in trying to challenge some of the predisposed assumptions that if it is online, it is true.

Historical controversies like those above, or such as the Hitler Diaries or Holocaust deniers, should be a staple part of any history course on historiography and methodology. Hoaxes and frauds in historical study are not new to the digital age, but the very ubiquity of online information and communication can mean that students, but also some academics, sometimes do not see the woods for the trees. These are exactly the sorts of questions, debates and discourses that we should be having in the digital age – not just with ourselves as professional scholars, but with our students as well.

Contributing chapters

Whilst each chapter can be read in isolation, holistically they offer a thought-provoking collection. As a discipline, History is constantly renewing itself and re-exploring the dynamic relationship between the past, the present and the future. Historians perhaps need to reconsider some of the things we have previously taken for granted. This collection encourages both the established and the emerging scholar, as well as the student of history in the digital age, to really question how the field of history is changing all around us and what the impact of this might be for the discipline. It includes international contributors from a variety of disciplines – History, English, Information and Archival Studies – and many of the chapters allow for a cross-national perspective (with focus on UK, American and Canadian practice) as well as a cross-disciplinary one to ensure that the discussion is as inclusive as possible. The digital age is one which requires a multi-disciplined approach. The book does not seek to either applaud or condemn digital technologies, but rather to take a more holistic view of how the field of history is changing in the digital age. Nor does it attempt to make distinctions between different types of electronic records or artefacts. Such 'semantic debates' are, as Kuny has argued, 'of questionable utility' in an age when 'digital' is so ubiquitous.[46]

This introduction has offered an overview of the changes and challenges the field is facing, exploring some of the literature and situating the chapters that follow. The book is divided into four interconnecting sections, each of which focuses on a particular aspect of history in the digital age: re-conceptualizing history, studying history, teaching history and the future of history in the digital age. Each chapter offers its own references and notes for further reading.

In the first section, *Re-conceptualizing history in the digital age*, the three chapters explore how the practice of history itself is changing thanks to the impact of digitization and digital technologies. David J. Bodenhamer (1) argues that the spatial humanities, specifically spatial history, are allowing new and innovative scholarship in the field to raise new questions about how space has influenced human behaviour and social, economic, political, and cultural development. This is followed by Luke Tredinnick's (2) chapter on remediating historicized experience. He suggests that one consequence of our everyday use of media digital technologies is the tendency for history to become a cultural artefact that is self-consciously manufactured through individual and collective participation. In so doing, they have collapsed the distinction between the present and the truly historical. This has, argues Tredinnick, profound consequences not only for how we think about the nature of history, but also for the ethical contexts within which historians and history pedagogues work. The third chapter in this section by William J. Turkel, Kevin Kee and Spencer Roberts (3), explores the ways in which historians, and students of history, need to reconsider traditional research methods whilst also making the vital point that the digital age is an age in flux. They make an argument which is fundamental to the purpose of this book as a whole; the onus should not be on prescribing which technologies or databases to use, but rather that scholars themselves should become 'more mindful about their method ... not as something that one acquires once and forgets about, but rather as something that one practices every day, making continuous small improvements over the course of a lifetime'.

The second section, *Studying history in the digital age*, develops some of these themes by considering history in practice. These chapters are not focused on digital technology *per se*, but rather use the authors' experience of digital technologies in order to pose important questions about how such resources can challenge our understanding of source material, historical practice and methodology. Jim Mussell (4) engages with the poignant thought that we are now so used to engaging with digital versions of printed objects, we no longer reflect seriously on the transformations necessary to get them from the archive to the monitor. He also notes, as do many of the contributors to this book, that material in digital form is not constant; it can be altered, amended, compressed and republished in ways that traditional sources cannot be, and most significantly, this can be done behind the scenes without a user necessarily registering that changes have taken place. Rosalind Crone and Katie Halsey (5) continue this argument in their exploration of the history of reading. Using the *Reading Experience Database*, or RED, as an example, they demonstrate the behind-the-scenes issues involved in creating a historical database – how source material is collected, edited and its provenance assured. Their argument shows that not only is serious historical consideration with the material vital, but new methodological questions and practices are created in the process. Historians are able to engage with traditional source material in totally new ways and, in so doing, create entirely new possibilities – and problems. They also ask the question of to what extent the actual process of online cataloguing and searching might inhibit initiative in historical scholarship and remove the serendipitous elements of research. In the final chapter in this section, Brian Maidment (6) takes a look at a less discussed aspect of digitization in history – that of the digital image. Scholarly digital repositories alongside the publicly accessible internet offer a vast opportunity for scholars to engage with visual material. However, as Maidment argues, the temptation to use images drawn from the web to 'illustrate' or confirm arguments derived from manuscript, printed or even oral sources without any consideration of the complex discourses through which prints are constructed, disseminated, 'read' and assimilated into cultural meaning remains omnipresent. The 'mis'-interpretation of images by print historians is a long-standing issue within historical discourse, but it takes on another dimension in the digital world. The appearance of a mass of graphic images in digital form adds yet other layers of mediation to an already highly mediated form of historical evidence.

The third section of the book focuses on *Teaching history in the digital age*, and offers chapters by first an experienced scholar and then, in contrast, a historian who is herself part of the 'digital born' generation. These two perspectives are interesting and important. Mark Sandle's (7) chapter discusses the extent to which digital technologies are fundamentally reconceptualizing the way history is encountered by students, of how technology mediates the past and of the benefits and pitfalls there are for lecturers in deploying these new approaches. Charlotte Lydia Riley (8) then explores this from the perspective of the student and the early career academics who have little or no experience of a world without digital technologies which offers some interesting comparisons to the preceding chapters.

The final section focuses on *The future of history* with regard to the impact of digital technologies and the increasing awareness of new conceptual and methodological questions within the historical community. David Thomas and Valerie Johnson (9) use their experience in the National Archives in London to suggest how the process of preserving the past and the ways in which historians interact with the past are presenting vital challenges not only to the field but also to the ways in which historians will ultimately be able to study the past. Digitization offers great opportunities in terms of preservation of traditional printed documents but there are entirely different questions to be asked about contemporary sources which are originally created in digital formats and which are vulnerable to deletion and permanent loss.

Finally, my conclusion (10) takes a holistic look back over the book and attempts to draw together some of the key themes which have emerged from the chapters. Although the contributors' disciplines, geographic locations and academic focus are different, there remains some significant parity between their arguments which offer some powerful ideas. No one can predict the future of historical research or the future of technological development, nor does this book attempt to do so. Instead, as noted in this introduction, it suggests that historians need to start thinking a little more conceptually and holistically about their own individual practice of research, teaching and methodology, and recognize that the field is, and continues to, change. We need to see past the everyday use of email, internet, Google, and the like and focus on what such interaction actually means for history. How we think of the past is changing. How we preserve historical documents is changing. How historical documents are created is changing. How students of history learn, research and think is becoming totally different to that of even one generation ago. This does not mean at all that traditional historical skills, resources or methodologies become any less important, but change should be recognized. This significance is easily overlooked or played down because such changes are so ubiquitous, so obvious almost, that they become invisible.

Historians must engage more fully with the conceptual questions and issues raised in this book if we are to fully acknowledge the changes, challenges and opportunities to the historical field in the digital age. It is not just about the practicalities of how, when and where material is to be stored, disseminated or preserved, or the technicalities of computer code or web browsers; there are also some quite fundamental questions about our conceptual relationship with the past in the twenty-first century, which apply to every historian and every student of history, no matter what their research interest or historical period of enquiry. This book hopes to offer some pause for thought for those students and scholars who do not consider themselves to be digital historians. As one historian has argued, 'the most important – yet difficult – skill is simply thinking: thinking in bold and creative ways'.[47] The past may be an undiscovered country, but the digital age demands its own bold historical exploration.

Notes

This chapter benefited greatly from the thoughts and comments of colleagues. To that end I would especially like to thank Chris Eldridge and Helen Yallop for their generous and insightful remarks.

This book cites more websites and online resources than your average history book. This is partly because much of what is being written and discussed on the subject is being done so in new digital formats, online articles, blogs and websites, rather than through traditional articles in journals or books which are much slower to publish. Much of the relevant literature is only available online. Of course, as this volume recognizes, URLs (Universal Resource Locators) may change over time and can be broken. The authors have tried therefore to ground their references as much as possible with full bibliographic information for any digitally referenced sources.

1 S. Ross, 'The expanding world of electronic information and the past's future', in E. Higgs (ed.), *History and Electronic Artefacts* (Oxford: Clarendon, 1998), p. 5.
2 T. Kuny, 'A digital dark age? Challenges in the preservation of electronic information', *63rd IFLA Council and General Conference*, 4 September 1997, p. 1.
3 W. J. Turkel in 'Interchange: the promise of digital history', *Journal of American History* (September 2008), 452–91. This quote from pp. 454–55.
4 R. Rosenzweig, 'Scarcity or abundance? Preserving the past in a digital era', *American Historical Review*, 108: 3 (2003), 735–62. Also online http://chnm.gmu.edu/essays-on-history-new-media/essays/?essayid=6 [accessed: 25 March 2012].
5 Rosenzweig, 'Scarcity or abundance?'.
6 G. Black, 'Museums, memory and history', *Cultural and Social History*, 8: 3 (2011), 415.
7 D. L. Andersen, *Digital Scholarship in the Tenure, Promotion, and Review Process* (New York: Sharpe, 2004), p. 10.
8 W. G. Thomas III in 'Interchange: the promise of digital history', *Journal of American History* (September 2008), 452–91. This quote from p. 454.
9 D. Cohen in 'Interchange: the promise of digital history', p. 455.
10 See, for example, the Roy Rosenzweig Center for History and New Media hosted at the George Mason University in Virginia, http://chnm.gmu.edu/essays-on-history-new-media/essays/ [accessed: 25 March 2012]. This is an excellent resource for contemporary online articles on digital history. Also the History News Network which lists historical blogs considered to be of particular note, http://hnn.us/blogs/entries/9665.html [accessed: 25 March 2012].
11 Rosenzweig, 'Scarcity or abundance?'.
12 Preface to Vol. 1 of the *Illustrated London News* (London: 1842). Discussed in T. Weller, 'Preserving knowledge through popular Victorian periodicals: an examination of *The Penny Magazine* and the *Illustrated London News*, 1842–43', *Library History*, 24: 3 (2008), 203.

13 S. Fleming, 'Time reckoning for the twentieth century', *Tracts on Chronology 1854–92* (Washington: Byron S. Adams, 1889), pp. 347, 348.
14 H. G. Wells, *World Brain* (London: Methuen, 1938).
15 Rosenzweig, 'Scarcity or abundance?'.
16 Rosenzweig, 'Scarcity or abundance?'.
17 M. McLuhan, *Understanding Media: The Extensions of Man* (New York: Mentor, 1964).
18 McLuhan, *Understanding Media*, p. 8.
19 J. Seely Brown and P. Duguid, *The Social Life of Information* (Massachusetts: Harvard Business School Press, 2000), pp. 173–74. Also discussed in W.J. Turkel, 'Intervention. Hacking history, from analogue to digital and back again', *Rethinking History*, 15: 2 (2011), 287–96.
20 W. J. Turkel, 'Intervention. Hacking history, from analogue to digital and back again', *Rethinking History*, 15: 2 (2011), 289. See also M. Strlic, J. Thomas, T. Trafela, L. Csefalvayova, I. Kralj Cigic, J. Kolar and M. Cassar, 'Material degradomics: on the smell of old books', *Analytical Chemistry*, 81: 20 (2009), 8617–22.
21 G. Black, 'Museums, memory and history', *Cultural and Social History*, 8: 3 (2011), 415.
22 K. F. Edge and F. H. Weiner, 'Collective memory and the museum', in I. Russell (ed.) *Images, Representations and Heritage: Moving Beyond Modern Approaches to Archaeology* (New York: Springer, 2006), p. 227.
23 Kuny, 'A digital dark age?'.
24 D. Cohen, 'Digital history: the raw and the cooked', *Rethinking History*, 8: 2 (2004), 339.
25 Rosenzweig, 'Scarcity or abundance?'.
26 E. Hampshire and V. Johnson, 'The digital world and the future of historical research', *Twentieth Century British History*, 20: 3 (2009), 396–414; Rosenzweig, 'Scarcity or abundance?'.
27 See, for example, A. Maxwell, 'Digital archives and history research: feedback from an end user', *Library Review*, 59: 1 (2010), 24–39. This quote from p. 25.
28 T. Weller, 'History in the Information Age: a mutable past and present?' Paper presented at the Twenty-Ninth Irish Conference of Historians; University of Limerick, Ireland, 12–14 June 2009.
29 Rosenzweig, 'Scarcity or abundance?'.
30 To give a sense of how quickly digital sources are growing, Pingdom estimated that there were nearly 40 million tweets *a day* in January 2010, http://www.pingdom.com [accessed: 25 March 2012].
31 See, for example, A. Maxwell, 'Digital archives and history research: feedback from an end user', *Library Review*, 59: 1 (2010), 24–39. This quote from p. 25.
32 Rosenzweig, 'Scarcity or abundance?'.
33 C. Edwards, 'File not found', *Engineering & Technology*, 6: 2 (March 2011), 48–50.
34 Edwards, 'File not found'.
35 N. Poyntz, 'History blogs', *History Today*, 60: 5 (2010), 37.
36 R. Rosenzweig, 'Can history be open source? *Wikipedia* and the future of the past', *Journal of American History*, 93: 1 (2006), 117.
37 J. Howard, 'Alternative teaching? Teaching by lying: professor unveils "last pirate" hoax', *The Chronicle of Higher Education*, 19 December 2008; Wikipedia entry on Edward Owens, http://en.wikipedia.org/wiki/Edward_Owens_(hoax) [accessed: 25 March 2012].
38 J. Howard, 'Alternative teaching? Teaching by lying: professor unveils "last pirate" hoax', *The Chronicle of Higher Education*, 19 December 2008. For more see T. Mills Kelly, 'Tomorrow's yesterdays: teaching history in the digital age', in M. Pegrum and J. Lockard (eds) *Brave New Classrooms: Educational Democracy and the Internet* (New York: Peter Lang, 2006), pp. 213–24.

39 M. Feldstein, 'The pirate hoax', *e-Literate*, 20 December 2008, http://mfeldstein.com/the-pirate-hoax/ [accessed: 25 March 2012].

40 J. Rodriguez, 'Viewpoint: the practice of manipulating images to emphasise some point or effect has a long and honourable history, and digital manipulation ought to be no different', *British Journal of Photography*, 7053 (1995), 10; L. Jordanova, *History in Practice* (London: Arnold, 2006); L. Jordanova, 'Image matters', *The Historical Journal*, 51: 3 (2008), 777–91; D. Ades, 'Objects of enquiry: an art historian's response to Peter Burke', *Cultural & Social History*, 7: 4 (2010), 445–52.

41 T. Weller, *The Victorians and Information: A Social and Cultural History* (Saarbruken: VDM Verlag, 2009), pp. 108–9.

42 H. Vizetelly, *Glances Back through Seventy Years: Autobiographical and other Reminiscences* (London: Kegan Paul, Trench, Trubner, 1893), p. 237.

43 U. Keller, *The Ultimate Spectacle: A Visual History of the Crimean War* (Abingdon: Routledge, 2001).

44 A. Conan Doyle, *The Coming of the Fairies* (New York: George H. Doran, 1922); F. M. Griffiths and C. Lynch, *Reflections on the Cottingley Fairies* (Wembley: JMJ Publications, 2009).

45 The clip can be viewed on YouTube at http://www.youtube.com/watch?v=fwYyFzhVtzE&NR=1&skipcontrinter=1 [accessed: 25 March 2012]. The clip was claimed to be a Nazi propaganda film from 1943. In fact, the first Winnie-the-Pooh animation was not made until the 1960s and was in colour, unlike the black and white of this clip.

46 Kuny, 'A digital dark age?'.

47 A. M. Taylor in 'Interchange: the promise of digital history', *Journal of American History* (September 2008), 452–91. This quote from p. 459.

Re-conceptualizing history in the digital age

1 The spatial humanities

Space, time and place in the new digital age

David J. Bodenhamer

If we live in a geographically ignorant society, as some observers claim, a remarkable array of spatial technologies are available to ensure that we never get lost. Numerous online services such as Google Maps and MapQuest provide instant directions to almost any location, with turn-by-turn instructions and even street-level views for an increasing number of cities around the world. Smart phones compete with each other, in part, based on the quality of their navigation software. The multi-fold paper road map, long a staple of travellers, may be on the verge of becoming an artefact, but technology-based guides to space are clearly popular in the marketplace. The impact of these geospatial technologies on government administration, industrial infrastructure, commerce, and academia has been nothing short of revolutionary, with their significance likened to earlier inventions such as the microscope, telescope, and printing press.

Interest in space also is in vogue among humanists. No matter which humanities discipline we explore, references to space and spatiality are common. Scholars today write as casually about landscapes of memory, cognitive mapping, place making, and geographical imagination as they once did about the influences of class or modernization. We have adopted the name, the spatial turn, given by social scientists to this phenomenon and have touted its ability to introduce new perspectives to our study of society and culture. But what is this spatial turn? When did it begin – and why? Finally, what impact has the spatial turn and its associated technologies made in the humanities, including history, and what is its potential to reorient our scholarship as dramatically as it has our everyday lives?

The phrase 'spatial turn' has a murky lineage but it has become common shorthand for the revival of interest in space as a way to understand society and culture. This reintroduction to space first occurred in the 1970s and 1980s, when a new critical geography began to emerge. Many people in the field 'sought alternative paths to rigorous geographical analysis that were not reducible to pure geometries', Edward Soja, a leading theorist noted. 'Rather than being seen only as a physical backdrop, container, or stage to human life', he argued, 'space is more insightfully viewed as a complex social formation, part of a dynamic process'.[1]

This notion of space as social process and not simply geography was part of a postmodern intellectual shift associated initially with French scholars such as

Jacques Derrida and Michel Foucault, who attacked long-standing claims of objectivity and neutrality in academic research. Postmodernists rejected the notion of an objectively superior culture – the best art, the greatest literature, and so forth – and refuted claims of a central hierarchy or organizing principle in society. The world did not divide neatly into free or not free, western and eastern, familiar and foreign, superior and inferior; instead, it embodied extreme complexity, contradiction, ambiguity, uncertainty, and diversity.

These ideas were not new – the nineteenth-century German philosopher Friedrich Nietzsche famously noted that 'whichever interpretation prevails at a given time is a function of power and not truth' – but postmodernism gave them a different expression.[2] For postmodernists, the way we see and define the world is unavoidably relative; in spatial terms, this stance meant that every society defined space differently according to its needs. The meaning of space depended upon such social and political forces as gender, class, and race, among other things, and it always revealed the role of power in society. In this view, nineteenth-century missionary efforts to declare lands ripe for conversion or the idea of a separate woman's sphere, for instance, represented the impulse of power masked in the language of concern and compassion. Although it is easy to exaggerate its influence, postmodernism invigorated a number of humanities disciplines to pay close attention to how societies had defined or constructed space.

Over the past two decades, the humanities and social sciences especially have advanced a more complex and nuanced understanding of space, or, as David N. Livingstone has written, 'there has been a remarkable "spatial turn" among students of society and culture'.[3] For non-geographers, this intellectual movement has been largely defined by a greater awareness of place, manifested in specific sites where human action takes place. Subject matter once organized largely by periods of time, with names such as the Great Depression or the Age of Discovery, now embraces themes of region, diaspora, colonial territory, and contact zones and rubrics such as 'border' and 'boundary'. The shift has been accompanied by and reinforced through an equivalent concern with material culture and built environment, in observations of local representation in dress, architecture, eating, music, and other cultural markers of space and place. Climate, topography, hydrology, and landscapes likewise have re-emerged as important considerations in the investigation of literatures, histories, and social and political life. As a result, our sense of space and place has become more complex and problematic, but in the process it has assumed a more interesting and active role in how we understand history and culture.[4]

Today, historians and other humanists are acutely aware of the social and political construction of space and its particular expression as place. Spaces are not simply the setting for historical action but are a significant product and determinant of change. They are not passive settings but the medium for the development of culture: 'space is not an empty dimension along which social groupings become structured', sociologist Anthony Giddens notes, 'but has to be considered in terms of its involvement in the constitution of systems of interaction'.[5] All spaces contain embedded stories based on what has happened there. These stories are both individual and collective, and each of them link geography (space) and history (time). More importantly, they all reflect the values and cultural codes present in the various political and social arrangements that provide structure to society. In this sense, then, the meaning of space, especially as place or landscape, is always being constructed through the various contests that occur over power. There is nothing new in this development – the earliest maps reveal the power arrangements of past societies – but humanities scholarship increasingly reflects what may in fact be the greatest legacy of postmodernism: the acknowledgement that our understanding of the physical world itself is socially constructed.

Increasingly, historical research focuses on ideas of movement and encounter, on what happens in the spaces between cultures, on processes of transculturation, and on how differently separate cultures perceive the worlds they inhabit. Like their fellow humanists in literature and cultural studies, historians also have turned attention to gendered and racialized spaces, as well as to the body in space. Scholars have found value in concepts of interior and intimate spaces. In each of these ways, we have asked new questions about human experiences and gained new perspectives.[6] In doing so, we have enriched our understanding by considering how a sense of space and spatiality has shaped both ourselves and the 'other'.

At its core, the spatial turn is about the particular and the local, without any supposition that one form of culture is better than another. It rejects grand narratives. Its claim is straightforward: to understand human society and culture we must understand how it developed in certain circumstances and in certain times and at certain places. From this knowledge, we can appreciate that the world is not flat but incredibly complicated and diverse. This view no longer seems new because humanists, including historians, have embraced it eagerly; now, we all recognize the particularity of space, the importance of place. But for all the uses we make of this insight – and for all its explanatory power – the concepts of space and place we employ frequently are metaphorical and not geographical. Far less often have we grappled with how the physical world has shaped us or how in turn we have shaped perceptions of our material environment.

New spatial technologies, especially Geographic Information Systems (GIS), are facilitating a (re)discovery of geographical space in the study of the past. GIS is software that captures, stores, manages, displays, and analyses information linked to a location on earth.[7] In this sense, it is a structured database that describes the world in geographical terms. It also is an intelligent or interactive map that allows users to query the database and see the results visualized. Finally it is a set of tools that allow data to be analysed spatially. Significantly, a spatial feature, location, is central to all three functions. This location may be a *point* expressed in terms of coordinates, latitude and longitude, derived from geometric measurements of the earth's surface, but it also may be a *line,* such as a river or road, or a *polygon*, an area with closed boundaries, such as a county, state, or defined market zone, among others. When we know where something comes from, we can use this location as a common identifier or marker for all other information from or about that particular space.

The power of GIS arises from its ability to relate different types of data – quantitative, textual, image, audio, and the like – to each other based on their shared location, regardless of format, as well as to manage vast quantities of these data within their spatial context. Equally important, it visualizes these relationships on a map of the geographical space in which they all occur, allowing users to see the information separately or together and to see it at different scales. GIS uses a series of transparent layers to manage this feat. It begins with a base layer of planet earth that is divided into a geometric grid of latitude and longitude. The software overlays other information – the locations of roads, schools, population, etc. – on this surface, using the same coordinate geometry to ensure that the location remains constant. It then provides users with the ability to turn these various layers on and off, thus allowing the data layers to be seen separately or in any number of combinations. With GIS, we can capture, manage, and visualize all the population, health, education, employment, and crime data from any area, for example, along the information on its roads and sidewalks, building locations, green spaces, historic photographs, oral histories, videos, and other information about the community – and display all of these items on a map of the common space they share. GIS is, in sum, the best tool we have for integrating information about a place and for allowing us to see and analyse it at different scales and in different ways.[8]

Even though GIS has revealed the power of the map in a new form, its use in studying society also has raised serious questions about the view of the world it presents. For all its capabilities, GIS suggests that the world is flat, at least metaphorically, by offering a view of the physical environment seemingly stripped of its cultural assumptions. It allows us to know where something occurs and to see what else is happening in the same space, but it tells us nothing about the meaning of what we see. As with many technologies, GIS promises to reinvigorate our description of the world through its manipulation and visualization of vast quantities of data by means previously beyond the reach of most scholars. In acting on this claim, we again run the risk of portraying the world uncritically, this time with a veneer of legitimacy that is more difficult to detect or penetrate. We have been swayed by the power of this seductive technology but have little knowledge of how it developed or why. Yet it is this history that makes us aware of both the limits and potential of GIS and other geospatial technologies for the humanities.

GIS emerged in the early 1960s as mapping-cum-analysis software. It sprang independently from both the Harvard Laboratory for Computer Graphics, which aimed to produce automated cartography, and the Canadian GIS, which developed computerized methods to map the land capability of Canada.[9] Its intellectual and methodological lineage is much longer than this recent past. The logical overlay technique, a key feature of GIS, existed as early as the eleventh century, and the nineteenth-century London physician John Snow famously used spatial techniques common to GIS to trace the source of cholera in a poor neighbourhood to a contaminated water pump.[10] What was new were powerful computers and an emergent demand from such widely distributed fields as environmental science, landscape architecture, and urban planning that prized its ability to overlay data on a map of the earth's surface. With the creation of ArcInfo®, the leading commercial package, in the 1980s, GIS quickly moved into the mainstream of computing applications and spawned a wide array of location-based services.[11]

For many historians, however, GIS was simply another software package, with little application to the cultural and social problems that attracted their attention. Perhaps surprisingly, even geographers found themselves divided over its value. GIS became the focus of quantitative geographers who saw its potential to solve spatial problems. The technology's capacity for managing large datasets and visualizing the results of spatial analysis was especially important to them: making data visual spurred intuitive interpretation – recognition of patterns, for instance – that remained hidden in statistical analyses. Human geographers, on the other hand, were unconvinced. As late as 1988 the president of the American Association of Geographers felt comfortable labelling GIS as 'a mere technique'. Tension existed between scholars who viewed the technology as the herald of a shift in scientific methodology and those who saw it as a vehicle for extending existing geographic concepts.[12]

The divide ran along a fault line increasingly known as Geographic Information Science, a critique that GIS, although well equipped to manage quantitative spatial data, rested on a positivist and naive empiricism and was incapable of knowledge production. Representing this view was *Ground Truth* (1995), a collection of essays edited by John Pickles, a prominent critic of GIS. Collectively, the essayists expressed several concerns that echoed postmodern thought: technological design inevitably favours certain conceptualizations of the world; GIS was a corporate product, designed to solve corporate problems, such as route logistics or market analysis; GIS employs a limited linear logic that is not adequate for understanding societal complexity, and as a consequence, it represents and perpetuates a particular view of political, economic, and social power.[13]

At its heart, the debate between advocates and opponents of GIS rested on epistemological and ontological differences that have implications for the construction of the spatial humanities.[14] In what became known as Critical GIS, scholars leery of the technology argued that it rested on a positivist epistemology that assumed an objective reality discoverable through scientific observation, measurement, and replication. But society and culture cannot be measured with such precision, these critics argued. Even calculations of the material world depended upon cultural assumptions; not every society accepted or used the precepts of Euclidian geometry. Also, GIS was a computing technology; it ingested quantitative data and parsed it with mathematical algorithms. Its operations could not accept uncertainty or fuzziness. It relied as well upon administrative data, or official representations of the world, a result that was highly problematic because this view reflected the influence of money and power. For purposes of economic development, for instance, local government could draw neighbourhood boundaries that bore little resemblance to the community identified by residents. Finally, its use of geometric space and Boolean logic – every position had to be known precisely and every element has only two values (yes or no, true or false, 0 or 1) – ruled out the possibility of alternate views of the world.[15]

In fact, critics claimed, evidence about the world depends upon the perspective of the observer, a distinction that GIS obscures. Two people who view the same object may interpret it quite differently because of their different assumptions and experiences. Consider: tribal societies in arid environments, such as the Navajo in the American southwest or the Yindjibarndi in Australia, have different conceptions of a river than people from wet regions; instead of a feature fundamentally composed of water but dry on occasion, these tribes view it as a dry course that sometimes contains water. Defenders of GIS responded that this difference does not matter because, regardless of name, the object remains the same. This position epistemologically is realism. It assumes that objects exist independently of the observer: the nouns creek, stream, and brook may tell us something about the observer but they still refer to the same thing – and we can use formal rules to parse when different words refer to the same object. But for critics of GIS, these epistemological and ontological differences were profound and raised serious doubt about the technology's usefulness outside of limited areas, such as transportation planning and route analysis.

The early part of the twenty-first century witnessed a slackening of the debate within geography as the two camps joined under the banner of GIS and Society in an effort to confront the issues raised by Critical GIS. This rapprochement has led to a common acknowledgement of problems in the way GIS represents the world. GIS delineates space as a set of coordinates with characteristics or attributes attached to an identified location, a cartographic concept, rather than as relational space that maps interdependencies linked to the location, a social concept. It also favours institutional or official databases as the primary source of information about the world. Both tendencies exclude non-Western conceptions of the world. American Indians, for example, defined the world as a set of interlinked phenomena, only some of which can be defined as geographic space.[16] Or, it is easier to understand ancient China dynasties when we see their definition of space as networks of places and actors rather than as prescribed jurisdictions with formal boundaries.[17] GIS currently has difficulty managing these different meanings of space. It remains, at heart, a tool for quantitative data, the type of evidence that admits at some level to a degree of measurement that can be replicated and verified. The precision that is necessary for statistical work does not admit readily the sort of evidence used by most humanists, and when it does, the result, usually in the form of maps, can be highly misleading, implying a certainty that the underlying data do not permit.

While geographers grappled with the theoretical and social implications of GIS, humanists were (re)discovering space, yet the two groups took divergent paths with only occasional intersections. Although the Annales School, most notably Fernand Braudel, its chief practitioner, had urged scholars since the 1930s to pay attention to *geohistoire*, the linkage of geography and history, most humanists paid much less attention to the environmental context for human behaviour and much more to the actions, associations, and attitudes that made a space particular, in short, a place. These places could even exist in imagined space or in memory. They also could be personal – emotional space or the body in space – and even metaphorical or fictional, a woman's place, for example, as in Virginia Woolf's story, *A Room of One's Own*. The spaces of interest to humanists bore little relationship to GIS, with its emphasis on physical or geographical space. Only in two areas of the humanities – archaeology and history – did scholars begin to apply the new spatial technology and, in the process, discover its potential and limits for their work.

Archaeologists came early to GIS, as well as to other spatial instruments such as Global Positioning Systems (GPS), in large measure because it provided a handy and more accurate tool kit for managing their research in familiar but speedier ways. Maps of uncovered human habitats were easier to chart with the survey-based techniques of GIS. Artefacts bore a spatial relationship that was important in interpreting the past, and it was the ability of GIS to visualize a spatially accurate physical and man-made environment quickly and with great ease that proved the attraction. Mapping a lost landscape, reconstructing historical view sheds, and traversing a highly detailed built environment were not new to the archaeologists' tool kit but the computing power brought by GIS was. The technology facilitated existing techniques.[18]

Historians also began to drift toward GIS, although more slowly than archaeologists. Early efforts centred on what came to be known as spatial infrastructure, that is, the development of large spatially enabled historical datasets, such as censuses, for use within a GIS. This development paralleled an emphasis in the nascent digital humanities on cyberinfrastructure (US) or e-Science (UK), which focused much of its energy on digitizing scholarly materials and the tools to use them. Within the spatial realm, national historical GIS projects emerged in Great Britain, Germany, the United States, China, and Russia, among others. None of these projects were inclusive of all historical periods, and many of them focused more on creating framework data for other scholars than on addressing research problems.

In practice, environmental specialists were among the first historians to use GIS by constructing a data landscape to tell a more complicated story than traditional methods allowed. Other historians took advantage of GIS to relate data of different formats based on their common location, at times using the internet to bring spatial and archival evidence together and allow readers to explore the evidence afresh, such as in the *Valley of the Shadow Project* or the *Salem Witchcraft Project*, both products of the University of Virginia digital humanities lab.[19] In most of these expressions, however, GIS was part of what might otherwise be called digital history rather than spatial history because the approach was fundamentally archival and textual rather than driven by questions about space or even by geographical information.

By the early twenty-first century, a distinct sub-field known as historical GIS and an associated literature was visible within the discipline. A minor flood of works included a practice guide (2003), two collections of essays, and, in 2007, Ian Gregory and Paul Ells' *Historical GIS*, the first book by a major university press on historical GIS as a distinct approach to scholarship.[20] Major conferences on the use of GIS in the humanities began to appear; a gathering at the University of Essex in 2008 had presentations on such topics as GIS and biblical research, the spread of disease in nineteenth-century Kyoto, and the financial geography of the US oil industry during the American Civil War, among dozens of other equally diverse subjects. Scholarly networks dedicated to historical GIS appeared in Europe and the United States, and funding agencies across the world financed important GIS projects in heritage and culture.[21] In 2010, the first book series appeared, but with a new emphasis: the inaugural title, *The Spatial Humanities*, which mimicked the series name, argued for a broader focus than GIS and history to include all humanities disciplines and for a wide range of geospatial technologies tailored to the needs of humanists.[22]

Anne Knowles, an early American advocate, has defined historical GIS as having the 'elements of *geohistoire*, historical geography, and spatial and digital history' and identified more by its characteristics than any theoretical approach or body of scholarship. Among these characteristics are the dominance of geographical questions and geographical information in framing inquiries, usually fashioned as patterns of change over time, and the use of maps to present its results.[23] But even though it is gaining use, most historians – indeed, most humanists – have not adopted GIS or, more fundamentally, found it helpful. What remains puzzling to its practitioners is why the technology is not finding its way into the tool kit of these scholars. After all, human activity is about time and space, and GIS provides a way to manage, relate, and query events, as well as to visualize them, that should be attractive to researchers.

Significantly, the standard characterizations of historical GIS suggest its limits, at least as currently practised. GIS fundamentally is about what happens in geographic space. It relies heavily on quantitative information for its representations and analyses and views its results as geographical maps. There is no question that this calculus is valid and valuable, and it forces attention to important considerations, such as scale and proximity, that too often are absent from humanities scholarship. But historians are drawn to questions and evidence that cannot be reduced easily to zeroes and ones. A mismatch exists, in short, between the positivist epistemology of GIS and the reflexive and recursive approaches favoured by historians who wrestle continually with ambiguous, uncertain, and imprecise evidence and who seek multivalent answers to their questions. The problem, it seems, is both foundational and technological: we do not yet have a well-articulated theory for the spatial humanities, nor do we have the tools sufficient to meet the needs of historians.

Yet the promise of GIS is so powerful – and the technology is becoming so ubiquitous – that we are loath to abandon it too soon. Perhaps we have been asking the wrong question. Instead of musing about how we can get historians to adopt GIS, it would be more fruitful to discover how to make GIS their helpmeet. Much of the work being done now fits neatly into what GIS was created to do. The real question is how do we as historians make GIS do what it was not intended to do, namely, represent the world as culture and not simply mapped locations? Achieving this goal requires us to re-conceptualize historical GIS as the spatial humanities, a term that captures a potentially rich interplay between Critical GIS, spatial science, spatial systems, and the panoply of highly nuanced humanist traditions, including history. The focus, in other words, must not be on accommodating our questions to a tool that does not fit our needs, but rather on how we can bend the tools to our need to explore space, time, and place creatively and constructively.

Addressing this need is at the heart of much current work in the spatial humanities and in spatial history, with the focus on four interrelated areas of research and development. First, researchers are exploring the epistemological frameworks of the humanities and GISci for the purpose of locating common ground on which the two can cooperate. This step is often overlooked in the rush to apply new technologies but it is the essential point of departure for any effort to bridge them. The aim is to expose humanities scholars to the breadth of geospatial technologies and subsequently for the technology itself to be interrogated as to its adaptability. Although epistemologically branded, geospatial technologies still offer potential for the humanities; they are more supple than their critics suggest. What is necessary is an appropriate intellectual grounding that will enable skilled historians and other humanities scholars to draw the technology further out of its positivistic homeland.[24]

The challenge is how to realize the promise of hybridity between humanistic critical discourses and the theoretical perspectives of Critical GIS. Humanists can give more thoughtful consideration to location and spatial relationality, and can take leads from visualizations of data such as self-organizing maps and Virtual GIS, which can capture complex data at the same time that they indicate relativity and ambiguity. The payoff for collaboration will be a historical scholarship that integrates insights gleaned from spatial information science and spatial theory into scaled narratives about human lives and culture. Such rewards are glimpsed, for example, in Mei-Po Kwan's and Guoxiang Ding's analysis of 'geo-narratives', assembled from oral history sources and a blend of other qualitative and quantitative data as a way to understand the lives of Muslim women in Columbus, Ohio after 9/11.[25]

Historians work largely with texts, and the majority of those texts take the form of language, alongside material artefacts, behavioural enactments, art, and the like. A key part of the challenge of thinking spatially and leveraging spatial technology is to design and frame narratives about individual and collective human experience that are spatially contextualized. At one level, the task involves reciprocal transformations from text to map and map to text.[26] More importantly, the humanities and social sciences must position themselves to exploit the Geospatial Semantic Web, which in its extraordinary complexity and massive volume, offers a rich data bed and functional platform to researchers to effectively mine it, organize the harvested data, and contextualize it within the spaces of culture.[27] The agenda here is to advance textual analysis that understands the bi-locality of text in both metaphorical space and geographic space. The payoff is potentially rich and extends the significant work on narrative topographies and novel mappings already underway in literary and cultural studies.[28]

An emphasis on absolute space based on Euclidean coordinate systems often frustrates the historian's effort to understand how spaces change over time, and how spatial relativities emerge and develop. There is an urgent need for the development, within GIS specifically and spatial technologies more generally, of spatio-temporal tools that will enable humanities scholars, social scientists, geographers, and others to incorporate time into analyses that are spatially contextualized. The increasing use of GIS by historians suggests that the historical interests in cause and effect, the development and alteration of networks, and the temporal patterning of events is served at least to some extent by current technologies. The fit is awkward because the technology treats time as categorical and discontinuous and defaults to a model that strings together spatio-temporal snapshots that approximate story-as-collage.[29] But, as sociologist Andrew Abbott reminds us, time is in fact a 'series of overlapping presents of various sizes, each organized around a particular location, and overlapping across the whole social process'.[30] The importance of narrative within history and the other humanities can stimulate the development of better spatial tools that incorporate time as well, just as spatial thinking and tools can encourage richer considerations of spatial relationships in narrative time.

Central to the emergence of the spatial humanities is a trust that the contingent, unpredictable, and ironic in history and culture can be embodied within a narrative context that incorporates space alongside of time. For the humanities it is above all the thick weave of events, locations, behaviours, and motivations that makes human experience of space into place. Place is the product of 'deep contingency' and of the human effort to render that experience meaningful in language, art, ritual, and in other ways.[31] Place is constructed out of the imagination as much as through what is visible and tangible in experience. Humanists, social scientists, and geographers, and all who are interested in seeing a spatial humanities mature, must build increasingly more complex maps of the personalities, emotions, values, and poetics, the visible and invisible aspects of a place. The spatial considerations remain the same, which is to say that geographic location, boundary, and landscape remain crucial, whether we are investigating a continental landmass or a community. What is added is a reflexivity that acknowledges how we create spatially framed identities and aspirations out of imagination and memory and how our multiple perspectives constitute a spatial narrative that complements the verbal narrative traditionally employed by humanists.

Here is where the concept of a deep map becomes important. An avant-garde technique first urged by the Situationists International in 1950s France, the approach 'attempts to record and represent the grain and patina of place through juxtapositions and interpenetrations of the historical and the contemporary, the political and the poetic, the discursive and the sensual.'[32] Its best form results in a subtle and multilayered view of a small area of the earth. As a new creative space, deep maps have several qualities well suited to a fresh conceptualization of GIS and other spatial technologies as they are applied to the humanities. They are meant to be visual, time-based, and structurally open. They are genuinely multi-media and multi-layered. They do not seek authority or objectivity but involve negotiation between insiders and outsiders, experts and contributors, over what is represented and how. Framed as a conversation and not a statement, deep maps are inherently unstable, continually unfolding and changing in response to new data, new perspectives, and new insights.

The analogue between a deep map and advanced spatial technologies seems evident. Geographic information systems operate as a series of layers, each representing a different theme and tied to a specific location on planet earth. These layers are transparent, although the user can make any layer or combination of layers opaque while leaving others visible. A deep map of heritage and culture, centred on memory and place, ideally would work in a similar fashion. The layers of a deep map need not be restricted to a known or discoverable documentary record but could be opened, wiki-like, to anyone with a memory or artefact to contribute. However structured, these layers would operate as do other layers within a GIS, viewed individually or collectively as a whole or within groups, but all tied to time and space that provide perspectives on the places that interest us. It is an open, visual, and experiential space, immersing users in a virtual world in which uncertainty, ambiguity, and contingency are ever-present but all are capable of being braided into a narrative that reveals the ways in which space and time influences and is influenced by social interaction. The deep map is one in which both horizontal and vertical movement is possible, with the horizontal providing the linear progression we associate with rational argument and vertical movement providing the depth, texture, tension, and resonance of experience.[33]

The coalescence of digital technologies over the past decade, especially seen in the tool kit of Web 2.0, makes it possible to envision how geospatial technologies might contribute to the formation of a deep map, just as the various theories about spatial narratives offer guidance on the structure they may take.[34] Archaeologists have used GIS and computer animations to reconstruct the Roman Forum, for example, creating a 3-D world that allows users to walk through buildings that no longer exist, except as ruins. We can experience these spaces at various times of the day and seasons of the year. We see more clearly a structure's mass and how it clustered with other forms to mould a dense urban space. In this virtual environment we gain an immediate, intuitive feel for proximity and power. This constructed memory of a lost space helps us recapture a sense of place that informs and enriches our understanding of lost places, such as ancient Rome (*Digital Roman Forum Project*).[35] In similar fashion, historians and material culturists have joined with archaeologists to fashion *Virtual Jamestown*.[36] This project, in turn, is a seed-bed for an even more ambitious attempt to push the technology toward the humanities by placing Jamestown at one vertex of Atlantic World encounters. Its goal is to repopulate a virtual world with the sense of possibilities embedded in the past, what Paul Carter has called 'intentional history'.[37] Viewed within the spatial context for their actions, which includes the presence of proximate cultures, whether indigenous tribes, Spanish,

Africans or Dutch, we then can understand better how contingencies became lost as they butted against the encountered realities within the space the English claimed in 1607. Another innovative effort, *HyperCities*, a GIS-based website, allows scholars to explore cities across time, using period maps overlaid on contemporary landscapes, viewing virtual buildings within their real-world context, and linking images and text to the locations they describe.[38]

A paradigm project underway at West Virginia University aims to go even further by combining immersive technologies with GIS to re-create a sense of nineteenth-century Morgantown. Working from digitized Sanborn maps and extant photographs of buildings and streets, users enter a CAVE, a projection-based virtual reality system, and find themselves in another time and place, with the ability to navigate through an environment of which they now are a part. Soon they will be able to enter and explore a building, moving from room to room and examining the material objects within it. By adding sounds, smells, and touch, all within the capability of existing technology, this virtual reconstruction would engage four primary senses, making the experience even more real for participants.[39] Once expensive, the costs of immersive environments are dropping rapidly, but, in fact, a CAVE is not essential for making an immersive environment open to humanists. As any parent of school-age children knows – or as any devotee of *Second Life* can testify – gaming technology already allows us to explore virtual worlds with a high degree both of verisimilitude and agency.

As these examples suggest, GIS is merging with other Web 2.0 technologies – for example, mash-ups, virtual research environments, augmented reality, among others – to move us beyond a map of geographical space into a richer, more evocative world of imagery based on history and memory. Over the past few years, GIS scientists have made advances in spatial multimedia, in GIS-enabled web services, geo-visualization, cyber geography, and virtual reality that provide capabilities far exceeding the abilities of GIS on its own. This convergence of technologies has the potential to revolutionize the role of space and place in the humanities by allowing us to move far beyond the static map, to shift from two dimensions to multidimensional representations, to develop interactive systems, and to explore space and place dynamically – in effect, to create virtual worlds embodying what we know about space and place.[40]

The use of appropriately cast spatial technologies within history and the humanities – in sum, the spatial humanities – promises to develop a unique postmodern scholarship, one that accommodates the contingent, fluid, and ambiguous nature of human beliefs and actions. The goal is not to sacrifice the rational, logical, and empirical approach to knowledge that has been the hallmark of the humanities since the Enlightenment, but rather to complement it with different ways of discovery. Geospatial technologies have such potential. They offer powerful platforms for interdisciplinary work, especially in its capacity to integrate information by location and to visualize the results for analysis and interpretation.

Ultimately the requirements for spatial humanities and for spatial history go well beyond technology, no matter how much it may enable our work. It also is about spatial thinking and infusing our work with complex spatial awareness. We must learn again how to think spatially and how to use spatial analysis to inform our research. Location is more than mere subtext, a geographic platform for events; it is the primary context for the events themselves. Geographical space, combined with time, becomes place, an analytical category that provides the context for our understanding of history and culture. As historians, we must learn to read and interpret this context with as much subtlety and sophistication as we do the time-centred rubric of cause and effect. Just as we fuse time and space seamlessly in the way we recount the stories of our personal lives, we also must bring these themes together once more in our historical and cultural narratives.

Ultimately these new geospatial technologies, linked to Web 2.0 (and, soon, Web 3.0) tools and methods and informed by critical spatial thinking, have the potential to revolutionize the role of place in history and the humanities by moving beyond the two-dimensional map to explore dynamic representations and interactive systems that will prompt an experiential, as well as rational, knowledge base. The notion of a richer, dynamic, and experiential GIS resonates with the evocative and thick descriptions of place and time that humanists have long favoured in their scholarship. The goal of this exploration is not to model or replicate the past but to complicate it. Questions drive historical scholarship, not hypotheses, and the questions that matter most address causation: why matters more than whom, what, or when, even though these latter questions are neither trivial nor easy to answer. The research goal is not to eliminate explanations or to disprove the hypothesis but to open the inquiry through whatever means are available and by whatever evidence may be found. Our approach is recursive, not linear: our goal is not so much to eliminate answers as to admit new perspectives. Such an approach to problems doubtless appears quixotic to non-humanists because it does not lead to finality. But for humanists, the goal is not proof but meaning. The challenge, then, for the spatial humanities is to use technology to probe, explore, challenge, and complicate, in sum, to allow us to see, experience, and understand human behaviour in all its complexity. As in traditional historical scholarship, the aim is less to produce an authoritative or ultimate answer than to prompt new questions, develop new perspectives, and advance new arguments or interpretations.

A spatial perspective and the use of spatial technologies, properly applied to the problems of history and the humanities, will satisfy this goal in ways that shift our ways of knowing from reason and logic alone to a more experiential understanding of the human condition as it differs from place to place. This perspective will be aided technically not through the use of GIS alone, which is a weak reed on which to base this shift, but rather through the continuing rapid convergence of technologies, operating in such a fashion as to blend space and time. In this view, space becomes an equal partner with time in providing the conceptual framework for the spatial humanities, which seeks above all to understand society and culture, past and present, in all their glorious complexities.

Notes

1 E. Soja, 'In different spaces: interpreting the spatial organization of societies', in *Proceedings*, 3rd International Space Syntax Symposium (Atlanta, 2001), http://www.centrostudiurbani.it/aree/citta/doc/SojaE.pdf [accessed: 25 March 2012].

2 Postmodernism's progenitors go well back to the first part of the twentieth century, for example, Dadaist efforts to destroy the categories of high and low culture, Heidegger's rejection of notions of objectivity and subjectivity, and existentialism's doubt, ambiguity, and uncertainty, among many others. For a brief critical overview, see C. Butler, *Postmodernism: A Very Short Introduction* (New York: Oxford University Press, 2003).

3 D. Livingston, 'Science, region, and religion: the reception of Darwin in Princeton, Belfast, & Edinburgh', in R. Numbers and J. Stenhouse (eds) *Disseminating Darwinism: The Role of Place, Race, Religion, and Gender* (Cambridge: Cambridge University Press, 2001), p. 7.

4 Denis Cosgrove discusses this spatial turn specifically in relation to landscapes, real and figurative, in 'Landscape and landschaft', *GHI Bulletin*, 35, Autumn (2004), 57–71. Also see K. Olwig, *Landscape, Nature and the Body Politic: From Britain's Renaissance to America's New World* (Madison: University of Wisconsin Press, 2002).

5 A. Giddens, *The Constitution of Society: Outline of the Theory of Structuation* (Oxford: Oxford University Press, 1984), p. 364.

6 Yi-Fu Tuan discusses the emotional and perceptual meanings of space in several books, including *Space and Place: The Perspective of Experience* (Minneapolis: University of Minnesota Press, 1977); *Place, Art, and Self* (Santa Fe: Center for American Places, 2004); and *Landscapes of Fear* (New York: Pantheon Books, 1979). A leading practitioner of the idea of gendered and racialized spaces is D. Massey, *Space, Place, and Gender* (Minneapolis, University of Minnesota Press, 1994), pp. 1–24.

7 For an excellent introduction to the technology and its epistemological underpinnings, see N. Schuurman, *GIS: A Short Introduction* (Oxford: Blackwell Publishing, 2004).

8 In the United States, a sizeable number of cities are using GIS to structure a wide array of information about the various jurisdictions (e.g. neighbourhoods, school districts, postal code areas, etc.) within their metropolitan areas for purposes of planning, service delivery, and public participation. For an example, see D. Bodenhamer, J. Colbert, K. Comer and S. Kandris, 'Developing and sustaining a community information system for Central Indiana: SAVI as a case study', in M. Sirgy, R. Phillips and D. Rahtz (eds) *Community Quality-of-Life Indicators: Best Cases V* (New York: Springer, 2011), pp. 21–46, which describes the nationally-leading community information system for the Indianapolis (Indiana) Metropolitan Statistical Area, an eleven-county region of 1.8 million people.

9 J. Coppock and D. Rhind, 'The history of GIS', in D. Maguire, M. Goodchild and D. Rhind (eds) *Geographical Information Systems: Principles and Applications. Volume I: Principles* (London: Longman Scientific and Technical, 1991), pp. 21–43.

10 S. Johnson, *The Ghost Map: The Story of London's Most Terrifying Epidemic – and How It Changed Science, Cities, and the Modern World* (New York: Riverhead Books, 2006).

11 T. Foresman, 'GIS early years and the threads of evolution', in T. Foresman (ed.) *The History of Geographic Information Systems: Perspectives from the Pioneers* (Upper Saddle River: Prentice Hall PTR, 1998), pp. 3–17.

12 N. Schuurman, 'Trouble in the heartland: GIS and its critics in the 1990s', *Progress in Human Geography*, 24: 4 (2000), 569–90.

13 J. Pickles (ed.), *Ground Truth: The Social Implications of Geographic Information Systems* (New York: The Guilford Press, 1995).

14 N. Schuurman, *GIS: A Short Introduction*, pp. 21–52.

15 E. Sheppard, 'Knowledge production through critical GIS: genealogy and prospects', *Cartographica*, 40: 4 (2005), 5–21.

16 R. Rundstrom, 'GIS, indigenous peoples, and epistemological diversity', *Cartography and Geographic Information Systems*, 22: 1 (1995), 45–57.

17 M. Berman, 'Boundaries or networks in historical GIS: concepts of measuring space and administrative boundaries in Chinese history', *Historical Geography*, 33 (2005), 118–33.

18 A good introduction, though now dated, is G. Lock (ed.), *Beyond the Map: Archaeology and Spatial Technologies* (Amsterdam: IOS Press, 2000).

19 *Valley of the Shadow: Two Communities in the American Civil War*, http://valley.lib.virginia.edu/; *Salem Witch Trials Documentary Archive and Transcription Project*, http://etext.virginia.edu/salem/witchcraft/ [both websites last accessed on 10 July 2011].

20 I. Gregory and P. Ell, *Historical GIS: Technologies, Methodologies and Scholarship* (Cambridge: Cambridge University Press, 2007), pp. 15–18.

21 For a survey of European activity in historical GIS, see I. Gregory, A. Kunz and D. Bodenhamer, 'A place in Europe: enhancing European collaboration in historical GIS', *International Journal of Humanities and Arts Computing*, 5: 1 (2011), 23–40. An important US initiative is the Stanford (University) Spatial History Project, funded by the Andrew Mellon Foundation, http://www.stanford.edu/group/spatialhistory/cgi-bin/site/index.php [accessed: 25 March 2012].

22 D. Bodenhamer, J. Corrigan and T. Harris (eds), *The Spatial Humanities: GIS and the Future of Humanities Scholarship* (Bloomington: Indiana University Press, 2010). The three scholars also serve as general editors of the series and formed as well the Virtual Center for Spatial Humanities to promote a broader focus.

23 A. Knowles, 'GIS and history', in A. Knowles (ed.) *Mapping the Past: How Maps, Spatial Data, and GIS Are Changing Historical Scholarship* (Redlands: ESRI Press, 2008), pp. 7–8.

24 A good introduction to the epistemological challenges is found in P. Ethington, 'Placing the past: groundwork for a spatial theory of history', *Rethinking History*, 11: 4 (2007), 465–93.

25 M. Kwan and G. Ding, 'Geo-narrative: extending information systems for narrative analysis in qualitative and mixed-method research', *The Professional Geographer*, 60: 4 (2008), 443–65.

26 See, for instance, M. Yuan, 'Mapping text', in D. Bodenhamer et al. *The Spatial Humanities*, pp. 109–23.

27 T. Harris, L. Rouse and S. Bergeron, 'The geospatial semantic web, Pareto GIS, and the humanities', in D. Bodenhamer et al. *The Spatial Humanities*, pp. 124–42. Also see A. Scharl and K. Tochtermann (eds), *The Geospatial Web: How Geobrowsers, Social Software and the Web 2.0 are Shaping the Network Society* (London: Springer, 2007), pp. 153–58; 'The spatial web: an Open GIS Consortium (OGC) White Paper', http://www.openGIS.org [accessed: 25 March 2012]; D. Butler, 'Virtual globes: the web-wide world,' *Nature*, 439 (2006), 776–78; M. Egenhofer, 'Toward the semantic geospatial web', GIS 2002 (ACM).

28 On 16 June (Bloomsday), 2008, Google unveiled an interactive map that allowed users to trace Leopold Bloom's wanderings around 1904 Dublin, with accompanying images and text, http://googlemapsmania.blogspot.com/2008/06/happy-bloomsday-on-google-maps.html [accessed: 25 March 2012]. Other examples include film studies and performance culture, as evidenced by P. Valiaho, *Mapping the Moving Image: Gesture, Thought and Cinema circa 1900* (Amsterdam: Amsterdam University Press, 2010), and literary and cultural studies, as in the pioneering work by F. Moretti, *Atlas of the European Novel, 1800–1900* (London: Verso, 1998). For the difficulties of

literary mapping, see B. Piatti, H. Bär, A. Reuschel, L. Hurni and W. Cartwright, 'Mapping literature: towards a geography of fiction', http://www.literaturatlas.eu/downloads/vienna_piatti-mapping_literature.pdf [accessed: 25 March 2012].

29 D. Peuquet, *Representations of Space and Time* (New York: The Guilford Press, 2002), pp. 12–15; D. Massey, 'Space-time, "science", and the relationship between physical and human geography', *Transactions of the British Geographical Society*, 24 (1999), 261–76; I. Gregory, 'Exploiting time and space: a challenge for GIS in the digital humanities', in D. Bodenhamer et al. *The Spatial Humanities*, pp. 58–75.

30 A. Abbott, *Time Matters: On Theory and Method* (Chicago: University of Chicago Press, 2001), p. 296. Also see E. Ayers, 'Mapping time', in M. Dear, J. Ketchum, S. Luria and D. Richardson (eds) *Geo-Humanities: Art, History, Text at the Edge of Place* (London: Routledge), pp. 215–25.

31 E. Ayers, 'Turning toward places, and time', in Bodenhamer et al. *The Spatial Humanities*, pp. 1–13.

32 M. Pearson and M. Shanks, *Theatre/Archaeology* (London: Routledge, 2001), pp. 64–65.

33 D. Bodenhamer, 'Creating a landscape of memory', *International Journal of Humanities and Arts Computing*, 1: 2 (2008), 97–110.

34 For an overview of the profound changes made possible by Web 2.0 technologies, see C. Leadbetter, *We Think: Mass Innovation, Not Mass Production* (London: Profile Books, 2008). Newcastle University Library has developed a useful online guide to Web 2.0 tools for humanities researchers, http://www.netvibes.com/nulibartsweb2#Welcome [accessed: 25 March 2012].

35 See http://dlib.etc.ucla.edu/projects/Forum/ [accessed: 25 March 2012].

36 See http://www.virtualjamestown.org [accessed: 25 March 2012].

37 P. Carter, *The Road to Botany Bay* (London: Faber and Faber, 1987), p. 3.

38 See http://www.HyperCities.com/ [accessed: 25 March 2012].

39 'Immersive visualization system promotes sense of being there', *ArcNews Online*, Winter (2006–7), http://www.esri.com/news/arcnews/winter0607articles/immersive-visualization. html [accessed: 25 March 2012]. T. Harris, S. Bergeron and L. Rouse, 'Humanities GIS: place, spatial storytelling and immersive visualization in the humanities', in M. Dear et al. *GeoHumanities*, pp. 226–40.

40 M. Dodge, R. Kitchin and C. Perkins (eds), *Rethinking Maps: New Frontiers in Cartographic Theory* (London: Routledge, 2009).

2 The making of history
Remediating historicized experience

Luke Tredinnick

What does the past look like through the lens of digital culture? This chapter recounts three moments during the last one hundred years that touch on the nature of historical consciousness: a theft, a death, and a disaster. These moments span a century of unprecedented change in media and communications technologies, from the beginnings of popular photography to the proliferation of social media. Nevertheless each was incidental to these changes. Nor are they related, other than being brought together here. Each stands in this chapter as only an illustration of the influence of technology on how we understand the past. Today, digital information technologies have helped open up history, exposing the mechanisms of its fabrication, and placing the historical past in the hands of the masses. By pluralizing access to primary historical materials, and to the means of making future historical records, they emphasize the highly partial and situated nature of the historical trace. Digital technologies also enable us to represent historical subject matter in new ways, through film, video games, and digital imaging. But in addition to the changing the craft of history, and the possibilities of historical representation, the proliferation of digital technologies may also help us recognize the historical past as a product of mediation. They may help us recognize historical subjectivity in the making of history.

In August 1911, Vincecenzo Peruggia emerged from a side entrance of the Musée du Louvre concealing a modest wooden panel beneath his clothes, and disappeared into the Paris crowds. While notable, the painting he spirited away was not yet the most famous object in the Louvre's collection. Indeed, its absence remained unnoticed until the next day. Nevertheless the theft of the *Mona Lisa* quickly became one of the most notorious crimes of the age. Even as Peruggia concealed the work behind the false bottom of a wooden trunk in his lodgings, the news had spread far and wide via newspapers, and the new media of the newsreel. Within weeks the event had captured the attention of a worldwide public. In Paris, crowds flocked to the scene of the crime. But the absence of the *Mona Lisa* from the Louvre collection did more than just excite the popular interest; in the wake of the crime the painting quickly became one of the most reproduced images in the world, more a symbol of the idea of art, than an artwork in its own right. The theft established a curious interaction between the artefact, and its innumerable copies; even Peruggia displayed postcard reproductions on his mantelpiece as he kept the original hidden out of sight. When the *Mona Lisa* was later recovered, its cultural significance had been entirely transformed.[1]

Almost exactly eighty-six years later in a nondescript road tunnel a little less than three kilometres from the Louvre, a paparazzi photographer captured one final image of 'the most photographed woman in the world.'[2] The image became notorious, not only because it recorded the drab circumstances of the death of Diana, Princess of Wales, slumped in the back seat of a crumpled black Mercedes, but because it appeared complicit in her death. Pursued by photographers from the Ritz, the accident in the tunnel seemed to be the inevitable consequence of a life lived through a camera lens. The connection was made explicit by Earl Spencer who stated that whilst 'I always believed the press would kill her in the end [...] not even I could imagine they would take such a direct hand in her death.'[3] In his eulogy he added that 'a girl given the name of an ancient goddess of hunting was the most hunted person of the modern age.'[4] Eight years later the photograph of Diana's final moments was published in an Italian magazine; the editor described it in fairytale terms picturing 'a sleeping princess.'[5] The publication was widely condemned; but the photograph itself was incidental to the legacy of Diana, and the way in which that legacy has been perpetuated and maintained. The world's most photographed woman has become more famous in her death, the subject of conspiracy theories, legal actions, and continued media attention, and a site of contested representation. The absence of the princess, like the absence of the smiling subject of Da Vinci's painting, only created an increased resonance to her image.

Today, there is another absence that haunts the public consciousness: a gap at the skyline of Lower Manhattan where once stood what were briefly the world's tallest man-made structures. When two Boeing 767 airliners ploughed into the buildings, at 8.46 and 9.03 on the morning of 11 September 2001, the world watched the events unfold in real-time. Within six and a half minutes, ABC News interrupted a commercial break to bring live coverage of the event.[6] That coverage included a video feed from a fixed camera position north of the tower, and a little while later from a second camera position across the East River in Brooklyn Heights.[7] The live video was rapidly supplemented by other news networks and news organizations, and the images were syndicated around the world. No other event of this kind was subject to such intense live coverage. As a consequence, its historical significance was immediately apparent. The concentration of media organizations in New York meant the attacks on the World Trade Center overshadowed the other events of the day. However, ultimately, it was not the fixed camera positions of the news networks that told the story of that day; handheld cameras and recording devices filled in the missing details both outside and inside the towers. Personal testimony poured out from innumerable sources, reflecting the experiences of both those personally involved in the tragedy, and those watching live in other parts of the globe. This was the first event of its kind in the communication of which the emerging technological platform of the World Wide Web would play a significant role.

These three otherwise unrelated events each represents one instance in the making of history. They share a number of common factors: the power of visual culture in defining historical significance, the proliferation of images through media and social networks, the role of the public in framing their interpretation, and the desire to bear witness to an absent space. Taken together they demonstrate the increasing speed at which information travels across the globe, from weeks, to hours, to minutes in under one hundred years. But the sequence of these events also tells another story, not one of the development of media and its influence on how we frame the significance of contemporary events, but a story about the changing nature of history itself throughout the twentieth century. Advancements in media and communications technology have shifted the site of history's making, transforming the public from spectators of historic events to participants in historical dramas. These changes have collapsed the distinction between the present, and the truly historical, such that we begin to interpret, frame and understand events as already historicized at the very moment that we experience them. They have allowed anachronism to emerge as a productive source of historical understanding. And they have perhaps altered the nature of history, from something vested in the scholarly activities of an elite cultural group, to a living and mutable, political and personal part of the wider social matrix. To tell that story, we need to understand how technology has problemetized the status of historical research, and undermined the relationship between the ostensibly knowable past, and the discourse of history. This challenge to the discourse of history concerns not merely the power of the visual image, but also the function of the written word within historical research.

Since its emergence as a scholarly discourse, history has relied on a quiet complicity with the written word, an intimate relationship that reveals itself in two important ways.[8] On the one hand, historical research has traditionally relied on written records of various kinds as testimony to past events and dead experiences.[9] Writing became the valorized form of historical evidence out of which the truths of past experience would be conjured. On the other hand, historical scholarship is also a predominantly literary activity, centred on the production of written texts.[10] Despite the innumerable possibilities suggested by media and information technologies, history remains largely a matter of rewriting the already written traces of the past. This complicity between writing and history inevitably invests the written record with a particular significance in delimiting the kinds of historical accounts that become possible. Mayhew has noted, for example, that 'both the message it embodies and the medium through which that embodiment occurs are themselves historically contingent.'[11] Similarly, the polemical postmodern history theorist Keith Jenkins has described the already 'historicised' nature of the record, highlighting its 'highly volatile and mutable' nature, and its ideological saturation.[12] For Jenkins the processes by which experiences come to be committed to record and transmitted through time provide the missing context for the kinds of histories that it is possible to write. History he suggests is made and maintained in the archive, before it is uncovered by the historian.

This idea of the already historicized record is provocative for digital history because the nature of recorded information has been subject to such tremendous and rapid change. This has led many to question the future of historical scholarship, a lingering doubt encapsulated in a curious paradox. On the one hand, the volatile and ephemeral nature of much digital information seemingly threatens an emerging dark age, in which the material records of contemporary culture will be irrevocably lost.[13] Vincent, for example, suggests that 'we may be on the verge of a new prehistory' and argues that 'electronic communication means no history. The fashion for open access means no history. The mass production of evidence, and its mass destruction on an industrial scale, means no history.'[14] On the other hand, as the volume of recorded information continues to grow exponentially,[15] an increasingly complete, complex and diverse record of contemporary experience is being laid down moment by moment. Mayer-Schonberger has suggested we live in a culture of 'perfect memory';[16] he argues that 'forgetting has become the exception, and remembering the default.'[17] The proliferation of recorded information creates its own challenges for the 'craft' of history;[18] Ross, for example, worries that 'swamping future historians with vast amounts of digital information may impede their research.'[19] Too much information is as problematic as too little.

Caught between these competing nightmares,[20] history is confronted with a looming crisis of relevance and legitimacy. In one possible future modernity succumbs to its forgetful dotage; in another it is reborn into chaotic and impressionistic infancy. Neither scenario allows historical scholarship to continue unchanged.[21] The discourse of history arguably became possible in a culture poised between remembrance, and forgetfulness, a culture that in its modernity embraced the administrative rationality that made it possible to spin out narratives from the surviving historical traces, but where the work of representing the past was already largely done in constituting the archive. It is conceivable that the idea of history marks a passing stage in the evolution of modernity, a momentary spark of what Tosh calls *historical consciousness*[22] before the murky darkness closes in again. As modernity declines, so perhaps will its defining cultural marker: a reflexive engagement with an objectively knowable past.

This is generally the way in which the dilemma of digital history has been framed. Yet there is something naive about these accounts and their preoccupation with the problems of digital preservation. Information saturates every aspect of our lives. We are surrounded by the historical record, not the dry, dusty archive of the past, but a living history created in our everyday online interaction. The duplicability of digital information and the proliferation of copies through its cycle of use has meant that while the media of storage may be more volatile in the digital age, much information is persistent, outlasting the original contexts for which it was created. The digital documentary record will not be preserved in central repositories, but through our use and exchange of information and knowledge. The real digital archive is not concentrated in formal mechanisms for legal deposit and preservation, but saturates the entire social network. And the irony is that this kind of distributed storage of the future records of the past represents the most robust preservation strategy possible, relatively invulnerable to the kinds of threats with which centralized repositories are confronted.[23]

Missing in these anxieties about digital preservation is the potential of digital technologies to create new kinds of histories, and a new kind of relationship with the past. Technological innovation has augured what Henry Jenkins has described as 'participatory' culture, in which individuals more actively intervene in the structure and make-up of cultural discourse, fashioning the stuff of culture in more personal, fragmented, and playful ways.[24] History is clearly succumbing to this participatory mode. It is not merely that the opening up of primary source materials, from census data, to genealogical records, has enabled individuals to construct their own disintermediated relationship with the past. It is also that the proliferation of popular histories, and a popular engagement with the past across both new and traditional media, creates a fertile interaction of the scholarly history and mass culture which cannot leave either unchanged. And there is something else missing from the dilemma of digital history, a legacy of history's preoccupation with the written record. They do not account for the immediacy of the visual image in creating a direct connection with a historical past that is nevertheless always situated and consumed within the present. Digital technologies perhaps offer the opportunity to reconfigure the idea of history in more strikingly visual terms.

The writer who has most explicitly explored this terrain has been Jerome de Groot, who has argued that while 'historians have kept much of their traditional legitimacy' in the information age, that cultural role has nevertheless 'been eroded due to shifts in technology, theory and access.'[25] Groot chronicles the explosion of history as both leisure pursuit and popular discourse during recent decades, and suggests that history has become a popular epistemology, and 'increasingly prevalent as a cultural, social and economic trope and genre.'[26] He explores this explosion of popular history through film, television, and video games, and suggests these 'challenge professional historians as they present some-thing of a dissident history.'[27] There is much about this analysis that is highly persuasive, particularly the hybrid nature of popular histories, and the ways in which they are seemingly untroubled by elements of anachronism. However, de Groot is largely concerned only with the ways in which the past and historians are represented within popular culture; he does not interrogate the consequences of this for the epistemological and ontological status of the historical past in contemporary society.

Of equal interest perhaps is the making of histories in digitally mediated contexts; it is not merely that an objectively knowable past is repurposed for changing cultural contexts, but that different kinds of historical discourses are mobilized within a more participatory mode of cultural engagement. This chapter explores how digital technologies change the way we understand history as a collective means of organizing and explaining shared experiences. It explores how technologies have helped transform both the structures of historical consciousness and the function of history within culture. In the immediacy of digital culture, history perhaps regains part of its mythapoic function. But the story of digital history is not invested in the nature of the electronic archive; the emerging historical consciousness of the twenty-first century has developed slowly from the changing relationship between the record and the history. Long before the invention of the computer, a curious incident in central Paris sent ripples through the rest of the century, and began to problemetize history's assumption of a knowable past.

Every day during the tourist season a dense crowd of onlookers gathers inside the Louvre, bristling with cameras, camera stands, and video recorders. Their common aim is ostensibly to capture another photograph of what is already one of the most reproduced images in contemporary culture. Yet so many people press against the low balustrade surrounding the painting, that it is rarely possible to find an uninterrupted view. The fate of the *Mona Lisa* in an age of popular photography has been the subject of some considerable lament. Writing only a few years after its installation in a new home intended to improve the visitor experience, the *Guardian* art critic Jonathan Jones complained that already 'the world's most renowned painting had fallen among enemies.'[28] For Jones, 'the memory you take away is of a crowd behaving grotesquely [...] one camera flash after another blasts its ugly reflection on the glass protecting the painting.'[29] Subsequent blog contributors tell scores of similar stories. For some the intrusion of the digital camera is a discourtesy, for others cultural vandalism, and for yet others merely a reflection of the unmerited status of the painting.

The growth of photography as a leisure pursuit throughout the twentieth century inevitably changed the way individuals encountered the material world around them, including those surviving traces of the past collected in museums and galleries. In 1936 the German cultural critic Walter Benjamin argued that however faithful the copy, it can never capture the aura of the artwork, its total impression deriving from both its aesthetic qualities and its material history as a cultural object of value.[30] For Benjamin, 'the presence of the original is a prerequisite to the concept of authenticity.'[31] Mechanical reproduction divorced the material history of the work of art from the context of its apprehension. Photography therefore replaced the unique material artefact with the generic copy, and in the process robbed both of their authenticity, resulting in 'a tremendous shattering of tradition.'[32] The fate of the *Mona Lisa* today perhaps epitomizes these effects. Leader has observed that the painting 'has spawned an industry of copies, in the form of posters, brooches, mugs, T-shirts, cigarette cases, lighters, scarves, and all manner of other objects' and highlights 'the painting's strange propensity to multiply itself.'[33] The image saturates culture, in its original form, and in parody and pastiche, such as Duchamp's *L.H.O.O.Q.*[34] In its commodification the image has perhaps lost the last vestiges of its authenticity. The violence perpetrated by the tourist camera is made all the more absurd by the perfect reproductions already widely available.

Yet this is not quite the whole story, because the site of the *Mona Lisa* is still saturated by events that took place a century ago. Until the middle of the nineteenth century, the *Mona Lisa* was hardly noteworthy amongst the Louvre collection. While not an insignificant work, and much cherished, its significance was overshadowed by other paintings in the gallery. Its current worldwide renown is largely the work of Vincecenzo Peruggia, who in August 1911 slipped the painting from its frame and disappeared into the Paris streets. The theft became a media sensation. Leader notes that as a consequence:

> It was impossible to escape the image of the kidnapped lady. There she was, on newsreels, chocolate boxes, postcards and billboards. Her iconic fame was suddenly transformed into that of filmstars and singers.[35]

In the wake of the theft, crowds flocked to gaze at the empty space where the painting had hung;[36] the absence of the painting fixed its image in popular culture. The *Mona Lisa* became a media phenomenon, before it became the iconic image of the painting itself. Since then the fame of the painting has been perpetuated by its proliferating image. It draws so many camera lenses today largely because of the renown that was earned during its absence in 1911, and the wide reproduction to which it was subjected as a consequence. Each additional photograph increases the desire to experience the object, and to capture that experience in a photographic trophy. It is therefore impossible to approach as an unmediated experience: it is always already framed by the camera lens. The painting today is a photograph before it is a work or art. It is framed by its history, by its absence from the gallery, and by the desire to bear witness to that absent space.

In many ways the crowds in the Louvre are still flocking to witness an empty space in the gallery. The *Mona Lisa* has been described as 'probably the single most disappointing piece of work in the entire world.'[37] The disappointment of the actual painting, its diminutive size, its faded appearance, its lack of lustre and vitality, and its over-familiarity, is testament to the myth of the aura, and the lack of any 'original' which exists only as an idea suggested by innumerable reproductions of an already absent work of art. The image now belongs in the context of mass reproduction. The authentic original was created as an ideal of an artefact already absent, an ideal subsequently propagated through mass reproduction, parody, and pastiche. The authenticity of the image is a consequence of its reproduction. What more appropriate way to respond to this absence than to reconstitute the painting in its authentic context: as a mediated product of mass reproduction?

This relationship between the material work and its reproduction reveals something about the relationship between the history, and the idea of the authentic past. Baudrillard described history as 'our lost referential, that is to say our myth.'[38] History, he suggests, slips away in a culture where the ever-present historical trope in popular culture, from Hollywood films to theme parks, supersedes the authentic past. The idea of history reproduced through mass culture becomes detached from 'the possibility of an "objective" enchainment of events and causes and the possibility of a narrative enchainment of discourses.'[39] And this suggests that the objective past in history, like the aura of the work of art, may always have been a myth: the missing referent of the simulacrum. In the presence of the *Mona Lisa*, it is easy to identify in the uses of digital photo-graphy the proliferation of images divorced from historical value and material context. The material history of the object seems undone by the cheap clone. Yet in this process, the painting has also gathered new meanings over time. The inauthentic copy is at the heart of the material history of the painting; in the case of the *Mona Lisa*, history cannot function solely in the presence of the original. The idea of the original already assumes the presence of the reproduction. This implies that mediation of material culture and material history plays a fundamental role in our apprehension of all kinds of ostensible non-mediated experiences.

The new media theorists Bolter and Grusin have described this kind of interaction as remediation. They have argued that:

> All mediation is remediation. We are not claiming this as an a priori truth, but rather arguing that at this extended historical moment, all current media function as remediators and that remediation offers us a means of interpreting the work of earlier media as well. Our culture conceives of each medium or constellation of media as it responds to, redeploys, competes with, and reforms other media. In the first instance, we may think of something like a historical progression, of newer media remediating older ones and in particular of digital media remediating their predecessors. But ours is a genealogy of affiliations, not a linear history, and in this genealogy, older media can also remediate newer ones.[40]

In the space of the gallery, the painting remediates the photograph just as much as the photograph remediates the painting. Our 'real' experience is framed by an already circulating image, but is no less real or authentic as a consequence. The camera testifies to experience by remediating the material world through the idea of the photograph, constructed a fabricated space of visual signs in which the fidelity of the image to an ostensible original hardly matters at all. The digital camera therefore hardly intrudes in the cultural space at all: it is always already present. Yet the encounter between the painting and the camera played out daily in the Louvre remains saturated with historicity; history is the defining idea at operation in the space of the gallery. The gallery is itself a remediation of the idea of history. History is both present in framing the work of art as an object of desire, and lost in the anachronistic apposition of technology and the persistent material traces of the past.

The complicity between the camera and the artwork in fabricating the idea of the always absent aura is of the same kind as the complicity between the writ-ten record and the written history in fabricating the idea of the always absent past. Benjamin's aura describes the material history of the artefact. Its absence is made obvious by the immediacy of digital photography; the instantly rendered image dissolves the distinction between the original in which the authenticity of the work is invested, and the reproduction that creates the spectacle of the work. That absence therefore also exposes the missing past in historical discourse. It suggests that the discourse of history literally fabricates the idea of an ostensibly knowable past out of the gap between the historical trace, and the written history. The immediacy of digital history, like the immediacy of the digital image, threatens to dissolve that gap between the past and the present.

It is easy to recognize that in the gallery, historical representation and historical record are not the independent spheres that they are sometimes assumed to be. The original and its copy, the record and the representation, interact in curious ways. It is more difficult to see this effect in historical scholarship. In the discourse of history this kind of interaction is concealed by the cultural lag between the chronicle and the history, and the assumed disinterest and impartiality of the historian. As a consequence the idea of the record seems inevitable to precede the idea of history, to become the thing consumed in subsequent historical representation, whether those acts of representation take place within popular culture or within the academy. But in contemporary culture, the past and the present, the record and history are converging. The past has saturated the present, and the two exhibit complex interaction in an already historicized present. This occurs because of the immediacy of the digital record, and the blurring of that distinction between a thing and its copy.[41] The historical consciousness of the digital age is perhaps changing.

Yet while the pursuit of a historical past made knowable through the meanings inscribed in its surviving material traces may reflect a dominant mode of historical scholarship, it is not the only kind of history that is possible. Indeed, this way of understanding the relationship between the past and the present is itself historically situated. What Tosh terms 'historical consciousness'[42] arguably germinated in late manuscript culture, when the expanding uses of literacy helped secure the past against the written record.[43] In fact, the histories written throughout the early modern period continued to be ecumenical about evidence, lacking later scholarship's rigorous classification of source materials, and frequently placing scripture, literature, myth and tradition on an equal footing in ways that reflected 'the Enlightenment's pre-historical notion of historical change.'[44] Even by the eighteenth century, 'in their contempt for basic scholarship and research [...] historians showed an unjustifiable carelessness.'[45] History 'continued to be marked by a combination of moral engagement and literary endeavour.'[46] The pursuit of an objectively knowable past emerged only in the nineteenth century. It reflected the investment of the past in a written archive that was itself governed by the contingencies of an emerging administrative rationality.[47]

The habits of digital culture in many ways recall older kinds of historicity, before the empirical rationality of Enlightenment thinking took hold, when the past was more pliable. The ways in which the digital camera maintains the cultural value of the original artefact through iteration recall the function of storytelling in maintaining the memories of oral cultures;[48] the desire to bear witness to which the camera testifies recalls the function of memory and personal testimony in rendering the past accessible.[49] History is perhaps becoming reintegrated into popular and folk traditions, not as a trope or episteme as Groot implies, but as a living relationship with the historical past played out in the present. The camera in this context mobilizes the past within the present; it takes the stuff of history and turns it into the stuff of experience, and uses it to maintain the historical idea of the past in the present. Both are caught in a cycle of dependence, drawing authenticity from a circulation of signs, a tiny eddy in the wider semiotics of culture.

Just as the historical narrative becomes open to intervention, so too does the maintenance of the record. While the material library or archive consolidates power within institutional context making presence in the record tantamount to present in history, the distributed nature of digital communications means that the maintenance of the historical records is pluralized. The role of the historian in creating the historical narrative out of the detritus of documentary culture is supplemented by the role of individuals in making their own sense of the past. The knowable past invested in the records of libraries and archives is supplemented by a kind of social historical process. The idea of history perhaps changes, less a dead record, and more an active engagement with the past out of which each of us makes our own sense, and out of which through dialogue in the digital sphere we come together to a shared sense of our relationship with the past.[50] Under assault by this complex interaction of the original and its reproduction is a spectator relationship to the work of art, and a spectator relationship to the history that it symbolizes. That spectator position is rewritten as a remediation of experience through already established historical narratives.

This projection of the present as an already historicized narrative is particularly evident in one of the more curious events of the late twentieth century. When news of the death of Diana, Princess of Wales, broke across the world in August 1997, it was not a single image that helped frame the historical significance of that event, but innumerable images proliferating through the mass media. The shared cultural experience that defined the wider public reaction did not take place in a road tunnel in the centre of Paris, or even on the streets in London, but through the television screen. For most people who watched the drama unfold, the death and funeral of Diana was experienced as a mediated event. The crowds that were drawn to London played out their part in concordance with the images already broadcast, and followed events using portable radios, and the relay screens that transmitted coverage of the funeral service. Just as in 1911, those crowds gathered to bear witness to an absent space. But in their desire to bear witness, they inserted themselves into the centre of the unfolding drama, consciously changing the perceived historical significance of those events even as they happened. To bear witness was also to participate in the making of history.

The significance of Diana's death was immediately apparent, and comparisons with other events in British history were quickly drawn. Writing in the *Guardian*, John Ezard described the news as 'more shatteringly felt than Earl Mountbatten's assassination in 1979, or even than Winston Churchill's long-expected passing in 1965.'[51] A few days later in the *Independent* John Walsh wrote that 'there's never been a moment in this country's history when such a huge, variegated, rainbow coalition of Britons collectively wrung their hearts over the loss of a human being – even Queen Victoria, even Churchill.'[52] These kinds of analogies were a common part of the coverage; from the outset Diana's death was remediated within a narrative of traditional political and royal history. When the BBC broke from normal programming to cover the news, it began the broadcast with the national anthem; Martyn Lewis interviewed a series of politicians, historians and journalists throughout the morning in keeping with the tone of the coverage.[53] The institutions of state were well prepared to channel the national mood and emotional outpouring into the kind of invented tradition that helped perpetuate the status quo through the regalia of state.[54]

There was also from the start an understanding about how the public reaction to the events would be framed. Comparisons with the assassination of Kennedy in 1969 situated Diana's death as one of those moments of acute public consciousness, in which the circumstances of hearing the news become imprinted on our personal memories. That idea, already overused, situated the public in a reflective spectator position to the events that were unfolding. The role of the public was in this context to insert the event into a personal social narrative, assuming a bystander position in relation to historical change. It was not to transform themselves into the nexus of that change.

However, the death of Diana involved a mass of contradictions that immediately problemetized that framing of events in this way. Here was a princess who had been stripped of royal designation after her divorce, who nevertheless aspired to becoming the 'queen of people's hearts,'[55] a 'people's princess'[56] who challenged and undermined the position of the monarchy. A member of the royal family, but not a royal, conventionally she was not entitled to a state funeral, but was nevertheless interred with all the trappings of a state event. Given this context, the trope of national mourning channelled through the symbolism of the state was clearly problematic, and sat incongruously with the tabloid dramas in which Diana's life had been situated. What emerged was a struggle for control over the discursive context of Diana's life and death. That struggle was situated in the mode of representation, of symbolism, and in the remediation of history and tradition through the cipher of popular culture. Increasingly the comparisons drawn were not with royal and political figures, but with celebrities: Marilyn Monroe; Grace Kelly; and James Dean. With breathtaking tastelessness, a song written for Monroe was hastily rededicated to Diana. Here was an event that was being remediated not through political history, but through celebrity culture. Instead of the contemplative and respectful tone that may have been anticipated, a mood of resentment and blame, targeted towards both the Royal family and the press, began to emerge.

The story quickly became not one about the life and death of Diana, but the strength of public feeling, and its catharsis in rejection of the traditional representations into which her image was being fitted. That reaction played out through the appropriation of various symbols and symbolic acts. As crowds flocked to pay tribute at Kensington Palace, Kitzinger noted that:

> Visual representations were central to the construction of this event. Within days the mass media were representing the 'strength of feeling' and 'national mourning' through capturing gestures and symbolism. Cameras

panned the carpets of floral tributes, focussing on the guttering flame of a candle, the poignant message, the gift of a teddy bear.[57]

The absence at the centre of the story was filled with the images of public grief, most notably the face of Diana herself, which was 'used by mourners to adorn the gates of the Palaces. It was reproduced on commemorative plates, posters and T-shirts.'[58] Like the image of the *Mona Lisa*, the image of Diana took on an iconic property in her absence, disconnected from the material conditions of her life, and rendered as a cultural commodity invested with new meanings. This became possible because like the *Mona Lisa*, Diana's image was easy to appropriate. Kitzinger notes that 'while Diana's image was repeatedly displayed, her voice was rarely heard. Footage of the princess was literally mute, in death, Diana, creature of the modern media, became a star of the silent screen.'[59] Helmer notes that 'Diana herself was, in life, speechless and inarticulate' and suggests that her 'body, once absent, provided the blank slate upon which the stories of the ordinary person could be written.'[60] Watson suggests her absence 'had the immediate effect of freezing and preserving these fleeting and inchoate images and giving the metamorphosis its definitive shape.'[61] Diana's image, more than her life, defined her place in history because her image was largely without voice, and therefore could cipher the various popular narratives that helped remediate the historical significance of her death.

The crowds initially drawn to London and that later lined the route of the funeral precession were aware of the historical relationship between Diana's death and their participation. In the *Independent*, Suzanne More wrote, 'every one of us knew why we were there. "For Diana, for history," as one so-called ordinary person put it to me yesterday.'[62] Decca Aitkenhead described people's 'desire to locate themselves in the spot where history will for once reach out to them [...] pluck them up, and bring them inside, gathered together in a collective historic experience.'[63] Aaronovitch described the reaction of a minicab driver who insisted 'that he would be standing on the route of the cortege, his young son's hand held tight, so that he too would be "a part of history."'[64] Jenkins and Wilkins interviewed mourners in the crowd, including the comment that 'this is history here in the making.'[65] The crowds who pressed in around Kensington Palace, and later lined the route of the funeral procession, were driven in part by a desire to witness history in the making, but also to remake history by bearing witness, and in doing so disrupt the incorporation of Diana's life and death into a historical tradition that was perceived to have done her such harm. The desire to bear witness was wrapped up in a desire to enforce a particular kind of narrative on to the life and death of Diana, and in a rejection of the preferred reading of events.

Within this, the crowd insisted on particular forms of public and private mourning. Kitzinger notes:

> Visible acts of mourning were not only volunteered by 'the common people' but demanded of the Royal Family. In response to 'public demand',

the union flag fluttered at half-mast at Buckingham Palace and television cameras focussed hungrily on the physical interaction between Prince Charles and his sons.[66]

The massed crowds demanded the return of the royal family from Scotland to respond to the national grief, hounded her young sons into offering public consolation, and insisted the royal standard be raised above the palace. The chutzpah of this appropriation of grief as essentially public property went largely unchallenged. When Earl Spencer delivered his eulogy at Diana's funeral, the applause started outside the Abbey, but was taken up by the assembled dignitaries and celebrities inside. The massed public were defining the emotional response to the service, and marking the eulogy's significance by forcing an incongruous scene upon the congregation – a profoundly uncanny moment. Most strikingly of all, the mounds of flowers that accreted in central London, and the bouquets that on the day of the funeral were tossed ineffectively at the funeral precession, marked the very different tone of the events, the way in which layers of tradition had been apparently swept aside. The crowd did not line the route in reverential silence; a backdrop to history like those who witnessed Churchill's funeral procession to which so many comparisons had prematurely been made. Instead they intervened, insisting on their presence in history through that strangely jarring applause, and the throwing of flowers. It was those images, rather than the carefully choreographed and symbolically laden procession and service, which came to define the day. This was not merely a desire to bear witness, but to intervene in the making of history, in the ways in which those events were framed, and in the documentary record on which future histories could be written.

In the wake of her death, the life of Diana was immediately recast in narrative form. Helmer suggests that:

> to a greater extent than any of her royal counterparts, however, Diana was embedded in common story forms, such as the romance of her marriage and the tragedy of her death, stories which serve to embed her character as a passive entity caught in an unforgiving plot.[67]

Geraghty has also explored the ways in which Diana's life was situated within narrative forms, from fairy-tale, to soap opera and tragedy.[68] In the months and years that followed, the legacy of Diana was also perpetuated through the web. Helmer notes that:

> Her death inspired many who perhaps would not typically publish to publish memorials, tributes, and commentary on the World Wide Web, which at one time hosted hundreds of continuously maintained web sites devoted to the memory of Diana.[69]

These electronic memorials 'indicate a conscious decision to find "a place in history," to witness, to provide testimony.'[70] This is not merely of finding the history of Diana's life, but of entwining the historical and the personal. Within hours of the news, conspiracy theories began to circulate via newsgroups, discussion forums and email.

The debate about the degree to which the media reflected, or fermented the public mood in the days following Diana's death lingers on. Perhaps it was neither one nor the other, but the interaction of the coverage and the public mood. It was not merely that the immediacy of the coverage allowed the resentment to spread through the crowd like a contagion, although that is certainly part of it. Rather, the death of Diana was from the start a media event; the material circumstances were less significant than the ways in which the event was represented on television, through the newspapers, and subsequently via the World Wide Web. As an already mediated event, Diana's death was *remediated* through innumerable other fictional and historical narratives, from the death of Kennedy, Churchill and Grace Kelly, through to the fairy-tale, romance and tragedy genres. There was a sense in which this drama had been played out in innumerable ways before, that individuals knew how to respond because their responses, from open displays of grief, to the pavement floral tributes, were existing tropes that simply required reassembling in novel ways. The symbolism of those days reflected a maudlin sentimentality.

This is part of the way in which the remediation of experience through historical narrative functions to influence our understanding of the world around us. The past as both objective period and series of tropes provides a ready stock of narrative models and symbolism on which to attach new meanings fitted to contemporary concerns. This can be done in a self-conscious way, such as with the Live Eight concerts of 2005 that knowingly exploited the historic status of the original concerts and appropriated its imagery and its meanings for a new set of political preoccupations. The sequel in history can play a similar role to the sequel in fiction and film. Alternatively, the remediation of experience through historical narratives can be done in less self-conscious ways, such as was the case with the death of Diana. Nevertheless it is the immediacy of digital culture and mass media, and the immediacy of the visual image's bridging of epochs, that allows this kind of appropriation of history as an explanatory model to explain and coordinate present experience in the moment of its occurrence. The historical event becomes part of the vocabulary for understanding and framing personal experience and contemporary events. More importantly this occurs not solely in the academic sphere, not solely in the public sphere, but in a negotiation between the two.

The death of Diana is an example of what might be termed instant history; events that are so recognizably significant that their status as history is already obvious at the moment of their occurrence, and as a consequence open to immediate remediation as historical narratives. With instant history, the future historical accounts are being moulded and contested even as events are unfolding. What marks these events out in contemporary culture is the immediacy of the interaction between media representation and public consumption. The cultural lag between the chronicle and the history is vanquished; history converges on the present. The most striking such event in recent years occurred in 2001, when the world's only remaining superpower was targeted by an attack as audacious as it was callous. Like the theft of the *Mona Lisa*, and the death of Diana, the terrorist attacks of 11 September were immediately recognized as historic moments, as the stuff of future historical study. Yet unlike the two other moments explored in this chapter, the story of those attacks unfolded in real-time, in front of a worldwide audience, and in awful, shocking detail.

It is hard not to be profoundly moved by images that emerged from New York on 11 September 2001. The event was filmed from beginning to end, the images endlessly repeated in the immediate aftermath, and every development subject to extended analysis. Yet it is important to recognize also that the cultural impact of those events was much to do with the spectacle. What set the attack on the World Trade Center apart from any other event of its kind was the sheer volume of images and video of the events, from every angle and from every perspective. The attack was described as 'the most momentous event ever seen live on television'[71] and most people experienced those events as television. In a book whose title echoes the work of Baudrillard, Žižec suggested:

> For the large majority of the public, the World Trade Centre explosions were events on the TV screen, and when we watched the oft-repeated shot of frightened people running towards the camera ahead of the giant cloud of dust from the collapsing tower, was the framing of the shot itself not reminiscent of the spectacular shots in catastrophe movies.[72]

The comparison with Hollywood films has been widely drawn. Yet in one sense our familiarity with ostensibly similar images from disaster movies like *Independence Day*[73] and *Armageddon*[74] made the real events seem all the more unreal.[75] The slow-motion collapse of the buildings in particular seemed unnatural to many, and conspiracy theories began to emerge within hours of the event. Writing on Usenet on the day of the attacks, one poster suggested: 'those collapses look really strange ... just as it looked like the one tower was OK to me, it went down. Nah, I'm not an architect – just a conspiracy theorist.'[76] Many still believe the collapse was the result of controlled demolition.[77] Conspiracy theories are the marker of instant history and remediated history; they indicate the contested nature of representation and interpretation, and struggle over control of the future historical narrative being laid down in the present.

Yet if the coverage was experienced as a remediation of Hollywood films, it was also experienced through the lens of the past. Chopra-Gant observes that 'there was an event of such self-evident historical significance that it was certain, almost from the outset, that its story would have an undeniable claim to a place in the discourse of recent American history even while the events were still taking place.'[78] He also suggested that 'those watching on television did not only see it live, but saw it live *as history*.'[79] Writing in *The Times* the day after the attacks, MacArthur observed that 'television cameras were not there to record the death of the Princess in 1997 but they were there yesterday as a live witness to the attack on America.'[80] For all the immediacy of the mass media age, the images that accompany contemporary events more often than not provide testimony after the fact. Yet here was an event not only witnessed live, but where the status of those images as historical record was immediately apparent. Writing two days later in the *Guardian*, Mark Lawson suggested of the saturation of images to come out of New York, 'these are the photographs that the history books will hold.'[81] There was a widespread feeling that the attacks marked a historical turning point, the dawn of a new era, and that the world would never be the same as a consequence.

From the outset, the events were situated within historical parallels, including Pearl Harbor, the Lockerbie Bombing, and the bombing of the World Trade Center complex in 1993, none of which seemed to capture the scale of the event. But the obviously historic nature of the attacks sent commentators looking back into history to find a way of expressing their importance. Writing two days after the attacks Mark Lawson observed:

> In 1929, stockbrokers threw themselves from banking towers because they had no desire to stay alive, a moment captured in iconic pictures of the depression. In 2001, financiers made the same Wall Street fall because it was their one forlorn chance of escaping death. The suicide of bankers and the homicide of bankers are joined in a visual time-loop.[82]

This is remediation in action; the one event becomes experienced through the cipher of the other. Experience is remade as an already written historical narrative. Although in this case the comparison is with a myth; the iconic pictures non-existent. But history was also self-consciously remediated to frame the significance of the events. In the early evening of 11 September, Thomas E. Franklin captured an image of three fire-fighters raising the American flag over the wreckage of the World Trade Center site. The image, entitled *Ground Zero Spirit*,[83] was used around the world to symbolize the events and their aftermath. It was subsequently used as the basis of the Heroes Stamp produced by the American postal service. But the image resonated largely because it recalls another photograph taken by Joe Rosenthal in 1945, a photograph rendered concrete in the US Marines War Memorial in Arlington, Virginia. *Raising the Flag on Iwo*[84] won the Pulitzer Photography prize in the same year and itself became the basis for a postage stamp released in 1945. The two images are now irrevocably tied by their compositional similarity, and by the resonance between them. The older photo remediates the newer just as much as the newer remediates the older. In 2006 another iconic photograph of the events of 11 September was published; a photograph of laconic New Yorkers relaxing and enjoying the sunshine while the towers burn in the background.[85] The formal composition of the image echoes the two other photographs, with the plume of smoke cutting across the scene like the American flag.

The events of that day and the days that followed were also framed by absences; the missing people symbolized by the photographs pinned to billboards, the gap in the New York skyline, and most significantly the absent president. In the weeks, months and years after the attacks, people travelled to see an absence at the heart of New York where what were briefly the world's tallest buildings once stood. In 2008 when James Marsh's *Man on Wire*[86] was released, documenting Philippe Petit's 1974 wire walk between the two towers, the power of the film derived partly from the destruction of the building. The images of Petit suspended between the twin towers recalled the images of office workers and city traders hanging out of the building, and falling to their deaths. The threat to Petit seemed all the more real because we had witnessed his fall before. The anchoring of wire to the buildings seemed unfeasibly insecure. Petit's movement now carved out a space in the skyline of New York that was impossible to recover. September 11 changed the vocabulary of the New York skyline.

The immediacy and intensity of the media coverage of the World Trade Center attacks has changed the ways in which the history of those events will come to be written. Inscribed in the databanks of digital culture are innumerable personal testimonies published on discussion forums and blogs, through email and instant messaging, from the appalled to the triumphant. Together they provide an insight into the emotional impact of the attack across the globe in diverse and vivid detail. The images and reports of professional media outlets have been supplemented by thousands of images and videos captured on personal recording devices. And this has perhaps begun to change how we think about the collective response to major world events. The US television series *Flash-forward*[87] provides a fictional account of the mediation of personal experience through technology; the mosaic project in the series gathers personal testimony of the flash-forward event. This is clearly reflecting and fictionalizing the experience of the 9/11 attacks, but it also suggests how the voices represented in the histories of the future will inevitably be more numerous, will inevitably reflect the experiences of ordinary people in more vivid detail than ever before.

In 2002, the attack on the World Trade Center was voted the most historic event of the last one hundred years. The death of Diana was voted the most historic British event during the same period.[88] The two events are incongruously tied by their resonance within popular culture. Yet it is difficult to imagine that the complicity between the media coverage of these events, and their incorporation into personal experiences has not played a significant role in their resonance. It is not merely that these were examples of instant history, but also that they were experienced as stories in our own lives. There significance as historical moments has already been carved out by their visibility within mediated culture.

The otherwise unrelated historical moments discussed in this chapter share a number of common factors. In each, visual culture played a significant role in the ways in which they were framed as historical events. In each, the iteration of images and proliferation played a significant role. And in each, people were drawn to witness an absent space where the material subject matter of an historical event had once been. They demonstrate how history is remediated within present experience, how the narratives and conventions of historical discourse are exploited to explain an organized collective experience. Advancements in media and digital technologies have collapsed the distinction between the present and the truly historical, such that we begin to interpret, frame and understand events as already historicized at the very moment that we experience them. They have altered the nature of history, from something vested in the scholarly activities of an elite cultural group, to a living and mutable, political and personal part of the wider social matrix. In this, the spectator position of traditional scholarly history, in which audiences consume the stuff of history, has been renegotiated as a participatory form of history-making, in the remediation of already historicized experience.

The presence of history in the lived experience of digitally mediated culture begins to problemetize both the discourse of history, and the craft of the history. It emphasizes the significant role of writing in the discourse of history – that complicity between the predominantly written historical source and predominantly written historical account. It exposes how historical distance has been constructed as an artificial distinction between source writing and historiography. This distinction is collapsed in those mediated moments which are at the same time both versions of history, and historical documents. The immediate representations of the death of Diana, the theft of the *Mona Lisa*, and the attack on the World Trade Center stand as not merely the first draft of history, but as historical documents in their own right. As versions of history they are immediately channelling experience through the conventions of historical discourse, confronting the past and the present in ways that allow anachronism to become a productive source of historical understanding. Within this it is clear that while scholarly history will still have an important role, it will lose its monopoly on historical consciousness and historical understanding, because it has lost its dominant position in historical representation. The histories of the digital age are likely to be increasingly plural and diverse.

Yet the events discussed in this chapter are not unique in this shift; while each is an example of spectacle created within media representation and perpetuated by the visual image, there are many other events of this kind. Many of the most notable events of the past hundred years were covered live or near live, from the assassination of Kennedy, to the moon landings, the loss of two space shuttles, wars in Iraq, Afghanistan, Yugoslavia, Libya, the Orange Revolution in Ukraine, and the Arab Spring across the Middle East. Many have been mediated by the visual image more than by the written word. As media culture continues to intensify through use of digital technologies, this by itself cannot but change the ways in which histories come to be written, not only the histories of the media age, but the histories of all ages. The new possibilities suggested by digital history highlight the paucity in the record of the past. It suggests the kinds of experience that have been excluded by the already historicized nature of the record and archive. If history was once inscribed in the archive before it was inscribed in the historical account, if presence in the archive was once tantamount to presence in history, then now the archive itself is as much the site of popular contestation and participation as the histories it generates.

There is furthermore a profound sense in which the historical is catching up with the present. The distance between the truly historical and the contemporary is being reduced such that contemporary events like the death of Diana or the attack on the World Trade Center are already historicized in the moment of their occurrence. The idea of history as retrospective is perhaps being overtaken by the idea of history in the making. History cannot function in the presence of the original; it requires an absent space on which to project a narrative of the past. It is only as experiences become rendered in the record that historical discourse can take hold. However, the immediacy of digital culture means that the record is already written in the moment of its experience, already understood as a property of mediation, already framed by the conventions of representation and narrative, and the conventions of history. The historical record does not always precede the historical account; sometimes both emerge in a single, already historicized moment.

Notes

1 Details concerning the theft of the *Mona Lisa* are taken from D. Leader, *Stealing the Mona Lisa: What Art Stops us from Seeing* (Washington: Shoemaker & Hoard, 2002).
2 J. Kitzinger, 'Image', *Screen*, 39: 1 (1998), 74.
3 M. Engel, 'Diana's body flown back to Britain; Matthew Engle on the tragedy that struck at the heart of a nation', *Guardian*, 1 September 2001, p. 1.
4 Earl Spencer, 'The most hunted person of the modern age', *Guardian*, 6 September 1997, available at: http://www.guardian.co.uk/theguardian/2007/may/04/greatspeeches [accessed: 25 March 2012].
5 R. Alleyne, 'Dying Diana picture a new low, say princes', *Daily Telegraph*, 15 July 2006, p. 1.
6 M. Chopra-Gant, 'Realismo narrativa y genero en la construccion de la historia del 11-S', in E. Gaytan, F. Gil and M. Ulled (eds), *Los Mensajeros Del Miedo: Las Imagenes Como Testigos Y Agentes Del Terrorismo* (Madrid: Ediciones Rialp, 2010).
7 Chopra-Gant, 'Realismo narrativa'.
8 See also L. Tredinnick (2010), 'Rewriting history: the information age and the knowable past', in T. Weller (ed.), *Information History in the Modern World* (Basingstoke: Palgrave Macmillan, 2010), pp. 175–98.
9 Tosh, for example, argues that 'the study of history has nearly always been based squarely on what the historian can read in documents or hear from informants. And ever since historical research was placed on a professional footing during Ranke's lifetime, the emphasis has fallen almost exclusively on the written rather than the spoken word. [...] For the vast majority of historians, research is confined to libraries and archives'; J. Tosh, *The Pursuit of History: Aims, Methods and New Directions in the Study of Modern History* (London and New York: Longman, 1991).
10 Hayden White described history's 'ineluctably poetic nature'. Ankersmit suggests 'that historical knowledge is as much "made" (by the historian's language) as it is "found" (in the archives).' Munslow says that 'history is best understood as what it plainly is – a narrative about the past'; F. R. Ankersmit, *Historical Representation* (Stanford, California: Stanford University Press, 2001); A. Munslow, *The New History* (London and New York: Pearson Education, 2003); H. White, *Metahistory: The Historical Imagination in Nineteenth-Century Europe* (Baltimore, Maryland: Johns Hopkins University Press, 1973).
11 R. Mayhew, 'Denaturalising print, historicising text: historical geography and the history of the book', in E. Gagen, H. Lorimer and A. Vasudevan, *Practicing the Archive: Reflections on Method and Practice in Historical Geography; Historical Geography Research Series 40* (London: Royal Geographic Society, 2007), pp. 23–36.

12 K. Jenkins, *On 'What is History?' From Carr and Elton to Rorty and White* (London and New York: Routledge, 1995), p. 17.

13 Stille has observed that 'while the late twentieth century will undoubtedly have recorded more data than any other period in history, it will also almost certainly have lost more information than any previous era' (A. Stille, *The Future of the Past: How the Information Age Threatens to Destroy our Cultural Heritage* (London, Basingstoke and Oxford: Picador, 2002), p. 300). Kuny suggests that 'we are, to my mind, living in the midst of a digital dark age' (T. Kuny, 'The digital dark ages? Challenges in the preservation of electronic information', *International Preservation News*, 17: May (1997), 8–13); Deegan and Tanner suggest: 'The Gutenberg printing revolution led Europe out of the Dark Ages – the loss of knowledge of the learning of the ancient Greeks and Romans. The digital revolution may land us in an age even darker if urgent action is not taken' (M. Deegan and S. Tanner, 'The digital dark ages', *Library and Information Update*, I: 2 (2002), 41–42). Trehub insists that it 'is not just a clever conceit; it is a real danger' (A. Trehub, 'Keeping it simple: the Alabama Digital Preservation Network', *Library Hi Tech*, 28: 2 (2010), 245–58).

14 J. Vincent, *History* (London and New York: Continuum, 2005), p. 19.

15 P. Conway, 'Preservation in the Digital World', *Council of Library and Information Resources*, http://www.clir.org/pubs/reports/conway2/ [accessed: 25 March 2012]; H. C. von Baeyer, *Information: The New Language of Science* (London: Weidenfeld & Nicolson, 2003).

16 V. Mayer-Schonberger, *Delete: The Virtue of Forgetting in the Digital Age* (Princeton and Oxford: Princeton University Press, 2009), p. 4.

17 Mayer-Schonberger, *Delete*, p. 2.

18 For the craft of history, see G. R. Elton, *The Practice of History* (Malden, Massachusetts and Oxford: Blackwell Publishing, 2002). Brand, for example, has suggested that by exploiting data-mining techniques, 'history will become a different discipline, closer to a science.' Similarly Ross suggests: 'the age of electronic records opens numerous possibilities that will enrich the understanding of contemporary culture' (Ross, 'The expanding world', p. 13) and that 'historians would be likely to "mine" this resource in different ways.' See: S. Brand, 'Escaping the digital dark age', *Library Journal*, 124: 2 (1999), 46–48; S. Ross, 'The expanding world of electronic information and the past's future', in E. Higgs (ed.), *History and Electronic Artefacts* (Oxford: Clarendon Press, 1998), pp. 5–28.

19 Ross, 'The expanding world', pp. 5–28.

20 R. J. Morris (1998), 'Electronic documents and the history of the late twentieth century: black holes of warehouses', in Higgs, *History and Electronic Artefacts*, pp. 31–48.

21 For reflections on this issue, see Higgs, *History and Electronic Artefacts*, pp. 31–48.

22 J. Tosh, *The Pursuit of History*.

23 See L. Tredinnick, *Digital Information Culture; The Individual and Society in the Digital Age* (Oxford: Chandos Publishing, 2008), pp. 135–47.

24 H. Jenkins, 'Quentin Tarantino's Star Wars?: Digital cinema, media convergence and participatory culture', in M. Durham, M. Gigi and D. Kellner, *Media and Cultural Studies KeyWorks* (Malden and Oxford: Blackwell Publishing, 2006), pp. 549–76.

25 J. de Groot, *Consuming History: Historians and Heritage in Contemporary Popular Culture* (London and New York: Routledge 2009), p. 1.

26 de Groot, *Consuming History*, p. 3.

27 de Groot, *Consuming History*, p. 6.

28 J. Jones, 'These tourist snappers are killing the *Mona Lisa*', *Guardian*, 9 March 2009, available at: http://www.guardian.co.uk/artanddesign/jonathanjonesblog/2009/mar/09/mona-lisa-tourist-snappers-louvre [accessed: 25 March 2012].

29 Jones, 'Killing the *Mona Lisa*'.

30 W. Benjamin, 'The work of art in the age of mechanical reproduction', in *Illuminations, edited by Hannah Arendt, translated by Harry Zorn* (London: Jonathon Cape, 1970), pp. 211–44. Originally published in 1936.
31 Benjamin, 'Mechanical reproduction'.
32 Benjamin, 'Mechanical reproduction'.
33 Leader, *Stealing the Mona Lisa*, p. 4.
34 M. Duchamp, 'L.H.O.O.Q.' [Postcard and pencil], (Musée National d'Art Moderne, Paris 1919).
35 Leader, *Stealing the Mona Lisa*, p. 2.
36 Leader, *Stealing the Mona Lisa*.
37 A. Gentleman, 'Smile please', *Guardian G2*, 19 October 2004, p. 2.
38 J. Baudrillard, *Simulacra and Simulation, Translated by Sheila Faria Glaser* (Michigan: University of Michigan Press, 1994), p. 43.
39 Baudrillard, *Simulacra and Simulation*, p. 47.
40 J. D. Bolter and R. Grusin, *Remediation: Understanding New Media* (Massachusetts and London: MIT Press, 2000), p. 55.
41 For an analogous argument, see R. Barthes, 'The discourse of history', in R. Barthes, *The Rustle of Language; translated by Richard Howard* (Berkeley and Los Angeles: University of California Press, 1989) pp. 127–40.
42 Tosh, *The Pursuit of History*.
43 See M. T. Clanchy, *From Memory to Written Record: England 1066–1307* (Oxford: Blackwell Publishing, 1993); S. Justice, *Writing and Rebellion – England in 1381* (Berkley and London: University of California Press, 1996).
44 Ankersmit, *Historical Representation*, p. 23.
45 A. Marwick, *The Nature of History* (Basingstoke: Macmillan Education, 1981), p. 35.
46 M. Fulbrook, *Historical Theory* (London and New York: Routledge, 2002), p. 13.
47 For the concept of administrative rationality, see M. Weber, 'Bureaucracy', in H. Gerth and C. Wright Mills (eds), *Max Weber* (Oxford and New York: Oxford University Press, 1946).
48 See M. J. Carruthers, *The Book of Memory: A Study of Memory in Medieval Culture* (Cambridge: Cambridge University Press, 1990); E. A. Havelock, *The Muse Learns to Write: Reflections on Orality and Literacy from Antiquity to the Present* (New Haven and London: Yale University Press, 1986); W. J. Ong, *Orality and Literature: The Technologizing of the Word* (London: Methuen & Co, 1982).
49 See Clanchy, *Memory to Written Record*.
50 See Tredinnick, *Digital Information Culture*, pp. 149–66.
51 J. Ezard, 'A legend perfected to reign forever', *Guardian*, 1 September 1997, p. 6.
52 J. Walsh, 'Diana – the last farewell: last journey for broken butterfly', *Independent*, 6 September 1997, p. D6.
53 M. Lawson, 'Sky and CNN were first, but a royal death is a BBC matter', *Guardian*, 1 September 1997, p. 7.
54 For the concept of invented traditions, see E. J. Hobsbawm and T. Ranger (eds), *The Invention of Tradition* (Cambridge: Cambridge University Press, 1983).
55 M. Basher, *Panorama: An Interview with Diana, Princess of Wales*, [Television programme], London: BBC, 20 November 1995.
56 J. McGuigan, 'British identity and "the People's Princess"', *The Sociological Review*, 48: 1 (2001), 1–18.
57 Kitzinger, 'Image', p. 73.
58 Kitzinger, 'Image', p. 74.
59 Kitzinger, 'Image', p. 74.
60 M. Helmer, 'Media, discourse, and the public sphere: electronic memorials to Diana, Princess of Wales', *College English*, 63: 4 (2001), 437–56.
61 C. W. Watson, '"Born a lady, became a princess, died a saint": the reaction to the death of Diana, Princess of Wales', *Anthropology Today*, 13: 6 (1997), 3–7.

62 S. Moore, 'Diana: unique, complex, extraordinary, irreplaceable', *Independent*, 1 September 1997, p. S1.

63 D. Aikenhead, 'This isn't grief, it's wanting to belong', *Guardian*, 5 September 1997, p. 17.

64 D. Aaronovitch, 'Comfort of strangers', *Guardian*, 6 September 1997, p. 13.

65 L. Jenkins and E. Wilkins, 'Overnight campers will be allowed into Royal Parks', *The Times*, 5 September 1997.

66 Kitzinger, 'Image', p. 74.

67 Helmer, 'Media, discourse'.

68 C. Geraghty, 'Story', *Screen*, 39: 1 (1998), 70–73.

69 Helmer, 'Media, discourse'.

70 Helmer, 'Media, discourse'.

71 B. MacArthur, 'Millions watched biggest live TV event in history', *The Times*, 12 September 2001.

72 S. Žižec, *Welcome to the Desert of the Real* (London: Verso, 2002), p. 11.

73 R. Emmerich [director], *Independence Day* [motion picture] (United States: Twentieth Century Fox, 1996).

74 M. Bay [director], *Armageddon* [motion picture] (United States: Touchstone Pictures, 1998).

75 See also M. Chopra-Gant, *Cinema and History: The Telling of Stories* (London: Wallflower, 2008).

76 Real@not.here, Untitled Post, *How Many Stories/Floors was the World Trade Centre? How Many People in it?* [alt.prophesies.nostradamus], 11 September 2001. Available at: http://groups.google.com/group/alt.prophecies.nostradamus/browse_thread/thread/f337f901af57812b/7915951b3a5cff59?hl=en&q=%22Those+collapses+look+really+strange%22#7915951b3a5cff59 [accessed: 25 March 2012].

77 For example, I. Henshall, *9/11: The New Evidence* (London: Robinson, 2007); B. Zwicker, *Towers of Deception: The Media Cover-Up of 9/11* (Gabriola Island, BC: New Society Publishers, 2006).

78 Chopra-Gant, 'Realismo narrativa'.

79 Chopra-Gant, 'Realismo narrativa'. Translation provided by the author.

80 MacArthur, 'Biggest live TV event in history'.

81 M. Lawson, 'The power of a picture: the devastation in America has produced photographs that will haunt the world for ever', *Guardian*, 13 September 2001, available at: http://www.guardian.co.uk/world/2001/sep/13/september11.usa53 [accessed: 25 March 2012].

82 M. Lawson, 'The power of a picture'.

83 T. E. Franklin [photographer], *Ground Zero Spirit* [photograph], first published on 12 September 2001.

84 J. Rosenthal [photographer], *Raising the Flag on Iwo* [photograph] (1945).

85 T. Hoepker [photographer], *Untitled photograph* [photograph] (2001).

86 J. Marsh [director], *Man On Wire* [motion picture], (United Kingdom and United States: Discovery Films, 2008).

87 B. Braga and D. S. Goya [creators], *Flashforward* [television series] (US: HBO Entertainment, 2009–10).

88 B. Sheppard, 'Death of Diana voted most memorable date in last 100 Years', *Express*, 23 August 2002, p. 21.

3   A method for navigating the infinite archive

William J. Turkel, Kevin Kee and Spencer Roberts

The transaction costs of traditional research methods

Although the conventions of historical research have evolved over the past century or so, until relatively recently most historians faced scarcity of information and limited access to sources. Most sources had to be consulted in person by visiting archives and libraries. Close reading, then as now, required a significant investment of human labour, as did the creation of indices, concordances, summaries, finding aids, and other scholarly apparatus that facilitated the discovery and use of new evidence for the past. Traditional scholarly conversations, at least those held in public, were conducted largely in journals and monographs, and unfolded over timelines typically measured in years.

As late as the 1980s and 1990s, two of us (Turkel and Kee) were taught the following method of research:

1. Do a systematic literature review.
2. Formulate question(s).
3. Do some combination of archival work, field work, or experimentation, depending on your discipline.[1]
4. Master your subject.
5. Write up your results (for most historians, a well-defined cycle of conference papers and journal articles, leading eventually to a monograph).
6. Review the recent literature for any late-breaking news that needs to be taken into account.
7. Publish the final product.

When we learned this traditional research method it was already of questionable utility. We will argue that it is now more-or-less useless, made obsolete by the events of the last few decades. Sadly, however, it is still being taught in college and university departments that continue to act as if they are preparing students for academic life in the mid-twentieth century.

In the 1960s, Gordon E. Moore (later one of the founders of semiconductor giant Intel, but then director of research and development at Fairchild Semiconductor) observed that the number of electronic components on an integrated circuit was doubling roughly every year and argued that 'over the short term this rate can be expected to continue, if not to increase'.[2] More than forty years later, 'Moore's Law' continues to hold, having become a self-fulfilling prophecy for the industry.[3] Computers and related electronic devices continue to become ever smaller, faster, more powerful and less expensive, digital storage becomes ever denser, and the number of devices connected to the internet continues to double at roughly the same pace.[4] Digital sources, both those that were digitized from analogue originals and those 'born digital', also proliferate at exponential rates.

One gets a vague impression of this runaway growth by conducting life online and by participating in social media. Each day, the number of Google searches, Yahoo! searches, Bing searches, emails sent, text messages sent and YouTube videos watched, all number in the billions.[5] We have a sense that the world online is big, probably in much the same way that a fish has the sense that the ocean is big: it seems unbounded in every direction. This local view, the view from a web browser, cannot really give us any idea of what is out there, however. In 2003, researchers at the University of California, Berkeley estimated that the amount of new information created the previous year was on the order of 5 exabytes (10^{18} bytes). If one megabyte (10^6 bytes) is printed as text, it takes about as much physical space as a traditional book. Five exabytes-worth of traditional books would fill 37,000 libraries the size of the US Library of Congress. Seven years later, a similar study estimated that Americans consumed about 3.6 zettabytes (10^{21} bytes) of information in 2008. Printed in traditional book form, this much information would blanket the United States and Alaska to a depth of about seven feet.[6] A number that could be visualized in terms of library buildings at the turn of the millennium requires a continent to imagine less than a decade later. If you hated mathematics in school, this is what the word 'exponential' means. 'When something grows exponentially, for a long time it may seem not to be changing at all', Abelson, Ledeen and Lewis write in a study of the 'digital explosion'. 'If we don't watch it steadily, it will seem as though something discontinuous and radical occurred while we weren't looking.'[7]

This glut has serious implications for the work of historians, as for every other kind of scholar. In a talk at Research Without Borders at Columbia University in 2011, Dan Cohen, Director of the Roy Rosenzweig Center for History and New Media at George Mason University, pointed out that a single historian might have been able to read and analyse the 40,000 memos issued at the White House during the Johnson administration, but that such a practice could never handle the 4 million email memos sent while Clinton was in office.[8] Our digital libraries are growing as fast as our digital archives. Google Books, an effort to digitize every book published in modern history, has completed more than fifteen million volumes in the first decade of the project, and the speed at which they are working continues to increase. The company estimates that there are about 130 million books in the world; it is not unreasonable to speculate that they might finish digitizing them all within the lifetime of our students, if not ourselves.[9]

The traditional research method that we described above is clearly inadequate for dealing with an archive that is instantly accessible, machine-readable, growing exponentially and constantly being reordered. Anyone who thinks that they are capable of doing a systematic literature review these days is mistaken, and anyone who thinks that they have mastered a subject is dangerously misguided. As one begins to learn about anything, the amount of new information on that subject will accumulate faster than it can be read or understood. The long-term projects that we have tended to favour as a discipline (especially the traditional monograph) are almost guaranteed to be way out-of-touch by the time that they reach print ... and still more so by the time that anyone has a chance to read or respond to them. What we need now are humility, curiosity and nimbleness; or to put it in the terms of Isaiah Berlin's classic work, we all need to be (or become) foxes rather than hedgehogs.[10]

But how do we research effectively, efficiently, and as comprehensively as possible in the infinite archive? We have no wish to throw out the skills that lie at the core of our discipline: there is no substitute for close and critical reading, for careful citation, or for reasoned judgement. At the same time, there is no point in wasting human care or attention on tasks that can be done much faster and more thoroughly by machine.

To date, humanists have shown little willingness to make use of new technologies. 'The professoriate may be more liberal politically than the most latte-filled ZIP code in San Francisco', Dan Cohen writes,

> but we are an extraordinarily conservative bunch when it comes to the progression and presentation of our own work. We have done far less than we should have by this point in imagining and enacting what academic work and communication might look like if it was digital first.[11]

Historical papers are mainly written with reference to previously published journal articles, books and chapters, most of which are either in print or else are digitized versions of the printed format. Most online journals imitate print versions without providing even rudimentary tools for social interaction. The situation is a lot like the televised radio shows that were produced at the birth of TV: new media, old mentality. The preferred format for publishing scholarly work, especially in history, continues to be printed journals or books. Though these media are perfectly acceptable, a reluctance to embrace alternatives such as web publishing will only hurt scholarship as years pass.

The problem lies not only with the traditional establishments, but also with the scholars themselves. Basic word processors such as Microsoft Word are mainly used as digital typewriters, with few instructors or students making use of powerful cross-referencing abilities or even built-in reviewing tools. Researchers may use a computer to download digital versions of journals or books, or to search library catalogues, but often fall back on exploring the stacks themselves in order to find the marginalia that makes or breaks a project. Technology is often used to make the traditional methods a little bit easier without challenging standards or creating alternative procedures and tactics.

Organizations that serve scholarship have also found themselves on the trailing edge of technological trends. Only in the past couple of years have the Modern Language Association and the *Chicago Manual of Style* updated their standards to accommodate the use of websites, online publication, blogs and databases. A related problem is that traditional history has largely been based in text. While digital history makes use of text, too, there are any number of other media available, including hyperlinks, images, videos, audio recordings, visualizations and sonifications, equations, code, server logs, and still more exotic forms.[12] In order to capitalize on these media, new and old, history needs to shift focus from text to more integrated means of conveying information. This is particularly important as society continues to move further from a text-based culture towards one that incorporates aural and visual displays. Humanists need to present their research and teaching in multiple channels simultaneously.

One real problem here is that lecturers and professors tend not to consider the learning and teaching of digital skills to be part of their mandate. The most foolish profess an asinine commitment to 'Luddism', but we have yet to meet anyone who knows what that word means and would also be willing to give up the technologies of reading, writing or publishing. Most also seem to be completely accepting of underwear, toothbrushes, electric lights, bicycles, buildings, microwave ovens and pharmaceuticals. Being a 'Luddite' in the academy turns out to be a weak and incoherent commitment. More charitably, many teachers subscribe to the myth of the 'digital native', assuming that their students are more technologically savvy than they are themselves. This, alas, turns out to be quite wide of the mark.[13] Many of those teachers who do value digital skills assume that it should be someone else's responsibility to teach them, although whose responsibility is not at all clear. In Canada, at least, the vast majority of students majoring in history have never taken a computer science or programming class at the university level. If we do not incorporate these skills and techniques into our own classrooms, there is no reason to expect the current situation to change.

A method for digital research

There are any number of advanced computational techniques that can be used in humanities research, including text mining, machine learning, social network analysis and dynamic visualization. There are also sophisticated tools such as databases, web crawlers, search platforms and geographic information systems. Researchers who identify themselves as 'digital humanists' or 'digital historians', and many who do not, are already putting these tools and techniques to good use. We believe, however, that the work of all humanists can benefit from the adoption of a simpler, more fundamental digital workflow. The processes and tools that we will describe are not more complicated than those used for email or word processing, and the benefits obtain for *any* project, not only those that necessitate a high-tech approach. The seven fundamental principles of this method are:[14]

1. Make everything digital.
2. Keep stuff in the cloud.

3. Manage citations in a database.
4. The information comes to you.
5. Attention is the scarcest resource.
6. Work with others.
7. Share.

1. Make everything digital

If you have never really worked with digital sources or tools (besides word processing or exchanging email) there are a number of gentle introductions. We like Lisa Spiro's *Getting Started in the Digital Humanities*, and the wiki of digital research tools which she edits.[15] On the latter site you will find step-by-step instructions for many common tasks: 'I want to … analyze data, analyze texts, author an interactive work, blog, brainstorm/generate ideas … .' The magic ingredient for any of these tasks is a digital source. Usually you can find digital sources easily; learning how to do advanced searching with the major search engines really pays off here. Of course, one always has to be on guard against the idea that if a source is not digital, it does not exist! When you cannot find a digital source, you should make one of your own. If you have to look at a traditional (analogue) source once, you should digitize it, so that your computer can help you to find it quickly if and when you need it again. Any article, photograph, map, letter or book can be digitized and made searchable through the use of Optical Character Recognition (OCR) software. Simply collecting digital sources and storing them on a hard drive is analogous to creating a library without a catalogue. If a source has been collected during research, it can and should be made accessible for all future purposes by taking a few extra minutes to run OCR on the text and add the metadata required to keep a digital database. The last thing you want to do is engage in long and fruitless searches for things that you know you read *somewhere*.

Software such as Adobe Acrobat Pro makes quick work of scanning, recognizing and adding metadata to a file that will allow your computer to retrieve the document when needed. Flatbed scanners are best used for books, larger media, and fragile objects such as photographs and slides. Printed documents can be easily scanned with an automatic document feeder that scans a stack of pages without user involvement. For short passages, handheld pen scanners are useful to trace over and capture the text, much the same way as a highlighting pen works. Photographs taken with a digital camera can also be recognized, and are particularly useful for capturing large or complex pieces. Improvements to camera phone technology make mobile devices a handy way to digitize a document and even the camera capabilities on the iPad are adequate for some documents, though you might have to play with lighting to ensure a clear picture. As a general rule, if a camera of any kind can take high-quality images of printed text, OCR software will be able to recognize it.[16]

Adobe's Portable Document Format (PDF) stores both an image of the page and, optionally, a layer of text that has been recognized with OCR. The former is used by humans for reading, the latter by computers for searching. Additionally, Adobe Acrobat (or similar programs) will usually prompt the user to enter metadata about the document to facilitate searching and citation. Basic meta-data such as author and title are crucial, but extended metadata help categorize and track documents. Some online content providers use OCR on their own documents to facilitate keyword searching, but strip out the text layer before providing it for download by the user. Acrobat Pro allows you to re-OCR the document, thus making it very much more useful.

Software such as DevonThink and Evernote allow you to create a library of digital sources that are organized by tags, categories or folders that are relevant for your own project. When searching for a term in DevonThink, for instance, a user can specify which folders to include in the search, expanding or limiting the scope of results. A user can also interact with digital sources through Acrobat or DevonThink in ways that are familiar from working with paper documents: adding comments and sticky notes, highlighting or underlining important passages, and the like.

2. Keep stuff in the cloud

One of the most important advantages of working solely with digital sources is that it is possible to duplicate your entire research project quickly and very inexpensively. Obviously you should do this for backup purposes: the time to create both local and offsite backups is before catastrophe strikes. If your research project is distributed across paper notebooks, physical books, photo-copies, microfilm, fiche, 3x5 cards, and so on, you cannot really create a complete backup. More than one scholar has lost years of work and had to abandon a monograph or dissertation when his or her house or office caught fire, and practically everyone who has done a large project has worried about such things.

Digital backups have additional advantages beyond what librarians refer to as the LOCKSS principle (Lots of Copies Keep Stuff Safe). One is version control. Programs like Apple's Time Machine allow you not only to recover lost files, but to revert to earlier versions of a particular text. A less fancy mechanism, but one that is just as serviceable, is to duplicate a file each time you edit it and add the date to the filename in the *YYYYMMDD* format. Dates in this format will auto-matically sort in the correct order in both Windows File Explorer and Mac OS X Finder, making it easy to trace a history of revisions through filenames alone.

Digital files are also easily, inexpensively and privately stored on servers maintained by third parties and accessed via a web browser. Such 'cloud' storage gives you access to your research from any computer that has an internet connection. Some of the best-known and most useful examples are Google Docs, Dropbox, Evernote and JungleDisk. A service like Google Docs provides scaled-down office software in the browser (word processor, spreadsheet, etc.) while allowing documents to be shared with and modified by collaborators. Dropbox is integrated with your own system of files and folders, making sharing as easy as dragging and dropping. (We wrote this paper together by sharing Scrivener and

Word files in a Dropbox folder, for example.) If you've ever been frustrated trying to coordinate a co-authored article or grant application by emailing attachments to your colleagues, give one of these services a try. Other cloud-based programs, such as Evernote, are designed to provide one place to store your notes so that they can be accessed on every internet-enabled device that you own. JungleDisk provides automated, inexpensive online backup that can be scheduled to run unattended.

3. Manage citations in a database

The necessity for keeping good metadata is one of the first principles that novice scholars learn. The proper place for such information is in a database that is specifically designed for it. Citation management systems include freely available programs such as Zotero and Mendeley, both of which allow cloud-based storage and collaboration, and commercial alternatives such as Sente, Endnote and RefWorks. Each of these programs has advantages and disadvantages. Zotero, for instance, can scrape metadata from sites like Google Books, Google Scholar, Open WorldCat or Amazon.com, and will automatically store URLs and page images for sources found online so that you can access the version that you consulted even if the online version changes. Many of these tools can export citations into word processors using pre-formatted style guides, and can automatically create bibliographies from the selected sources.

4. The information comes to you

Think of a search as an activity that you do once, when you are looking for something in particular: a name, a date, a fact. When you find what you are looking for, you skim the results, make a note of the source, and, perhaps, book-mark the site if you think that it will be useful in the future. When you want to keep up with the news on a topic, or want a steady stream of results, it is usually better to pursue a strategy that Tara Calishain calls 'information trapping'.[17] Major search engines like Google and Yahoo! provide mechanisms for creating RSS feeds from searches. When you subscribe to an RSS feed (for 'RDF Site Summary' or 'Really Simple Syndication'), your computer is notified whenever something changes. By monitoring RSS feeds from searches using a program called a feed reader or feed aggregator, you get a steady stream of news about your topic, combined into a single report. You can use a desktop application like NetNewsWire on the Mac or an online service like Google Reader.

Additional techniques can make this strategy even more powerful. First of all, it is possible to use a service like Feed43 to create RSS feeds for any webpage. This has a bit more of a learning curve, but it allows you to monitor anything on the web. Second, Yahoo! Pipes provides a mechanism for combing RSS feeds with other kinds of computational processing. Again, there is a learning curve, but it is well worth it. Finally, other tools called crawlers, spiders or bots search the internet for specific content and download or index it. Crawlers can be coded from scratch, but for those without programming skills, programs such as DevonAgent offer significant modularity and depth. The major benefit of these tools is that they can be set up and then left to run while you work on other tasks.[18]

5. Attention is the scarcest resource

As the late Roy Rosenzweig argued, historians now face a culture of abundance.[19] The scarcest resource in your research process is always going to be your own time. Ideally, then, you only want to pay attention to those things which absolutely require it, and to hand everything else over to computer programs. Software tools help to focus attention through indexing, concordance, visualization, clustering and relating. DevonThink, for instance, can index documents in a collection to create a concordance. Terms can be sorted by weight or frequency, excluded, or used to compare documents. Proprietary algorithms analyze documents or passages to automatically cluster them by similarity, summarize them, or find other sources that are most closely related. Computationally sophisticated researchers can write their own programs for text mining or machine learning, but tools like DevonThink bring those abilities within reach of non-programmers.

Another way to highlight otherwise obscure connections is to use visualization tools such as Stéfan Sinclair's Voyant or the IBM web service ManyEyes. Kee and Roberts ran a set of digital humanities syllabi through a visualization program to identify which authors were read most often and which university courses required students to read similar material. Such work can be done the hard way, of course, but digital tools expedite the process and allow the researcher to focus on questions and interpretation, rather than bean counting.

6. Work with others

Social media such as blogs and forums provide the glue that holds together large communities of people interested in any given topic, whether paid professionals or amateur enthusiasts. These communities provide a wealth of knowledge and expertise, opportunity to engage in public history, and a collective intelligence that can be leveraged to solve problems outside the scope of any single individual. As our colleague Shawn Graham discovered during his attempt to implement history learning through the commercial game *Civilization IV*, the most knowledgeable communities are often found in unlikely spaces. The CivFanatics Forum provided for Graham a wealth of knowledge about how gamers modify the parameters of the software to replicate historical events, but also demonstrated a depth of historical knowledge about the ancient world that surpassed the content of many university-level courses.[20] Alternate Reality Games (ARGs) demonstrate how communities working in unison can solve problems that otherwise defy solution. When Jane McGonigal helped to build an ARG for the release of *Halo 2*, she could not have envisioned that the players would become so adept at solving the problems designed by the game team. Collective intelligence worked so well that 'as the players invented smarter strategies and honed their coordination skills to meet these challenges, the designers were pushed to imagine future challenges even more difficult and confounding'.[21] Though ARGs have not yet been used extensively for answering research questions, historians, such as our colleague Rob MacDougall, have begun to experiment with the capabilities of communities engaged in investigating historical events.[22]

7. *Share*

Many of the communication barriers that prevented wide-scale collaboration have been eliminated in the digital age. When physical travel or paper publication costs limited opportunities for the public sharing of research results, they could only be presented intermittently. Content can now be shared much more regularly, and the costs of not doing so outweigh any benefit to sitting on results. Many scholars find that posting to research weblogs help them to clarify their own ideas, while putting them in touch with potential collaborators, informants, readers, would-be students, journalists and others. Communities that use sites like Twitter can instantly share job, grant and conference announcements, links to articles and news, information about databases or new repositories of sources, and the like. Research results published online in an open access venue reach the widest possible audience, and highlight the importance of *post hoc* peer review. For better or for worse, they also make scholarship much more interactive and dynamic, linking researchers to much wider communities of participation.

The method hits the road

Turkel and Kee were both on sabbatical in 2010–11, giving them time to experiment with processes of research and teaching. Looking for a faster way to research and write a monograph – the previous one took him seven years – Turkel found Steven Johnson's and Chad Black's articles on the Macintosh program DevonThink.[23] He realized that by using all digital sources and combining a number of off-the-shelf programs (including DevonThink) he could work much more efficiently. As a result of using a collection of programs to find, harvest, cluster, excerpt and keep track of digital sources, Turkel's second monograph took about ten months to research, write and submit to a publisher.[24] When Kee found out about this, he decided to try teaching the method to graduate students (and Roberts was one of them). We briefly report on the results of that experiment here.

The method was introduced to the students in the context of an introductory course on the digital humanities.[25] The course honoured convention, requiring that students *think about* digital humanities through definitions, theoretical problems and examples. It also required that students *think with* digital humanities, exploring the ways in which computing could support their conventional research agendas (ranging, for example, from studies of fifteenth-century Norse manuscripts to eighteenth-century New England fashion), and transform their established research practices. For the students, digital humanities thus became the process of incorporating computing into their own humanistic practice.

Each week the students examined a research process, and then experimented with using a specific tool to make that process more efficient. To support their exploration they were given blog posts about digital methods, tutorials created by the makers of each tool, and in some cases supplemental tutorials written by Kee and Roberts. During the first week, they backed up their files, used Dropbox to access and exchange course-related material, and installed Zotero to manage their own citations (as well as access the references for the course). In addition, they accessed and contributed to course content via a Wiki (and began learning to use a simple mark-up language related to HTML).

Building on this foundation, they then turned their attention to social media. Each student created a blog, where he or she was required to comment on class readings, in-class discussion, Wiki discussion, the blog posts of classmates, and the blog and Twitter feeds followed by the student. Each also created his or her own Twitter feed, and set up an RSS aggregator such as Google Reader. During the third and fourth weeks, students were required to become conversant with HTML, and to do some very basic text analysis with Wordle and the Google Ngram Viewer. The fifth week provided a bit of a respite, during which the students used Adobe Acrobat Pro and learned about doing OCR (Optical Character Recognition). During the last half of the course, the focus shifted to research tools and the organization and analysis of research notes. The students worked with Google Advanced Search and DevonAgent, Evernote, DevonThink (or similar tool for the PC) and Scrivener. In the final week of their abbreviated introduction to this method they were encouraged to explore a software tool of their choice.

During the last two weeks of the course, the eleven students were asked to reflect on their use of the method in their blogs, and to comment specifically on the processes and tools that they found the most, and the least, helpful. According to many of the students, the use of these processes and tools was transformative. While a professor needs to approach students' praise of an assignment with healthy scepticism, the level of engagement was obvious and genuine throughout the term. At the same time, to the considerable credit of the students, they were very frank with their criticism.

Some complaints were unavoidable. Windows users were understandably frustrated that tools such as DevonThink and Scrivener were only available on the Macintosh operating system. In some cases, students found themselves overwhelmed by a surfeit of new interfaces and possibilities. DevonThink, in particular, came under withering criticism for an inordinate number of options and uses. One student captured the feeling of several classmates when she recalled 'looking at the screen and feeling lost'.

In some cases, students were overwhelmed by assignments that required them to rebuild their research practices at the same time that they were being challenged to rethink, in this and other courses, how they conceptualized the humanities. In the midst of this storm, some held fast to the familiar. 'Once I have something which works why should I change it?' one student asked. If the usefulness of a tool was not obvious or demonstrable, many understandably rejected it. The foray into the use of HTML, for example, elicited near-uniform dismay. This technology was viewed by many students to be the domain of computer programmers whose job it is to design and develop websites. 'Don't get me wrong', one student remarked, 'I would love to be technologically gifted, but I'm not'.[26] Many students thought it would be best to focus on their own areas of competence or specialization, and to build collaborative relationships whenever they needed to create something outside their own abilities.

Not surprisingly, time-starved graduate students most appreciated processes and tools that enabled them to do that which they had been assigned (in their several courses) more efficiently. As one noted, 'overall, I am in favour of practical tools which help me organize, sort, and speed up my research. ... I need organization, efficiency, and reliability.' 'With these tools I can get through the drudgy bits a lot quicker', said another. Connecting with scholarly communities, doing research for specific projects, organizing sources, reading more efficiently, writing more effectively and managing citations were their highest priorities.

Social media tools brought them into contact with scholars with similar research interests. Twitter was especially helpful here. Many of the students took to Twitter grudgingly, viewing it as a space best left to celebrities and people who want to microblog what they ate for lunch. They quickly became converts after finding, to their considerable surprise, active researchers working in their own domains. 'I began by just browsing twitter accounts that I could follow', one medievalist in training wrote, 'ByzantinePhil, Medievalists.net, Early Scottish History, etc. I then followed what they tweeted ... and boy, am I glad I took notice. Medievalists.net especially allowed me access to various articles on medieval topics. Want to learn about Icelandic horses or medicine during the Crusades? ... twitter [*sic*] has your fix. ... Twitter has offered me a great wealth of information.' More often than not, students were happy to lurk; few commented on the relationships that they had formed via Twitter. In the majority of cases, the students were only a few weeks into their graduate careers (nine of the eleven were MA students), and were more comfortable playing the role of learner, rather than contributor, in these virtual research communities.[27]

Once they became aware of new sources, students used Evernote to sort them. This cloud-based application makes it easier to manage incoming streams of sources because it can be accessed by laptop, smart phone or tablet ... any device with a web browser. As one noted, the 'ability to just throw things into Evernote means I don't forget/misplace/lose any valuable information I come across'. The task of determining which resources deserved attention was made easier with tools like Adobe Acrobat Pro and DevonThink. Several especially resourceful students also used the software to keep up with their assigned class readings for every course. 'Acrobat Pro helps with, and even improves, my readings of assigned texts', one student confessed, 'which has been particularly useful during those weekends when I have hundreds of pages to get through for upcoming seminars and want to do a good job understanding them'. 'Though I hesitate to admit the following', confessed another, 'I can use the concordance tool [of DevonThink] to see which words occur most frequently in a document, filter them by word length, and very quickly get an idea of what the document is about and what terms are significant to the author'.

Another key component of graduate studies in the humanities – the writing of essays – was also reconsidered and, for many students, altered. The majority adopted Scrivener, a new writing tool. For some, it was a friend: 'it goes out of its way to make my life easier'. 'It allows me to build my paper as I always should have', remarked another, 'in sections specifically related to topics and parts of my argument and then look at the flow of my writing and seamlessly rearrange the parts to fit together in a more cohesive fashion'. The only software that rivalled Scrivener in terms of popularity was Zotero. By the end of the first month, many students were using Zotero to handle their citations in all of their courses. 'As the semester is quickly winding down', one student remarked, 'the bibliographies I've put together in Zotero have proved vital for me in terms of my ability to complete all upcoming papers successfully and on time'. Returning to the utility of social media for researchers, many students quickly came to appreciate the benefits of Zotero Groups, which as one noted, 'connects me to bibliographies that I no longer have to spend hours in the library trying to find (if indeed I find them all anyway). So here at the end of this course I can definitely say that Zotero will continue to be a part of my life and work, both inside and outside academia.'

Students had to use Zotero to access the sources for the course, and this requirement may have made early converts. In most cases, however, the limits of the academic calendar meant less time to experiment with method. As a result, a fast learning curve was key for the adoption of particular tools. Evernote required almost no preparation: within five minutes of installing the software, students were using most of its affordances. The multiple options of other tools, however, required a commitment that some were unwilling to make. At the same time, several students acknowledged that their patience had been rewarded; accidental discoveries (and last-moment conversions) were not uncommon.

According to their own testimony, a small percentage finished the course relieved that the experiment was over. Others, however, found that their workflows had been fundamentally altered. They were employing novel ways of thinking and new kinds of reading, such as using software to 'read' papers that had been assigned in their classes. One student moved beyond a piecemeal adoption of certain tools to a complete commitment to the method, and especially to DevonThink. 'Quite simply', he noted, 'DevonThink has revolutionized the way I research, organize, read, and study. I no longer print articles, but rather download or scan them, run them through an OCR process, and add them to my DT library. ... After only four months of use, my DT library has 400 unique items,

100,000 unique words, and over 2.6 million words total, all of which can be searched and related within groups of documents.' This tool enabled him to combine source materials in a way that had previously not been possible. 'I can merge multiple documents and perform a similar analysis, identifying the common terms among a selection of sources.' As a result, he was able to see connections that had before remained hidden, and ask questions that had not previously occurred to him. 'Without DevonThink, such work would be preventatively painstaking and tedious; with this tool, however, I find myself uncovering deeper connections and asking important questions because I can focus on interpretation and synthesis.'

Perhaps the most compelling reflection, however, came not in response to a specific piece of software. According to one student, 'there was something more important that I took away from the tools as a whole, not just with regards to the trajectory of an individual method'. Instead, she noted that

> the fact that I was exposed to so many different types of methods … and that some of them … actually turned out to be useful without being scary is really important to me. Not only do I now have some new tools to use while I'm doing research … I'm also more open-minded towards using them in the first place and really trying to engage with them, rather than brushing them off.

Helping these emerging humanists take a more experimental stance towards computing may be the most important outcome of this course.

In conclusion, we need to be clear. We do not think you should adopt the method that we presented in this chapter. By the time you read this, after all, many of our processes will have been refined and some of our tools superseded by better ones. Other people in our community will have adapted versions of the method that are more suitable for particular tasks, and a few generations of students will have helped us to figure out what is working and what is not. As with everything now, all is flux. What we do think is that any scholar or student can benefit from becoming more mindful about their method … not as something that one acquires once and forgets about, but rather as something that one practises every day, making continuous small improvements over the course of a lifetime. Method is like historiography: when it stops changing, it is effectively dead. We need to keep changing, too.

Notes

1 Obviously history favours the former, although subfields like environmental history, the history of technology and public history often involve more hands-on work.
2 G. E. Moore, 'Cramming more components onto integrated circuits', *Electronics*, 38: 8 (19 April 1965), 114–17. This quote on p. 115.
3 P. E. Ceruzzi, 'Moore's law and technological determinism: reflections on the history of technology', *Technology and Culture*, 46: 3 (2005), 584–93.
4 J. D. Cressler, *Silicon Earth: Introduction to the Microelectronics and Nanotechnology Revolution* (New York: Cambridge University Press, 2009).

5 M. McGee, 'By the numbers: Twitter vs. Facebook vs. Google Buzz', *Search Engine Land* (23 February 2010), http://searchengineland.com/by-the-numbers-twitter-vs-facebook-vs-google-buzz-36709 [accessed: 25 March 2012]; CTIA: The Wireless Association, *Semi-Annual Wireless Industry Survey Results* (7 October 2009), http://www.businesswire.com/portal/site/google/?ndmViewId=news_view&newsId=200910 07006200 [accessed: 25 March 2012]; H. Walk, 'Great Scott! Over 35 hours of video uploaded every minute to YouTube', *Broadcasting Ourselves: The Official YouTube Blog* (10 November 2010), http://youtube-global.blogspot.com/2010/11/great-scott-over-35-hours-of-video.html [accessed: 25 March 2012].

6 P. Lyman and H. R. Varian, *How Much Information?* (School of Information Management and Systems, University of California, Berkeley, 2003), http://www2.sims.berkeley.edu/research/projects/how-much-info-2003/ [accessed: 25 March 2012]; R. E. Bohn and J. E. Short, *How Much Information? A Report on American Consumers* (Global Information Industry Center, University of California, San Diego, 2009), http://hmi.ucsd.edu/pdf/HMI_2009_ConsumerReport_Dec9_2009.pdf [accessed: 25 March 2012].

7 H. Abelson, K. Ledeen and H. Lewis, *Blown to Bits: Your Life, Liberty, and Happiness after the Digital Explosion* (Upper Saddle River, NJ: Addison-Wesley, 2008), p. 9.

8 D. Cohen, 'Defining the digital humanities', Research Without Borders Conference, Columbia University (6 April 2011), http://scholcomm.columbia.edu/2011/02/10/defining-the-digital-humanities/ [accessed: 25 March 2012].

9 J. Crawford, *On the Future of Books* (14 October 2010), http://booksearch.blogspot.com/2010/10/on-future-of-books.html [accessed: 25 March 2012]; B. Parr, 'Google: There are 129,864,880 books in the entire world', *Mashable* (6 August 2010), http://mashable.com/2010/08/06/number-of-books-in-the-world/ [accessed: 25 March 2012].

10 I. Berlin, *The Hedgehog and the Fox: An Essay on Tolstoy's View of History* (Chicago: Ivan R. Dee, 1993).

11 D. Cohen, *The Ivory Tower and the Open Web: Introduction: Burritos, Browsers, and Books* [Draft], (26 July 2011) http://www.dancohen.org/2011/07/26/the-ivory-tower-and-the-open-web-introduction-burritos-browsers-and-books-draft/ [accessed: 25 March 2008].

12 W. J. Turkel, 'Hacking history, from analog to digital and back again', *Rethinking History*, 15: 2 (2011), 287–96.

13 See, for example, S. Vaidhyanathan, 'Generational myth', *Chronicle of Higher Education* (19 September 2008). Our own experience with teaching both undergraduate and graduate students is that they tend to be similarly unprepared for digital work from one year to the next.

14 This is adapted from W. J. Turkel, *A Workflow for Digital Research Using Off-the-Shelf Tools* (15 March–5 April, 2011), http://williamjturkel.net/how-to/ [accessed: 25 March 2012].

15 L. Spiro, *Getting Started in the Digital Humanities* (14 October 2011), http://digitalscholarship.wordpress.com/2011/10/14/getting-started-in-the-digital-humanities/ [accessed: 25 March 2012]; Bamboo DiRT: Digital Research Tools wiki, http://dirt.projectbamboo.org/ [accessed: 25 March 2012]; see also W. J. Turkel, *Going Digital* (15 March 2011), http://williamjturkel.net/2011/03/15/going-digital/ [accessed: 25 March 2012].

16 Handwritten text continues to elude OCR. If you are not going to type a full transcription, add a handful of keywords to the metadata.

17 T. Calishain, *Information Trapping: Real-Time Research on the Web* (Berkeley: New Riders, 2007).

18 Many historians are (rightly) suspicious that automated searching often fails to turn up crucial evidence because present-day technology is insensitive to nuance, fails to understand various kinds of circumlocution, does not deal gracefully with ambiguity, synonymy, metaphorical usage, etc. All of these concerns are valid. The best way to address them is to become a more sophisticated user or creator of technology, rather

than abandoning it altogether. The time that you spend carefully reading one document is time that you do not spend scanning through others.

19 R. Rosenzweig, 'Scarcity or abundance? Preserving the past in a digital era', *American Historical Review*, 108: 3 (2003), 735–62.

20 S. Graham, *Re-Playing History: The Year of the Four Emperors and Civilization IV*, Subject Centre for History, Classics, and Archaeology, The Higher Education Academy.

21 J. McGonigal, 'Why I love bees: a case study in collective intelligence gaming', in K. Salen (ed.), *The Ecology of Games: Connecting Youth, Games, and Learning* (Cambridge, MA: MIT Press, 2007), p. 221.

22 T. Compeau and R. MacDougall, 'Tecumseh lies here: goals and challenges for a pervasive history game in progress', in K. Kee (ed.), *Pastplay: Teaching and Learning History with Technology* (forthcoming).

23 S. Johnson, 'Tool for thought', *New York Times* (30 January 2005), http://www.nytimes.com/2005/01/30/books/review/30JOHNSON.html?_r=1&oref=login [accessed: 25 March 2012]; *More Information*, stevenberlinjohnson.com (29 January 2005), http://www.stevenberlinjohnson.com/movabletype/archives/000230.html [accessed: 25 March 2012]; and 'DIY: how to write a book', *BoingBoing* (27 January 2009), http://www.boingboing.net/2009/01/27/diy-how-to-write-a-b.html [accessed: 25 March 2012]; C. Black, 'DevonThink and other Mac Apps for history and humanities research', *Parezco Y Digo* (12 November 2008), http://parezcoydigo.wordpress.com/2008/11/12/devonthink-and-other-mac-apps-for-history-and-humanities-research/ [accessed: 25 March 2012]; 'DevonThink for historical research, Part II', *Parezco Y Digo* (13 November 2008), http://parezcoydigo.wordpress.com/2008/11/13/devonthink-for-historical-research-part-ii/ [accessed: 25 March 2012]; and 'DevonThink for historical research, Part III', *Parezco Y Digo* (29 November 2008), http://parezcoydigo.wordpress.com/2008/11/29/devonthink-for-historical-research-iii/ [accessed: 25 March 2012]. See also C. Black, 'Update on the ever-changing method', *Parezco Y Digo* (14 March 2011), http://parezcoydigo.wordpress.com/2011/03/14/update-on-the-ever-changing-workflow/ [accessed: 25 March 2012].

24 This was the so-called 'super-secret monograph'. See W. J. Turkel, 'On operating in stealth mode' (21 February 2011), http://williamjturkel.net/2011/02/21/stealth-mode/ [accessed: 25 March 2012]. Note that not all of the sources used for this project were 'born digital'. Many were digitized as part of the process of research and writing.

25 HUMA/HIST 5V71: humanities computing, Brock University, Fall 2011. The course outline, including an abridged version of the method, can be found at http://kevinkee.ca/www.kevinkee.ca/wp-content/uploads/Courseoutline_blog.pdf [accessed: 25 March 2012].

26 Turkel has had more luck introducing his graduate students to HTML, CSS and simple coding, although in a different context (interactive exhibit design). The utility of HTML is not nearly as evident in the research workflow that we describe here, although we would argue that *some* familiarity with markup languages is a crucial component of twenty-first-century literacy.

27 Turkel has had similar experiences assigning student blogging and tweeting as required coursework for public history graduate students: it takes them a while to get used to the idea that they are going to have to start 'doing history' in the public eye. They are usually much easier to convince than members of their 'regular history' graduate cohort, however.

Studying history in the digital age

4 Doing and making

History as digital practice

Jim Mussell

> Like all media revolutions, the first wave of the digital revolution looked back-
> ward as it moved forward. Just as early codices mirrored oratorical practices,
> print initially mirrored the practices of high medieval manuscript culture, and
> film mirrored the techniques of theater, the digital first wave replicated the
> world of scholarly communications that print gradually codified over the course
> of five centuries: a world where textuality was primary and visuality and sound
> were secondary (and subordinated to text), even as it vastly accelerated the
> search and retrieval of documents, enhanced access, and altered mental habits.
> Now it must shape a future in which the medium-specific features of digital
> technologies become its core and in which print is absorbed into new hybrid
> modes of communication.[1]

In *A Digital Humanities Manifesto 2.0*, the authors argue that the digital revolution has entered a second phase, in which digital objects (and environments,
tools and technologies) are considered on their own terms, rather than as deri-
vatives or surrogates for those from the non-digital world. In the first phase, the
manifesto suggests, the digital revolution reproduced versions of print forms
and the disciplinary apparatus that sustained them and gave them meaning. The
second phase, alive to the specificities of different media (and the technologies
upon which they depend), decentres print and so reconfigures the conditions
under which the disciplines produce and codify knowledge. In this chapter, I
examine how historians might engage with and benefit from this next phase of
the digital revolution. Historians of all kinds already practise digital scholarship,
whether this is composing papers using word processors, communicating via email
and Twitter, or using digital resources to locate and access documents of various kinds. Historians are also actively building resources, perhaps collaborating
with or identifying themselves as digital humanists. Digital resources, tools and
technologies have become integral instruments through which we interrogate and
understand the past. As these instruments continue to change, so too does the
practice of history.

The manifesto is a necessarily provocative document that heralds the digital
humanities as the set of methodologies necessary to reimagine scholarship in the
digital age. One of its authors, Todd Presner, calls the rejuvenated digital

humanities, liberated from their previously servile position, the 'digital humanities 2.0'.[2] While wary of such predictions, I think there is a case for imagining a corresponding 'digital history 2.0'. The manifesto posits a world in which print 'is no longer the exclusive or the normative medium in which knowledge is produced and/or disseminated' and 'digital tools, techniques, and media have altered the production and dissemination of knowledge in the arts, human and social sciences.'[3] While the digital humanities, described by the manifesto as 'an array of convergent practices', are undoubtedly well placed to interrogate and participate in such a world, the manifesto, in its bid for disciplinary space, overlooks the extent to which other disciplines have a stake in the digital and can offer frameworks within which its significance and meaning can be understood.[4] This revolution is, after all, an historical event, its momentum sustained by a set of contingent circumstances that are open to analysis. It is the transformation of our heritage accomplished through media transformation, a process subject to scrutiny in a number of humanities disciplines. If the digital humanities are to have an influence upon the more established disciplines in the humanities, it can only be through collaboration and this means that influence will work in both directions. The transformation from digital humanities 1.0 to 2.0 was initiated by broader shifts in digital culture but it is sustained by continued interactions with the older disciplines of the humanities. Rather than a messianic digital humanities 2.0 rejuvenating these disciplines for a new era, I see digital humanities 2.0 as one of the many disciplinary transformations that will result when existing expertise is brought to bear on new objects and methods.

In what follows I assume that digital resources of various kinds are already integral to historical practice but argue that if the discipline is to take full advantages of the digital revolution, then it must engage more closely with the digital properties that give these resources their character. If the first phase of the digital revolution focused on the computer's capacity for simulation, then the next phase will be the result of once more making it strange. The chapter is arranged in two parts. In the first I describe what I understand as digital history 1.0 and set out how this would differ from digital history 2.0. Taking my own field, nineteenth-century media history, as an example, I describe this transition as one predicated on a shift from documents to data. In the second part, I turn to the resources that will effect this transition, arguing that they are not just tools but legitimate objects of historical enquiry in themselves. One of the questions raised by the shift from documents to data concerns the status of the archive. As long as the archive is considered distinct from historical practice, a static set of documents against which history refines itself, then digital resources can only ever be instruments that provide access. However, if we recognize that in transforming the archive and rendering it processable it becomes something different, then these resources become constitutive parts of the archive and so subject to analysis in their own right. At stake in the shift from digital history 1.0 to 2.0 is the recognition that the traditional techniques of historical scholarship remain relevant, but that they are also necessarily transformed by the radical reconstitution of the archive. The name 'digital history 2.0' marks a break from digital history 1.0, but it remains history nonetheless.

From documents to data

The shift to history 2.0 requires a change in focus from document to data. It is the ability of the digital to sufficiently represent other media while bestowing upon them a particular form of materiality that has ensured digital resources are widely used in the humanities. However, the facility with which digital media can simulate non-digital forms means that it is easy to overlook the extent this depends upon digital properties. As N. Katherine Hayles has argued in a discussion of digital editions of printed texts, this amazing capacity for simulation is only possible because the computer is 'completely unlike print in its architecture and functioning'.[5] The more successful the reproduction, the easier it is to be seduced by the simulation and so treat the simulated media as if it was the non-digital material. The same might also be said for born-digital objects. As many applications exploit a repertoire of learned behaviour online, resources tend to correspond to recognized genres in order not to bewilder their users. Just as those resources that translate non-digital material attempt to reproduce their corresponding – and so familiar – patterns of use into the digital environment, so resources using born-digital material appropriate and exploit conventions from the digital environment and beyond in order to create a recognizable interface. The shift to history 2.0 depends, to an extent, on using digital resources against the grain of their interfaces in order to access the data they contain. It is a shift that depends upon defamiliarization, on recognizing what is distinct about digital media and technologies and then exploiting this digital difference for scholarly ends.

My field, nineteenth-century media history, is very much entrenched in digital history 1.0. The industrialized presses of the nineteenth century produced an enormous amount of material, in a wide range of forms, issued in single editions, in parts and in reprints, for a variety of audiences. Large amounts of this material have survived in the archive, but in a fragmentary condition. Despite some Herculean bibliographic work (the *Wellesley Index*, the various series of the *Waterloo Directory*, the *Dictionary of Nineteenth-Century Journalism*),[6] the archive remains difficult to work with. Many publications survive in runs too long to read; they are almost always incomplete, perhaps because not all issues survive, but also because they were routinely transformed on accession; and all periodicals and newspapers demand a high degree of contextual knowledge from the researcher, often requiring them to work between and across disciplines with a diverse and nearly always unsigned text. As a result, research into the press has necessarily been patchy, focusing on particular publications or people and relying upon existing disciplinary structures (certain authors, types of text, key events, etc.), at the expense of a rigorous analysis of the mechanisms of journalism or publishing more broadly.[7]

Digital resources of nineteenth-century newspapers and periodicals have existed online since the publication of resources such as Cornell University's and the University of Michigan's *Making of America* (1995), ProQuest's *Periodicals Contents Index* (1997), the *Internet Library of Early Journals* (ILEJ, 1999) and

Heritage Microfilm's *newspaperARCHIVE* (1999). Many of these early resources were ambitious in scope, but they have been surpassed by more recent resources such as ProQuest's *ProQuest Historical Newspapers* (2001–) and *British Periodicals* (2007), the British Library's *British Newspapers 1800–1900* (published by Gale Cengage (2007) and also called *Nineteenth Century British Library Newspapers*), and Gale Cengage's *Nineteenth Century UK Periodicals* (2007). More recently, the British Library and Brightsolid have published the *British Newspaper Archive* (2011–), providing access (at a cost) to four million pages, with more to come up to a projected forty million. Over the last twenty years we have gained access to hundreds of publications from anywhere with a web browser (and, in most cases listed above, appropriate access rights).

These digital resources have transformed the field by altering the conditions of access to its primary materials. Built around searchable keyword indices, nearly always developed from uncorrected transcripts produced from Optical Character Recognition (OCR) technologies, these resources subject the archive to a degree of bibliographic control. Not only do they render individual publications searchable but, by using text as the basis for the index, create the conditions for a cross-searchable database that can open up the press as a whole. There were printed reference resources that provided a degree of access across the archive, and many individual publications produced indices for volumes of periodicals as they were produced, but there was nothing like the coverage provided by a single one of the new digital resources. The ability to cross-search not only makes it easy to locate content, but also allows it to be traced across publications, exposing many of the connections occluded when reading one publication at a time. Although users might be drawn towards certain events or historical figures, the search engine's algorithms will return hits that it predicts are relevant, often returning familiar figures in unfamiliar contexts or providing articles that supply an unexpected perspective on an event. Search can disrupt existing hierarchies, complementing major figures, events or themes with a host of others who might otherwise be overlooked. As the search engine does not discriminate between types of content (unless instructed by the user), it also has the potential to displace or supplement existing canons of periodicals or newspapers, reminding users, for instance, of the diversity of periodical publication, or the importance of the provincial press. As portions of page images are returned (to compensate for the errors in the transcript), the resources reproduce the bibliographic codes on the page, providing access to the typeface, layout and any other visual features that constitute the printed text. By making its verbal content processable, these resources manage the scale and complexity of the print archive. They are designed to allow researchers to locate and recover articles in a form that reproduces the appearance of the printed page. The principal gains are efficiency and access: tasks that would have been prohibitively labour-intensive are routine; and the archive itself is now available to more people, in many more locations.

Digitization is a radical transformation of material form and so takes place in an economy of loss and gain. However, the rhetoric of surrogacy that underpins many of these resources masks the extent to which they differ from the printed material in the archives. There is much that can be learned about the press through the process of digitization, but for users, who are often positioned as passive consumers of content, there is little that could not be learned from looking at the appropriate hard copy. In fact, as is frequently noted, there are aspects of printed media such as weight, texture, smell and (to an extent) size that can only be appreciated by considering the material in the archives. In exchange for the non- or partial representation of various material aspects of printed objects, the user gains considerable increases in searchability and accessibility. These gains are predicated on the material properties of the digital objects produced during digitization, but the user is not in a position to evaluate these processes or their efficiency. For instance, as is well recognized, OCR, despite the claims of its vendors, rarely achieves the success rates in recognizing text from historical newspapers, usually due to the condition of the surviving hard copy.[8] This means that the searchable index only provides a partial representation of the text printed upon the page and reproduced on the scanned facsimile images. Yet very few resources allow users to see the OCR-generated transcript upon which their search queries are executed. Equally, even though many resources compete on scope, the corpus of publications that make up their contents is skewed towards certain types of publications in certain types of institution. Again, despite this, commercial vendors seldom provide information about the derivation of the content in resources and rarely provide contents lists so that users can ascertain what, exactly, they are searching. In both cases this data is present but is withheld from users so that they can get on with searching for and reading articles, one by one. These resources are designed to mimic (a version of) the print object upon which they are based and so, often deliberately, do not allow their users to take full advantage of the data that they contain.

Despite the long-standing interest in this material (because it is free of troublesome rights issues), the core methodology and functionality of the resulting digital resources have remained remarkably consistent for almost twenty years. Nearly every single resource offering access to nineteenth-century British newspapers and periodicals privileges search over browse, redefining the serials on the library shelves as a database of discrete articles. This means that users are expected to be looking for something and that this can be mapped to the occurrence of words in a transcript and described in a search query. Serendipity still applies, as the scale of the archive means that the user, with little sense of the archive as a whole and restricted to browsing lists of metadata to determine which hits to read, will probably be surprised at what has been returned. Yet restricting the use of the underlying data to an index, which can only be queried in ways delimited by the interface in order to return articles, limits the interpretive potential of this data.

Print has a foundational relationship with repetition, and so printed objects lend themselves to computational analysis. Corpus linguistics has been connected with humanities computing since the work of Father Busa in the 1940s, but its techniques and methods have been marginalized in media history, particularly that carried out in English departments.[9] Wedded to close reading yet aware of the abundance of material in the archive, research has proceeded via detailed analyses of isolated case studies, whose significance is evaluated against an extrapolated print culture. This is not to suggest that quantitative analyses have had no effect on media history, or that digital resources and tools have not played a part in the analysis.[10] Rather, there has been an institutionalized preference for the exceptional – what makes a particular text or publication important or different – over the repetitive and generic. Like the historiographical preference for the study of great men or the emphasis on particular social classes, this methodological bias has ensured that some printed objects are preserved over others, and of these, a select few deemed worthy of analysis within the academy. Yet without the tools and methodologies to interrogate the repetitive (and so the generic and the abundant), analysis is restricted to generalizations based on the exceptional without really establishing the grounds for exceptionality within the culture of the period.

Such an orientation makes it difficult to understand the patterns that characterized both the production of journalism and the textuality of print culture. Corpus linguistics is usually concerned with naturally occurring language, but the marked-up verbal content that underpins large digital resources of newspapers and periodicals can be mined to reveal things about print culture more broadly. The neglect of the tools and techniques of computational linguistics by those in literary studies has often been noted, but Franco Moretti's call for 'distant reading' has usefully turned the attention of the discipline to the bulk of material that necessarily remains unread.[11] If literary texts offer a rich ground for statistical analysis, then journalistic texts, published systematically in serial parts, provide an even better dataset.[12] As many scholars have noted, newspapers and periodicals negotiate between novelty and familiarity in order to satisfy the demands of their readers. Each issue offers something new, but this novelty was tempered by familiarity: what was provided must be more of the same. As Margaret Beetham has put it, each 'number is different, but it is the same periodical'.[13] The repetition of various features, article to article and issue to issue, created a formal identity for a publication that enabled it to transcend its particular instantiation, reassuring readers that they were still reading the same title despite changing content. Recurring features such as mastheads, layout, typeface created a visual consistency that linked articles and issues and the reappearance of certain types of articles in regular positions, whether on the page or in the issue, further entrenched the identity of the publication. Although these repetitions were intended to mark the identity of an individual title, they were themselves part of larger patterns, identifying the style of contributing authors, situating articles within textual genres, and publications within the wider market. Statistical analysis allows us, for the first time, to map the interplay of print and textual genres that enabled newspapers and periodicals to function as commodities in the competitive market for nineteenth-century print.

The digitization of the archive has produced a corpus of data large enough to reveal this systemacity while compensating for errors contained in the transcripts. At the moment, scholars can interrogate the transcripts and readily get a sense of how textual repetition operates within the archive, but only one search at a time and with no easy way to visualize the results. These resources are designed to delimit the archive, providing the 'right' article for the individual user. However, the archive itself constitutes a large dataset, and would be profitably approached as such. Whereas individual scholars can search for phrases that reveal how content was reproduced across the press, or how articles or sections recur issue after issue, such relationships could be easily mapped and then visualized over time and space. There are a number of ways this data could be usefully explored. The metadata, predominantly used to structure search queries and assist users browsing lists of results, might be interrogated for what it can reveal, for instance, about the amount of articles published per issue (or issues per volume, or volumes per year); periodicities; characteristic titles for articles, sections, publications; structure; relative page spans, etc. This data could be mapped in order to provide a better understanding of different genres in the marketplace, as well as how new publications were situated with regard to their competitors. Or the textual information within individual articles might be compared to examine the operation of genre, exposing how different types of article were deployed in particular publications and how these varied according to print genre. Given that issues of periodicals and newspapers are marked with a date, it would be straightforward to explore how publications reacted to changes in the marketplace, perhaps due to the introduction of new technology, significant public events, or shifts in the market. Equally, as nearly all publications are also marked with a place of publication, it would be easy to examine the print trade in different places, as well as the way these different markets depended on one another for content. These sorts of analyses, crucial for an understanding of the interconnected nature of print culture and the operation of the market, can only be accomplished by manipulating processable data.

At present, scholars are restricted to mining the data, query after query, in order to read articles, one by one. There has, however, been some work on processing the textual transcripts in order to refine the data that they contain. The *Nineteenth-Century Serials Edition* (*ncse*), of which I was one of the editors, used text-mining techniques to identify the names of persons, places and institutions within the textual transcripts and apply rudimentary semantic tags to articles.[14] This resource published six nineteenth-century newspapers and periodicals – *Monthly Repository* (1806–38), *Northern Star* (1837–52), *Leader* (1850–60), *English Woman's Journal* (1858–64), *Tomahawk* (1867–71), *Publisher's Circular* (1880–90) – constituting a corpus of just over one hundred thousand pages and organized into around five hundred thousand individual textual components. Recognizing that this represented too much to read, the process of marking up the content of the articles (and other textual components) had to be passed to the machine. In an example of the sorts of collaborations required to do this work, the project was a partnership between experts in print culture at Birkbeck College and King's College London; the British Library, who provided the bulk of the material; a private software company, Olive Software, who delivered a web application and server-side architecture; and the Centre for Computing in the Humanities (CCH, now Department of Digital Humanities) at King's College

London, who oversaw the implementation of the Olive product while carrying out experimental work in data mining. As the project unfolded, it became apparent that there was too much material to process by hand and so computational methods were adopted instead. Scholars at CCH used GATE (General Architecture for Text Engineering) to identify and extract named entities from the transcripts and then a set of gazetteers and further post-processing to refine the proper nouns and resolve possible contradictions. This produced lists of persons, places and institutions from the transcripts that could be appended as processable metadata, providing a searchable field that complemented free-text queries with a more reliable and easily refined dataset while also permitting navigation through cross-reference.[15] The application of semantic tags was more experimental. In collaboration with the University Centre for Computer Corpus Research on Language (UCREL) at Lancaster University, semantic tags were applied to articles according to the frequency and deployment of words and multi-word expressions.[16] This produced a list of tags, derived from a hierarchy of 232 category labels organized under 21 major discourse fields, for each article.[17] As the tags were derived from this ontology, it was possible to present them in a faceted browse interface, allowing users to navigate the materials by adding and removing terms from the hierarchy. The results were mixed: for instance, delimiting the articles by 'the body and the individual', 'health and disease', and 'disease' provides 23,452 hits, the first ten of which are for various proprietary medicines advertised in the press. If the role of the interface is to provide articles about disease, then users need to exploit the granularity of the data and drill down to something relevant. However, as a way of discovering something about print culture, the interface is very useful, in this case exposing the reliance of the press on advertisements for drugs and treatments of various kinds.

A more recent example is *Connected Histories*, a JISC-funded resource produced in collaboration between the Universities of Hertfordshire, London and Sheffield, launched in 2011.[18] *Connected Histories* is a portal and research space that allows cross-searching of eleven different resources (at the time of writing) dedicated to British history, 1500–1900. By treating the contents of these different resources as processable (textual) data, the project was able to generate its own indices and so link them together. Like *ncse*, *Connected Histories* used techniques from computational linguistics to identify named entities and then sort them into lists.[19] The interface allows users to construct searches across four separate indices: one consisting of all the words from the constituent resources; and three processed lists of names of people, places and dates. *Connected Histories* overcomes the divisions between the different digital resources, allowing users to navigate their diverse historical content, but it does so by interrogating something they all have in common, a set of processable data that, with differing degrees of accuracy, represents their verbal text.

These projects exploit the properties of data so that users can access and manipulate historical information in ways that otherwise would be too laborious or outright impossible. They join the many other digital resources more explicitly oriented around historical data.[20] For instance, *The French Book Trade in*

Enlightenment Europe is in the final stages of creating a database derived from the business records of the Société Typographique de Neuchâtel, a Swiss publishing house that operated from 1769 to 1794.[21] Although these records have been used for studies in the past, as processable encoded data they can be queried in a variety of ways, scaled up or down, and presented as visualizations or lists of figures. Further examples can be found at Stanford's *Spatial History Project*, where historical tabulated data is combined with geographical information in order to model cultural space.[22] Like all historical knowledge, that produced from encounters with these resources depends upon the manipulation of evidence; however, the power of these resources comes from the imposition of a layer of processable data that allows evidence to be repurposed, often in radical ways. Not only does this allow the historian to work with datasets that might be otherwise too large, complex or distinct; it is also generative, producing new bodies of evidence as they are transformed for analysis, and iterative, as datasets are adapted, supplemented and transformed anew.[23]

It is here that interdisciplinary collaboration becomes vital. Historians must account for the transformation of the evidence base in their analysis, and this necessitates understanding the methodologies and technologies responsible for these transformations. In nineteenth-century media history, such collaboration is undermined by a publishing model that positions the researcher in the role of passive client. Rather than collaborate and innovate, experimenting with data and working it against its grain (what Stephen Ramsay calls the 'hermeneutics of screwing around'),[24] the researcher must be content with programmatic, goal-oriented resources that guard their data and mask their methodologies. Scholarship in media history has tended to generalize about the press from the close reading of select publications. The success of these generalizations has rested on a growing scholarly consensus, recorded in books and journals, and reaffirmed, implicitly, by delegates at numerous conferences. Approaching digital resources as data-processing devices (of considerable power) rather than delivery mechanisms for facsimile reproductions will allow us to model and explore this consensus, to probe our assumptions about the field and, certainly, prompt questions that, at the moment, cannot be thought. However, at present media historians remain content to be seduced by the simulations onscreen, bewildered by the riches of a new archive that continues, resolutely, to serve old methodologies.

Aren't these just tools?

What is at stake in the shift towards history 2.0 is the status of the archive. No serious historian would deny that history is a process and its findings contingent, but often the admission of history's dynamism depends on the tacit assumption that the archive remains static, a fixed point of reference through which history corrects itself. Yet this interpretation depends upon locating the primary materials of history solely within the historical objects that survive. This material is obviously central to historical study, but its significance does not lie locked within the objects and documents on the shelves of libraries and archives.

Rather, what appears to be of latent significance is the product of critical engagement, where scholars return to objects with revised analytical frameworks, whether derived from new theoretical positions, different sets of data, or simply from a different historical moment. This is not to deny that some frameworks are more durable than others, but that historical significance is a product of discourse rather than intrinsic to anything we inherit from the past.

It is overconfidence in the integrity of historical artefacts that results in the common accusation that digital resources are simply tools. Such comments have dogged digital scholarship for years, judging its outputs by a set of utilitarian criteria that are seldom applied to more traditional scholarly publications. The UCLA manifesto (2.0) has a section addressed 'to the great **diminishers**', those who disparage digital scholarship (practice or product) as '*just* a tool […] *just* a repository […] *just* pedagogy', but doesn't offer a critique of this criticism in return. From the entrenched perspective of disciplines whose products are narrative accounts, published in stable (because familiar) print publications, it can be easy to overdetermine the division between primary and secondary material. If primary material is imagined as stable, curated in libraries and archives, and impervious to the changing interpretations of scholars, then digital resources created from this material will always be secondary, useful for access or analysis but unworthy of study in their own right. It can be tempting to rely on this distinction to enforce disciplinary boundaries, with history concerned with the objects and documents mediated by digital resources and the digital humanities in the digital aspects of the resources themselves. Yet if digital resources (and what researchers do with them) are understood as constitutive parts of the framework through which historical objects become primary sources, then digital technologies and methods become part of historical studies more broadly. There is still disciplinary space for the digital humanities, but given the widespread digitization of our cultural heritage, none of the established disciplines of the humanities can afford to ignore the digital – whether in terms of resources, technology, methodology or pedagogy – or designate it the sole intellectual terrain of this emerging discipline.

The study of digital data does not take history away from primary sources but rather provides a new context in which these sources might be encountered. This idea is a common one in textual scholarship, a discipline concerned with the transmission of texts and, because of its concerns with scholarly editing, closely connected with the digital humanities. Textual scholarship might be committed to transmission, passing text from one generation to another, but it is nevertheless always interpretive and generative, revealing new things about the text even as it remains putatively the same.[25] To produce the iterative text – a text that declares its prior existence in older print and manuscript forms – it must be carefully produced, its previous documentary witnesses sifted, and its final (but contingent) presentation carefully controlled. Print provides an often unremarked field of continuity for textual transmission, helping to support textual features through the recurrence of certain formal and material conventions. In *Radiant Textuality*, Jerome McGann argues that all editions make embodied arguments about their contents, but digital editions, because of the different way in which they model text, can lead editors to imagine what they did not know.[26] For McGann, digital publication can expose hitherto unthinkable aspects of textuality as modelled by the printed codex because digital editions 'can be designed for complex interactive transformations'.[27] However, this works both ways: digital publication might liberate editors from the demands of the codex, but it imposes its own material conditions upon textuality that, while opening up/closing down possibilities of representation, reveal hitherto unsuspected aspects of both types of media, print and digital, and their respective relations to textuality. This knowledge might be dialectical, generated through difference but, as McGann notes, it can only be realized in practice.

McGann suggests that textual editing illustrates the 'pragmatics of theory', arguing that editions constitute a form of 'poesis' rather than a more speculative, conceptual 'gnosis'.[28] Edited works thus embody a form of applied theory, like works of art or engineering projects. At the same time as providing access to content, these editions reflexively interrogate the problems of mediation while nevertheless recognizing its necessity. For McGann, one of the main contributions digital textualities offer humanities disciplines is this 'poesis-as-theory': the recognition of the intellectual (and creative) work of modelling, mapping, reconstructing and editing.[29] All of these processes are in some way transformative, situating whatever is being represented – whether a document, object, set of historical data or event – in a digital environment in order to learn something about it. Our cultural heritage, as it survives, is always already abstract, separated from the historical culture within which it was produced and had significance. What digital technologies allow scholars to do is provide new contexts within which this material can function. As programmable, dynamic and responsive environments, they permit scholars to study the emergence of different, unsuspected properties as they emerge in response to changing conditions, or the relationships between different entities as they unfold in time. These digital environments might be considered abstract or artificial, but only if we respect the surviving condition of historical objects as somehow natural. It is the role of historians to make absent contexts tangible, to make the imagined virtual, in order to reconstruct the significance of material from the past. Digital technologies provide powerful instruments that do just this, transforming material so that it can function in new environments, exposing both unrealized aspects of this material and the unthought assumptions that have hitherto structured our engagement with it.

Digital tools and techniques make apparent the changing condition of historical evidence. Even though scholars are prepared to acknowledge the constitutive role of cultural relations, there is a tendency to consider the archive as a hermetically sealed space in which historical material can be preserved untouched. The aura of authenticity is cherished as it promises an illusory historicity: by respecting the integrity of historical objects they appear to offer direct access to the past; yet this can only ever be achieved indirectly, by an engagement with the object in the present that, necessarily, changes what it means. This paradox is enacted in the architecture of the museum, where one department imposes stasis whilst another reinterprets content for changing social conditions. Tim Hitchcock, one of the creators of *Connected Histories*, engaged with precisely this division in his lecture at the launch of the resource in 2011. *Connected Histories* is a direct response to the problem of the 'silo': digital resources that republish historical content in such a way that it is not interoperable with other resources, restricting access to their own respective interfaces.[30] For Hitchcock, though, the most insidious silo is the one that 'suggests that information itself is something to be consulted and collected; that it is an unchanging object of study, rather than a pool of constantly changing stuff that can be interrogated from any angle, and pursued along any trajectory'.[31] *Connected Histories*, he argues, addresses the division between 'traditional forms of criticism and scholarship that assume we can contain data in an internally structured and divided, "library"; and the emerging world of text and data mining, that sees data as a process – something to be played with and analysed on a massive scale, across boundaries of genre and type'.[32] As described above, the resource fully achieves this aim, using the techniques of computational linguistics to provide an added layer of functionality to a set of resources that could otherwise only be consulted individually. It is perfectly possible for users to treat its content as surrogates for the historical material it republishes, carrying out fairly traditional research as if the resource was not there (but hopefully citing it nevertheless). However, the project's plans to publish an application programming interface (API), a piece of software that will make its contents machine-readable, demonstrates its commitment to the idea of history as practice and evidence as dynamic. The API means that others will be able to interrogate the *Connected Histories* indices, reconceiving the data in ways unimagined by the creators of *Connected Histories* and its contributing resources. Not only does this recognize that the objects in the constitutive resources can mean different things in juxtaposition, with *Connected Histories* offering itself as a 'work site' through which these objects can establish themselves and their relation to one another; it also acknowledges that the presentation of these objects in *Connected Histories* is not the final or definitive representation of this content.[33] By opening up the data within the resource to other uses, the creators of *Connected Histories* imply that this material is not finished, its potential for meaning not restricted to this particular configuration of resources in this particular digital environment.

Connected Histories provides a good example of a central trend of digital scholarship that has been adopted from the culture of the web more broadly: publish openly and rapidly and then iterate to perfection.[34] Digital resources might provide a rich environment within which to manipulate data, but it is only one environment and will have been designed to model data in particular ways. By publishing the data, especially in machine-readable formats, it can be taken up and reused by other resources, placing it in new contexts that can reveal unexpected properties and relationships. These transformative uses will inevitably provide new perspectives on the data, perspectives currently unimaginable because the environments within which data becomes meaningful do not yet exist. The challenge for the historian in the digital age is to understand these uses and reuses and account for them. The digital historian 1.0, using a digital resource to access representations of historical objects or documents, must be able to understand why data performs as it does, why certain material is returned and what might be done with it. This is a process of reconstruction, of compensating for the way the digital resource misrepresents the authentic original. The digital historian 2.0 requires a more advanced understanding of the affordances of the digital in order to perform more advanced research. In manipulating data from multiple resources, modelling their relationships and so exposing facets hitherto unrealized, the historian moves from simulation to simulacra, to validating representations against reified originals to producing analyses of phenomena, objects and relationships that belong to the past. History concerns the evaluation of evidence, using objects to posit their relationships in a past that is inaccessible to us. The historian's traditional skills are still necessary, but the focus on practice – on doing things with data – extends their application, forcing a recognition of the constructed nature of evidence and its relation to the absent past. Necessarily speculative, the historian must bring his or her expertise to bear on these digital environments and evaluate the plausibility of what they both embody and imply.

Conclusion: documenting the data

The first draft of the UCLA manifesto claimed that the first wave of the digital revolution 'replicated a world where print was primary and visuality was secondary, while vastly accelerating search and retrieval'.[35] The identification of print with verbal text betrays a bias towards the verbal in scholarly accounts of print culture even while claiming to move towards a more sensitive treatment of media fostered by the second digital revolution. Print has always been a visual medium and layout and typography, not to mention the printed image, were (and continue to be) central to print culture. In the second iteration of the manifesto, quoted as the epigraph at the head of this chapter, the sentence has been changed to 'replicated the world of scholarly communications that print gradually codified over the course of five centuries: a world where textuality was primary and visuality and sound were secondary (and subordinated to text), even as it vastly accelerated the search and retrieval of documents, enhanced access, and altered mental habits.'[36] The substitution is a telling one, distinguishing between print and text (while acknowledging the former privileges the latter) but inserting 'scholarly publication' as the paradigmatic print genre. Given that the manifesto addresses the digital humanities as a (revolutionary) academic discipline this insertion is sensible; yet it also makes a more subtle change, moving the discussion from the republication of primary materials to the scholarly publication of secondary materials. This shift is telling as it recognizes the interpretive work of the edition.

Scholarship has always been uneasy with contingency, preferring the myths of the definitive edition or monograph, the finished output over the work in progress, to acknowledging the integral role played by provisionality in advancing debate. The entire apparatus of the academy – from the way work is reviewed and published to how it is archived and referenced – is oriented towards finished works, even if these are to be superseded by the other finished works they prompt.[37] What is never finished is our understanding of the past. As scholarly debate moves on, output by output, our sense of the past changes as we revisit the evidence anew. The status of this evidence – belonging to the past, and so finished and appropriately archived – is not fixed, but changes as we approach it in new ways. Digital publications make this mutability explicit by encoding it in the performance of resources. Manipulating the properties of data, these resources make it easy for historical objects to function in new contexts, demonstrating unexpected behaviour and allowing us to test suspected relationships. This practice – experimental, speculative, concerned with data, but nevertheless historical – must be written up and disseminated. Traditional scholarly outputs such as monographs and journal articles will continue to serve a purpose, providing an institutionally validated and accessible way for this research to reach a wider (and hopefully interested) audience. Where such work will really become important is in digital-first scholarly publications that can handle the visualizations necessary to narrate data. These publications, usually open access, are poised to respond to the dynamic world of digital research, often providing useful data of their own for reuse elsewhere. Finally, of course, the resources themselves must be curated. These are both archives of primary material, sites of scholarly practice, and arguments in their own right. They demand curation not just to preserve their content but to enable continued exploration, reuse and reconfiguration. Libraries and archives must also enable practice, not just memorialize product.[38]

Archivists and librarians are used to thinking about data and have considerable expertise in responding to the requirements of diverse sets of objects. Nevertheless, there are challenges to digital history 2.0. An important barrier to this type of scholarship is in the way resources are constructed. The Linked Data movement makes it easy for the creators of resources to share their content, encoding it in such a way that it is machine-readable and redistributable.[39] Yet there are those who are resistant to the idea of reuse: the emphasis on output in the humanities has encouraged scholars to be secretive, hoarding evidence until they are prepared to publish; commercial vendors also have an interest in intellectual property, and will not publish anything that might jeopardize their place in the market. Yet what the digitization of our cultural heritage has made clear is that the past is processable and, with the tools and technologies developed by the digital humanities, often in collaboration with scholars from across the academy, we can model these processes, building them into the sites where we carry out historical practice. The *Digital Humanities Manifesto* is iterative: so too is history.

Notes

1 T. Presner and J. Schnapp, 'A Digital Humanities Manifesto 2.0' (2009), http://jeffrey schnapp.com/wp-content/uploads/2011/10/Manifesto_V2.pdf [accessed: 25 March 2012].

2 T. Presner, 'Digital Humanities 2.0: a report on knowledge', *Emerging Disciplines* (Houston: Rice University Press, 2010), http://cnx.org/content/m34246/latest/ [accessed: 20 August 2011].

3 Presner and Schnapp, 'Digital Humanities Manifesto', unpaginated.

4 Presner and Schnapp, 'Digital Humanities Manifesto', unpaginated.

5 N. Katherine Hayles, 'Translating media: why we should rethink textuality', *The Yale Journal of Criticism*, 16 (2003), 264.

6 W. E. Houghton (ed.), *Wellesley Index to Victorian Periodicals, 1824–1900* (Toronto: University of Toronto Press, 1966–79); J. S. North (ed.), *Waterloo Directory of English Newspapers and Periodicals, 1800–1900, first series* (Waterloo: North Waterloo Academic Press, 1994); J. North (ed.), *Waterloo Directory of English Newspapers and Periodicals: 1800–1900, second series* (Waterloo: North Waterloo Academic Press, 2003), http://www.victorianperiodicals.com/ [accessed: 25 March 2012]; L. Brake and M. Demoor (eds), *The Dictionary of Nineteenth-Century Journalism* (Gent and London: Academia Press and the British Library, 2009).

7 One of the strengths of the field is its methodological reflexivity and these bibliographic challenges are well documented. See, for instance, M. Wolff, 'Charting the golden stream: thoughts on a directory of Victorian periodicals', *Victorian Periodicals Review*, 13 (1971), 23–28; S. Bennett, 'The bibliographic control of Victorian periodicals', in J. D. Vann and R. T. VanArsdel (eds), *Victorian Periodicals: A Guide to Research* (New York: Modern Language Association, 1978), 21–51; J. Shattock and M. Wolff, 'Introduction', in J. Shattock and M. Wolff (eds), *The Victorian Periodical Press: Samplings and Soundings* (Leicester: Leicester University Press, 1982), pp. xiii–xix; L. Brake, A. Jones and L. Madden, 'Introduction: defining the field', in L. Brake, A. Jones and L. Madden (eds), *Investigating Victorian Journalism* (Basingstoke: Macmillan, 1990), pp. xi–xiv; L. Brake, 'Tacking: nineteenth-century print culture and its readers', *Romanticism and Victorianism on the Net*, 55: August (2009), 1–44, http://www.erudit.org/revue/ravon/2009/v/n55/039555ar.html [accessed: 25 March 2012].

8 S. Tanner, T. Munoz and P. H. Ros, 'Measuring mass text digitization quality and usefulness: lessons learned from assessing the OCR accuracy of the British Library's 19th century online newspaper archive', *D-Lib Magazine*, 15 (2009), unpaginated, http://www.dlib.org/dlib/july09/munoz/07munoz.html [accessed: 25 March 2012].

9 For the history of humanities computing see S. Hockey, 'A history of humanities computing', in S. Schreibman, R. Siemens and J. Unsworth (eds), *A Companion to Digital Humanities* (Oxford: Blackwell, 2004), pp. 3–19, http://www.digitalhumanities.org/companion/view?docId=blackwell/9781405103213/9781405103213.xml&chunk.id=ss1-2-1 [accessed: 25 March 2012].

10 See, for instance, S. Eliot, 'Some trends in British book publication, 1800–1919', in J. O. Jordan and R. L. Patten (eds), *Literature and the Marketplace* (Cambridge: Cambridge University Press, 1995), pp. 19–43; W. St Clair, *The Reading Nation in the Romantic Period* (Cambridge: Cambridge University Press, 2004).

11 F. Moretti, 'Conjectures on world literature', *New Left Review*, 1 (2000), 54–68, http://www.newleftreview.org/A2094 [accessed: 25 March 2012].

12 J. Burrows, 'Never say never again: reflections on the numbers game', in W. McCarty (ed.), *Text and Genre in Reconstruction: Effects of Digitalization on Ideas, Behaviours, Products and Institutions* (Cambridge: Open Book Publishers, 2010), pp. 13–36.

13 M. Beetham, 'Towards a theory of the periodical as publishing genre', in Brake et al., *Investigating Victorian Journalism*, p. 28.

14 *Nineteenth-Century Serials Edition (ncse)*, (2008), http://www.ncse.ac.uk [accessed: 25 March 2012].

15 'Technical introduction', *Nineteenth-Century Serials Edition*, unpaginated. For details of the research see M. Christodoulakis and G. Brey, 'Edit distance with combinations and splits and its applications in OCR name matching', *International Journal of Foundations of Computer Science (IJFCS)*, 20 (2009), 1047–68; M. Christodoulakis, G. Brey and R. A. Uppal, 'Evaluation of approximate pattern matching algorithms for OCR texts', in R. Perryman et al. (eds), *Proceedings of the 4th Advances in Computing and Technology Conference (AC&T)* (London: ISGES, 2009), pp. 35–42; M. Christodoulakis and G. Brey, 'Edit distance with single-symbol combinations and

splits', in J. Holub and J. Zdárek (eds), *Proceedings of the Prague Stringology Conference* (Prague: Czech Technical University, 2008), pp. 208–17.

16 'Technical introduction', *Nineteenth-Century Serials Edition*, unpaginated.

17 'UCREL Semantic Analysis System (USAS)', *UCREL Home Page* (University of Lancaster), http://ucrel.lancs.ac.uk/usas/ [accessed: 25 March 2012].

18 *Connected Histories*, http://www.connectedhistories.org/ [accessed: 25 March 2012].

19 The project used ANNIE, http://www.aktors.org/technologies/annie/, an information extraction system and GATE plugin, to identify named entities and then various gazeteers to refine and sort the indices. See 'About this project', *Connected Histories*, http://www.connectedhistories.org/ [accessed: 25 March 2012]. T. Hitchcock, 'Towards a new history lab for the digital past', (Institute of Historical Research, 2011), http://sas-space.sas.ac.uk/2854/1/Hitchcock–Towards_a_new_History_Lab.pdf [accessed: 25 March 2012]. A talk delivered at the launch of *Connected Histories* at the Institute for Historical Research, London, 31 March 2011.

20 A good overview can be found in D. Seefeldt and W. G. Thomas III, 'What is digital history? A look at some exemplar projects', *Perspectives on History* (2009), 1–7, http://digitalcommons.unl.edu/historyfacpub/98/ [accessed: 25 March 2012].

21 'About the project', *The French Book Trade in Enlightenment Europe, 1769–1794: Mapping the Trade of the Société Typographique de Neuchâtel* (2011), http://chop.leeds.ac.uk/stn/about.html [accessed: 25 March 2012].

22 *Stanford Spatial History Project* (2007), http://www.stanford.edu/group/spatialhistory [accessed: 25 March 2012].

23 See, for instance, P. White, 'What is spatial history?', *Spatial History Lab: Working Paper*, 36 (2010), http://www.stanford.edu/group/spatialhistory/cgi-bin/site/pub.php?id=29 [accessed: 25 March 2012].

24 S. Ramsay, 'The hermeneutics of screwing around; or what you do with a million books' (unpublished book chapter, 2010), http://www.playingwithhistory.com/ [accessed: 25 March 2012].

25 See P. Shillingsburg, *From Gutenberg to Google: Electronic Representations of Literary Texts* (Cambridge: Cambridge University Press, 2006), pp. 12–24.

26 J. McGann, *Radiant Textuality: Literature After the World Wide Web* (Basingstoke: Palgrave, 2001), pp. 81–82.

27 McGann, *Radiant Textuality*, p. 81.

28 McGann, *Radiant Textuality*, p. 83.

29 McGann, *Radiant Textuality*, p. 83.

30 See J. McGann, 'Culture and technology: the way we live now, what is to be done', *New Literary History*, 36 (2005), 71–82; Presner, 'A report on knowledge', unpaginated.

31 Hitchcock, 'Towards a new history lab for the digital past', unpaginated.

32 Hitchcock, 'Towards a new history lab for the digital past', unpaginated.

33 See P. Eggert, 'The book, the E-text and the "work-site"', in M. Deegan and K. Sutherland (eds), *Text Editing, Print and the Digital World* (Farnham: Ashgate, 2009), pp. 63–82.

34 D. Cohen, 'The ivory tower and the open web: introduction: burritos, browsers, and books [Draft]', *Dan Cohen's Digital Humanities Blog* (26 July 2011), http://www.dancohen.org/2011/07/26/the-ivory-tower-and-the-open-web-introduction-burritos-browsers-and-books-draft/ [accessed: 25 March 2012].

35 Presner and Schnapp, 'Digital Humanities Manifesto'.

36 Presner and Schnapp, 'Digital Humanities Manifesto', unpaginated.

37 See S. Brown et al., 'Published yet never done: the tension between projection and completion in digital humanities research', *Digital Humanities Quarterly*, 3 (2009), http://www.digitalhumanities.org/dhq/vol/3/2/000040.html [accessed: 25 March 2012].

38 See B. Nowviskie, 'A skunk in the library', *Bethany Nowviskie*, 28 June 2011, http://nowviskie.org/2011/a-skunk-in-the-library/ [accessed: 25 March 2012].

39 See, for instance, *Linked Data: Connect Distributed Data Across the Web*, http://www.linkeddata.org [accessed: 25 March 2012].

5 On collecting, cataloguing and collating the evidence of reading

The 'RED movement' and its implications for digital scholarship

Rosalind Crone and Katie Halsey

For the most part, the history of reading as a field has been (necessarily) dominated by a series of studies that focus on discrete collections of physical evidence.[1] We know a great deal about the reading of particular individuals in the past who left diaries or wrote notes in the pages of the books they read. Similarly, groups of readers in specific localities who made use of their local libraries or organized themselves into communities for the intensive examination of texts have often been discussed. These specific studies have been used to support, or sometimes challenge at the level of exception, a series of grand narratives or theories about the practice of reading over the *longue durée*: namely, the decisive shift from reading aloud to reading silently, and from intensive to extensive reading, between the post-Gutenberg proliferation of print and the beginning of the rise of mass literacy in the early nineteenth century.[2] As William St Clair suggests, the evidence base for these theories has always been, at best, shaky, especially as qualitative (anecdotal sources) and quantitative data (print runs and library borrowing records) have often demonstrated significant divergence.[3]

To solve this problem, some years ago scholars began to turn towards a well-established if under-exploited tool: the electronic database. This technology can deal with a large mass of information and highlight patterns across a large body of material in a way that individual researchers, immersed in archives, cannot. Databases have most often been used by historians to deal with hard evidence, that is, quantitative social and economic data. However, in the construction of the *Reading Experience Database* (RED), a new methodology was adopted: through the collection of reading experiences (recorded engagements with texts), qualitative evidence (of the kind that historians had previously dismissed as anecdotal or too fragmented to be useful) was to be analysed quantitatively. In 2011, with over 30,000 entries, RED has become a freely accessible repository searchable in many different ways – by keyword; by the name, gender, religion, nationality, age or occupation of the reader; by the author, title, form, genre or provenance of the text read; or by the type of reading experience. The latest incarnation, version three, launched in February 2011, comprises a series of national reading databases hosted at academic institutions across the world with an overarching or federated search facility which enables users to locate specific keywords in defined fields (name of reader, name of author and title of text read) in all the linked databases simultaneously. As part of this, the former *Reading Experience Database, 1450–1945* was rebranded as UK RED,[4] and the global search page has been given the name *Reading Experience Database* (RED).[5] The aim of the RED project has been, from the beginning, to collect and disseminate as much information as possible about the reading habits and practices of men, women and children in the past.

Scholars are thus able to present a number of different research questions to the same data and to discover new areas for further research. As this chapter will show, fifteen years of development, redevelopment and expansion (in several senses) have meant that RED not only provides a useful example of how digital technologies can reshape a sub-discipline, but also an illustration of the pleasures and pitfalls inherent in the use of computers and the internet for research and teaching. The extremely wide remit of the project has presented, and continues to present, methodological challenges, some of which are unique to this particular project, while others are symptomatic of wider questions involved in the study of history in the digital age. For better or for worse, digital resources can change our view of history, not just by making widely accessible material that was previously known only to a few, but also, crucially, by organizing this material in particular ways. The decisions made by scholars about collecting, collating and cataloguing material are invisible to front-end users of the resources, but nonetheless structure our understanding of the information presented, and, sometimes, just as in the case of more traditional historical scholarship, create a specific narrative about it. Such narratives may be either explicit or, more commonly, implicit, and this fact has important implications. Users frequently consider material found in online databases as 'raw' data, and hence treat it accordingly, but this is not, strictly speaking, true. The invisible processes of selection, collation and presentation strongly affect the ways in which the data is perceived and used, even though users may not be aware either of this fact, or of the principles behind the choices. This chapter will chart and interrogate the tasks involved in constructing digital databases and interpreting the results they present, beginning with the work of collecting the material.

Collecting

It is impossible for any researcher in the field of the history of reading to ignore the fact that the act of reading is very rarely recorded. As Simon Eliot puts it, 'any reading recorded in an historically recoverable way is, almost by definition, an exceptional recording of an uncharacteristic event by an untypical person.'[6] In other words, scholars are dependent on the survival of records of reading that are skewed in terms of gender, social class and historical period. Moreover, such records are also often partial, sketchy or liable to misinterpretation. They are also difficult to find. Eliot writes:

> [T]he evidence for reading is obscure, hidden, scattered and fragmentary. Its discovery is often a matter of serendipity. Again and again some of the

best evidence for the history of reading tends to be the by-product of other research: one stumbles over an extensively glossed book, a diary entry reveals a day devoted to specific reading with comments attached, a public library report refers to the odd reading habits of a counting-house clerk, and so on. On their own they are nothing more than picturesque anecdotes, listed together they seem too disparate to mean much.[7]

For many years, therefore, historians tended to dismiss these records as being unrepresentative and/or unreliable. The opportunity presented by a database management system, which could bring together enough of these 'picturesque anecdotes' to make analysis meaningful, was thus clearly valuable, but also, by its very nature, difficult and complicated, giving rise to a series of questions. What were the principles of selection and the criteria for inclusion and exclusion of material? How and where would the material be sourced? Who would find it? What volume of material would constitute a large enough sample on which to begin analysis? How could the reliability of the sources be tested? Collection and selection are issues that confront all creators of electronic resources, and the answers to the questions above (as well as many others) obviously affect the eventual shape of the data, as well as the kinds of interpretation that are possible. They hence also invisibly manipulate the kinds of research questions and answers that arise from the data.

Criteria for inclusion and exclusion were hammered out by the UK RED project team in the 1990s. The time period 1450 to 1945 (from the invention of printing to the time when radio and television began to displace print as the primary form of mass communication) was chosen. A 'reading experience' was defined as 'a recorded engagement with a written or printed text – beyond the mere fact of possession'.[8] This definition excludes evidence of ownership or acquirement which is not supported by evidence of reading, for example, sources such as library catalogues, receipts for book purchases, and the contents of private libraries. It also limits the parameters of 'reading' to print culture, rather than thinking in terms of the 'critical reading' of a play or film, or other theories of reading. The reading of music is, for now, proscribed. So too is evidence of professional public readings (such as Charles Dickens's), and reading carried out by professional reviewers, as not only is this available elsewhere (for example, in databases containing a large number of nineteenth-century periodicals and newspapers), but it was felt that the sheer quantity of this evidence could overwhelm any attempt to analyse the more everyday experiences. For similar reasons, fictional depictions of reading are excluded. And finally, graphic evidence of reading, often found in woodcuts, engravings, illustrations, paintings and photographs, is not yet recorded in UK RED. However, within such parameters there still remains an enormous diversity of material, and a substantial difference in the level of detail within that material. For example, the database includes both extremely detailed entries from daily journals, such as Samuel Pepys's and Elizabeth Barrett Browning's, and very minimal records, such as the observation of an anonymous man reading an unnamed newspaper on a certain date in a particular public house. The differing level of detail makes interpretative comparative analysis difficult and sometimes impossible. Yet even some very minimal records still provide statistical evidence that allows for particular kinds of quantitative analysis. In the last example, that we know the reader was male, reading a newspaper, in a particular public space is valuable information which can be compared with other similarly sketchy or detailed evidence in order to construct some kind of picture of reading in the past. The difficulty for users of the database is that they cannot always know in advance which kind of analysis will be most useful.

The principles of selection were crucial in attempting to ensure that the data was as representative as possible, within the constraints already outlined above. Traditionally, historians of reading had tended to use a combination of statistical evidence (such as booksellers' records) and case studies of particular readers (using their diaries, letters, memoirs, autobiographies and marginalia as evidence). Drawing on existing scholarship, a list of diaries, letters, memoirs, autobiographies and known marginalia, as well as secondary sources dealing with the history of reading was compiled, with the object of working through these sources to find the information about reading experiences in them. Researchers on the project attempted to address the skewing of surviving data towards elite male readers, and towards the end of the period under consideration, by searching out previously unknown or unused sources (such as prison records; trial transcripts; scrapbooks and commonplace books; book club records; the marginalia of unidentified readers; manuscript letters and diaries of family members that remained in private ownership and had never previously been published; mass observation surveys; and oral testimony). Nonetheless, the surviving records of servants and other working-class readers, of women, and from the period 1450 to 1750, are simply far less common, though they do sometimes exist. Analysis of the data by class and gender must therefore always take account of the gaps in the data caused by the lacunae in the historical record, but this depends on the user of the resource already having some level of knowledge about this issue. The presentation of the data in an open-access database is inherently problematic in this sense, as it can seem to present a false equivalence to users of the resource who do not have any background in the discipline. More broadly, this is a problem that applies across the digital sphere. The skills of evaluation and interpretation are crucial to understanding material discovered online, but are generally under-deployed in a culture that values fast information in the same way that it values fast food.

Pragmatically, in order to collect the volume of data that was needed to provide even a minimally representative sample (25,000 records), and ideologically, because the project members believed in the value of the social construction of knowledge, it was also necessary to employ crowd-sourcing techniques. From its inception, the UK RED project encouraged members of the academic community and the general public to contribute to the database through an online contribution form. In principle, this allowed both a wider selection and a greater volume of material to be entered. This was certainly true to some extent, as members of the public contributed the manuscript letters and diaries of ancestors and relatives who were quite unknown to the wider world, as well as marginalia and annotations in their book collections, and many volunteers alerted the project team to rich veins of material. Fascinating information about the habits of ordinary readers which would otherwise have remained locked in trunks and attics is thus now in the public domain. However, the collection of data was also shaped in part according to the interests of those who contributed, which sometimes worked against the attempt to create a representative sample. Members of author societies, for example, were generally interested in entering details of the reading of 'their' author. The database currently contains 405 records about Robert Louis Stevenson's reading, all of which were entered by members of the Stevenson Society. These records are immensely valuable in what they tell us about Stevenson's responses to texts, from which one can extrapolate many different kinds of argument, but the emphasis on one particular reader can distort the possibilities for quantitative analysis across the data in the database. Stevenson's contemporary, Arthur Conan Doyle, for example, has only one entry. This is clearly not illustrative of the different reading habits of the two men (other sources, including his own autobiography, *Memories and Adventures* (1924), show us that Conan Doyle was a voracious reader), but instead, of the interest of Stevensonians in the UK RED project. Nonetheless, when the database is searched in different ways, such as by keyword, or by the title of the text read, the presence of the Stevenson data is extremely valuable, as it provides the opportunity to compare the responses of other readers of the same text over a wide historical period. What is lost in the possibility for quantitative analysis is gained in the benefit to qualitative analysis.

The Stevenson case provides an example of a potential problem in the use of digital resources more broadly. Digitization projects inevitably direct students and researchers towards particular archives, material, or kinds of data at the expense of others, and encourage pockets of research in specific fields. Reputable websites usually provide clear statements about their principles of selection, and trained historians will almost always investigate potential bias in their sources, but even when explanations exist on the website, some students and researchers do not always either read them, or have the in-depth contextual knowledge that would make the disclaimers properly comprehensible to them. In this particular example, beginning research into Stevenson's reading is now much simpler than starting an investigation into Conan Doyle's, as all the information needed to start a Stevenson project is available at the click of a mouse, whereas a researcher would need to comb through a variety of print sources before arriving at a similar starting point for Conan Doyle. The danger is that in studies that take a wide look at reading in the nineteenth century, Stevenson's reading will feature much more heavily and so seem to be more important than Conan Doyle's, though this is not in any way objectively true. Because of the sheer scale – and the constant updating – of the RED project, it is impossible to name all specific examples of bias in the data on the website, though a researcher who looked closely at the pages dedicated to volunteers and contribution[9] would be able to glean the necessary information from them. To give another example, the online availability of the *Old Bailey Sessions Papers*[10] makes it far easier and less time-consuming to research criminal practices in London than in other large British cities, or rural regions, with the result that a body of research relating to these papers has been built up. The resource is extremely useful to crime historians, and we in no way wish to denigrate its importance or usefulness, but its very excellence has the potential to intensify the already metropolitan bias of narratives of British history, presenting a version of history based on information from London that may, in fact, not hold true in regional cities, or the rural areas of the British Isles. There is a very real danger that, through sheer weight of numbers, partial versions of history will start to become accepted as universal. Better training for students and researchers in identifying the inherent biases in digital sources would go some way towards solving this problem.

Unlike many digital projects, such as Wikipedia, the UK RED project team employed a traditional editorial approach towards the data, deciding that it was important to verify all the entries contributed to test their reliability, as well as to weed out potential duplication of information. While many would advocate a more wiki-style resource, the project team believed that only this level of editorial involvement could guarantee the eventual consistency and usefulness of the resource. Such debates are in no way limited to this single project, and raise the wider question of how and why information is controlled in the digital age. With respect to research resources, it remains unclear whether the onus for establishing the veracity of a piece of data should rest with the creators or the users of the resource. If it is to be the latter, then greater openness about the collection and structure of data by creators needs to be combined with better teaching of students in their use of the World Wide Web and the growing number of electronic resources which now exist for studying the past.

In the case of UK RED, the decisions imposed a heavy editorial burden, which is ongoing since the project is, at least in theory, never-ending. Records continue to be collected and stored as they are contributed by the project team and external contributors. To some extent, this suggests that the material in the database will always reflect the current state of scholarship, following rather than setting trends. On the other hand, the discoveries facilitated by the juxtaposition of very diverse material can and do lead to new ways of thinking about the discipline. A comparative methodology is made possible by the technology, so that existing scholarship can be taken in new directions. The organization of the data, through cataloguing and collating, is thus a crucial step in facilitating new kinds of research.

Cataloguing

Evidence of reading found by project staff or volunteers is entered into the database through an online contribution form. At present, this form is designed to handle textual evidence only; pictorial or audio evidence, such as photographs or interviews, cannot be entered into the database at this time. UK RED thus has a textual bias, containing only evidence of reading written down in the historical record in either print or manuscript. Moreover, UK RED is not a 'traditional' digitization project. Where other digital projects produce online replicas of archives, by uploading high-quality images of the primary sources, contributors to UK RED are essentially asked to describe their finds using the online form. In other words, contributors are asked to transcribe the evidence from the original source, preferably by directly quoting from it. The remaining fields on the form are then used to provide the context for that quotation, or to tag the quotation with useful metadata using the fields provided.

The result is that through this process the evidence of reading is fragmented and reassembled into a form that bears no resemblance to the original. This high degree of editorial intervention in the process of digitization means that UK RED looks very much like a traditional secondary source, describing evidence and presenting results of research rather than directly incentivizing users to examine the evidence for themselves. For instance, as research-active historians and teachers we uphold certain standards of critical source analysis, which include a thorough assessment of the primary source. The physical properties of the source do matter – its overall size, the fonts used, the inclusion of any non-textual matter, and the location of the piece of evidence within the textual layout of the page or the whole document. UK RED rarely provides that level of detail for any piece of evidence.

The reason for this is largely financial. High-quality digital images are expensive, as are the rights to reproduce material from archives and printed books. UK RED not only contains a great quantity of data assembled from such a large number of sources, however, but because the collection of this data is potentially infinite, and relies on contributions from volunteers, it is impossible to predict financial outlay and compile budgets. Thus even if a way is found to incorporate visual and audio evidence, so that users can view a photograph of the original manuscript or annotated page, or listen to an interview about someone's reading during the 1940s, UK RED will probably never be able to provide access to complete original textual primary sources.[11] This does not mean that UK RED is of less value or inferior standing when compared with those resources which have reproduced original sources, because, despite appearances, no digital archive is an exact replica of the original. What appears onscreen has always undergone a number of editorial interventions, mainly to do with selection and presentation. In many cases, not every item within an archive is digitized. Sometimes this is the result of funding constraints, whereby certain parts of the archive are photographed and released in different stages.[12] Other times, there are items within archives that are too fragile for this type of handling. For example, in the case of the *Victorian Plays Project: A digital archive of selected plays from T.H. Lacy's Acting Edition of Victorian Plays (1848–1873)*, 400 plays of a potential 1,500 were marked for digitization, but out of those a significant number had deteriorated to the extent that ink from the verso of the leaves was showing through, making reproduction difficult and the OCR conversion process impossible. These plays were thus excluded from the online resource.[13]

Recent collections of digitized newspapers present another instructive example. As newspaper historians are aware, newspapers can be unstable texts: one issue might be represented by several editions. In the case of nineteenth-century metropolitan mass circulation weekly newspapers such as *Lloyd's Weekly Newspaper* and *Reynolds's Newspaper,* several editions of the issue sold on the Sunday were printed in order to cater for geographically dispersed readers and last-minute breaking news. However, the reproduction of these newspapers in the *19th Century British Library Newspapers* does not seem to take this issue into consideration. For example, while one of the authors of this chapter was researching crime news published in *Lloyd's Weekly Newspaper* between 1840 and 1870, she often found that reports contained in the microfilm edition of the newspaper did not match those in the digitized copies online. For instance, many articles on famous metropolitan murders in the digitized version were incomplete, excluding crucial reports received by editors late in the week, and columns on intelligence from London's police courts were, at times, missing altogether, suggesting that different editions were being consulted. In defence of the producers of this valuable digital resource, it can be difficult to distinguish between editions – only some newspapers list the edition number, while others provide clues deeply buried in the columns of news. In the case of *Lloyd's Weekly News,* often when reports on murders were incomplete a small notice was printed at the end of the shortened (digitized) reports, explaining that the edition had been printed early for provincial readers and that any further reports would appear in next week's issue. Moreover, not every edition survives. However, by not being upfront about this, there is a danger that researchers could make important but false conclusions based on assumptions about the readership or dissemination of a particular piece of news contained in an edition.

Digitization manipulates in other crucial ways which are often much less apparent when digital images of the original sources are presented on the screen. Because contributors to UK RED are asked to transcribe the evidence of reading into the database, errors undoubtedly occur. Some of these are picked up and corrected by the database editors, for instance, simple typing errors. However, of concern is when such errors are corrected even though they existed in the original source, or when more fundamental errors in transcriptions are not detected at all. It is all too easy when rapidly transcribing texts to accidentally supplement a crucial word for one that was not in the original. The danger lies in the use of that evidence to support fundamental conclusions about reading in the past. But, in resources such as UK RED where the process of transcription is made obvious to users, thereby providing a direct encouragement to users to either revisit the original source or at least make reference to the digital resource in their notes, this situation might actually be less likely to occur.

Many other resources which contain images of the original documents also subject those sources to a form of transcription, but this is often hidden from public view. Optical Character Recognition, or OCR, transforms the original scanned document into machine encoded text. Essentially, that transcription is what is analysed when keyword searches are performed on these documents.

It is promising technology that has revolutionized the digitization of historical texts. However, OCR is not error free. The result is that either many hours are spent attempting to correct errors in the transcription or a far from ideal resource is produced in which adequately decoded text is available, but access to the collection as a whole (sometimes the majority) is restricted. In the case of the latter it is a highly frustrating situation, because the application of various electronic methodologies to analyse those documents is futile, and scholars who use these resources are forced back into the use of traditional methodologies, which challenges the rationale behind digitization.

Finally, it would be naive to suggest that those resources that include images of original documents necessarily encourage more expert engagement with sources. It is true that where images have been digitized, technology can assist greatly in their analysis and interpretation, for example, through the ability to zoom in very closely on particular sections. With regard to textually rich sources, such as newspapers, transcripts of criminal court trials, and even early published books, the way in which material is presented discourages examination of the physical form of the source. The *Old Bailey Online* presents users with a transcript of a trial with an option to view the original source – it would be interesting to know how many people actually use that option, and how many base their conclusions on the transcript. Similarly, newspaper databases, such as *The Times Digital Archive* and *Nineteenth Century British Library Newspapers*, attempt to force users to go straight to articles which contain specific keywords and are detached from the issues in which they appeared. In both resources, it is very difficult to move from the relevant article to the page and to the whole issue, which assists in the misinterpretation of these fragments by scholars.[14]

If the fragmentation of primary sources by UK RED and other digital resources on the one hand hampers traditional methods of source analysis, on the other hand the process facilitates the use of new technological methods that help us to examine large collections of sources and reveal new insights into the past. It is only by breaking sources down into a number of descriptive fields that these sources can be compared and patterns between them illuminated. As stated above, contributors to UK RED not only transcribe the evidence of reading (the quotation from the original source) into one field of the database, they are also requested to supply as much information as possible on the identity of the reader, the text being read, and the circumstances of the reading experience. However, because UK RED is based on a wide variety of qualitative evidence, which comes from an extremely diverse set of sources, problems in the cataloguing of that evidence immediately arise.

The first is that not every field in the database can be completed for every entry. In fact, virtually every entry in the database has data missing from at least one field, and often in more than one. UK RED thus sits a little uneasily amongst other resources which appear to be much more complete. For instance, in the case of the *Old Bailey Online*, which is composed of just one source, the *Old Bailey Sessions Papers*, the data looks much more stable and assessable. After all, every trial has a defendant, victim, indictment and verdict, and this certainly gives users confidence in using the *Old Bailey Online* for charting patterns of criminal activity in the metropolis, or at least that which came before this criminal court. In UK RED some of the evidence is as thin as the observation of an anonymous person, with no recorded gender, reading an unidentified text. And yet, as suggested above, the fact that this particular reading experience was recorded leads the editors of the database to argue that its inclusion is important for the purposes of analysis.

The second difficulty is that because UK RED charts experiences of reading over such a long time period, many of the categories used to describe reading experiences are fluid which means that it can be very difficult to insert any kind of authority control into various fields. When control is asserted, the results are often imperfect. For instance, terms currently offered to contributors to describe the socio-economic group of the reader are essentially derived from a nineteenth-century social hierarchy, and thus imperfectly reflect the social structures of the preceding and subsequent centuries. Yet to do away with these would be to limit any possibility of tracking the reading skill and reading taste amongst particular social groups. The list of countries from which contributors are asked to specify the place of reading experience is similarly unsatisfactory. Not only do names of countries change over time, but borders also shift, making any *longue durée* assessment of the reading of Britons in particular foreign countries rather difficult to achieve.

The problems of fluidity spill over to those reading experiences which are confined by time and place. Qualitative evidence so often defies any attempt to catalogue it rigidly. There is an ever-present danger in UK RED of providing either too little or too much contextual data on each reading experience. In other words, what we often consider as vital in assessing a qualitative source is not at all useful in the process of cataloguing that source. For example, in the case of readers contained in UK RED, there is a competing need to pin down these individuals by providing data about their lives and to describe the context of their reading experiences. The individual, say a nineteenth-century professional male, for whom we have many reading experiences but who has also, naturally, undergone a number of shifts in his life, presents a problem for UK RED. It is prudent to know that at the time of reading *Great Expectations* this man was a teacher, and by assigning that occupation to him we can compare his experience of reading this book with that of other male teachers. However, this man in fact began life as a milkman. Ordinarily, in assessing the reading of this individual, we would regard this information as important, that it may have a potential impact on his reading of *Great Expectations*. However, finding ways to adequately represent this in a database structure does pose difficulties. For the time being it has been solved by assigning occupations both to individuals (for the purposes of dis-ambiguation) and to reading experiences. The challenge rests in the communication of the complexity of this data to users of UK RED.

UK RED is therefore a useful example of the complexity involved in the process of digitizing qualitative evidence. Attempts to extract meaningful data from these sources which can shed light on patterns of experience can lead to reductionism. But if the process of cataloguing this evidence is not approached with some rigour, and tough decisions on descriptive categories avoided, then potential uses of this data are destroyed, and databases such as UK RED are confined to serving the role of an index to sources. This will not do.

Collating

The key to avoiding this situation lies in the collation of data, bringing the digitized data together in meaningful ways in order to push the boundaries of scholarship. That, after all, should be the *raison d'être* of digitization, because what we lose from digitizing the original source we gain in terms of new methods of analysis. In the first instance, UK RED, like many other electronic resources in the humanities, offers access to its collection of reading experiences through keyword searching, either within specific fields or across all fields of the database. Although this method of access does encourage the type of fragmented analysis described above, as users are presented with a 'Google-style' list of hits, or a summary of those entries which contain the relevant keywords, more sophisticated use of the structured query language (SQL) that sits behind the search can expose patterns in the data.

For example, it is possible to use UK RED to track reading tastes. The database can provide an answer to those 'million-dollar' questions about the popularity of particular titles and authors. Structured queries interrogating the nineteenth-century data reveal that the book most often read in that period was the Bible, and that the most popular author was Sir Walter Scott, closely followed by William Shakespeare.[15] But the examination does not end there. When we look a little more closely at the results from these queries, we find that while there are close to 400 records of Bible reading, around 370 instances of engagement with Scott's poems or novels, and 340 reading experiences of Shakespeare's works, these entries combined make up less than 7 per cent of the total nineteenth-century data in UK RED. In terms of named works, including those for which we have no title but can attribute to an author, there are close to 10,000 represented in UK RED, and nearly every one of those has fewer than 50 records associated with it. In fact, 90 per cent of these texts are represented by fewer than 10 records. We could say that UK RED thus provides some confirmation of the trend in studies of reading to emphasize the great diversity of reading diets in the nineteenth century.

Alternatively, we could argue that these results expose significant problems with using essentially quantitative methods to analyse qualitative sources, and even more than that, a variety of different qualitative sources in the same query. As stated above, the evidence of reading is necessarily patchy, which tends to leave many blank spaces in the database. Can we chart patterns across a database when large quantities of data are missing? Queries can of course be narrowed to look at relative examples – the presence of Walter Scott amongst those entries where the name of the author was given, for instance. But, given that such a method restricts enquiries to a select number of sources, to what extent does this perpetuate the problems that exist in traditional studies of reading, which resort again and again to the same rich sources to make conclusions about reading tastes and practices in the past?

The value of UK RED lies in its collection of evidence of reading from non-traditional sources alongside those we have known about for a long time, and the challenge lies in the appropriate exposure of that evidence. At present it tends to be overwhelmed by the traditional sources, namely the letters and diaries of famous individuals. So Elizabeth Barrett Browning (in her single and married state) has close to 600 reading experiences recorded in UK RED. Over 400 reading experiences are attributed to George Eliot, and Lord Byron is represented by around 266 entries. Diaries and journals, which, requiring more time, commitment and financial outlay, tend to be written by those of the higher classes, might give an account of every single day that a text was read. In contrast, the memoir (the writing of which became popular in the nineteenth century across a far wider social spectrum than the diary)[16] will provide a list of works read over the course of a lifetime. The memoir will generate one entry, the diary perhaps ten or more, depending on the speed and commitment of the reader. Even if differences between diaries and memoirs can be balanced out in the database over time, it is much more difficult to achieve a similar equilibrium with respect to those sources which provide snapshots of the reading habits of ordinary people. UK RED contains data from a number of socio-logical surveys or observational studies, not to mention criminal court records, in which disclosure about reading is largely incidental. It may be that evidence derived from these sources points at much more common practices than those sources which describe at length the role of reading in the life of an individual.[17] However, the way that SQL functions means that all these sources are considered as equal, even though as historians we know that some sources are more equal than others.

In this way, UK RED might offer some useful lessons to those scholars currently engaged in linked data projects. By focusing on the theme of reading, and collecting a diverse range of evidence that connects with that theme, UK RED is, in many ways, doing at the micro level what other projects are seeking to do at the macro level. For some years now, scholars in the digital humanities have been increasingly aware that the creation of e-resources has not reflected the practice of research within disciplines. In other words, projects have tended to focus on the digitization of defined sets of sources, but in compiling an article or book, historians often consult several different sets of sources, bringing the results of their analysis together. Projects such as *Mapping Crime*,[18] and, more recently, *Connected Histories*,[19] have attempted not only to replicate that research process, but in so doing, to expose new connections between sources to the extent that the data derived from the sources becomes much more important than the individual sources. In other words, with the launch of *Connected Histories* we are approaching the point where thousands of pieces of data extracted from hundreds of sources are reassembled in order to tell us about the past while little time is spent agonizing over the relative merits of the different sources from which this data was derived.[20] What UK RED can bring to the table in this discussion is a reminder about the gaps and silences in historical evidence. Approximately 90 per cent of the nineteenth-century records in UK RED relate to the reading of printed matter, and of these, 78 per cent describe the reading of books, while only 9 and 7 per cent of entries provide an account of the reading of serials and newspapers, respectively. And yet, attention to the sources in our analysis of the history of reading suggests that newspaper reading, often an everyday activity rarely recorded in memoirs and even diaries, may have been more common than book reading in this period.

This is not to say that more qualitative methods of analysing the links between data derived from different sources should not be attempted. On the contrary, the employment of a range of different methods to study links between data might actually help us to overcome obstacles posed by the relative merits of each source. So, for example, in the case of UK RED some use of social network analysis, which models links between texts and readers, might help to expose the ways in which communities form around texts, the emphasis being on the replication of patterns, and the connections between these patterns, rather than on particular titles that attracted lots of readers. Similarly, techniques of text mining and semantic analysis should provide a different perspective, for example, patterns in the ways in which people discuss their interactions with the written word, and hence how they conceptualize the act of reading. Very frequently, for example, readers describe either their books or the authors of the books as 'friends'. In his biography of his uncle, Lord Macaulay, Sir George Otto Trevelyan described his uncle's relationship with books as follows:

> His way of life would have been deemed solitary by others, but it was not solitary to him. While he had a volume in his hands he never could be without a quaint companion to laugh with or laugh at, an adversary to stimulate his combativeness; a counsellor to suggest wise or lofty thoughts, and a friend with whom to share them. When he opened for the tenth or fifteenth time some history, or memoir, or romance, – every incident and almost every sentence of which he had by heart, – his feeling was precisely that which we experience on meeting an old comrade [...] There was no society in London so agreeable that Macaulay would have preferred it at breakfast, or at dinner to the company of Sterne, or Fielding, or Horace Walpole, or Boswell ... [21]

Similarly, another nephew-biographer, James Edward Austen-Leigh, wrote in his 1870 *Memoir* of Jane Austen's knowledge of Richardson's novels that '[e]very circumstance narrated in *Sir Charles Grandison*, all that was ever said or done in the cedar parlour, was familiar to her; and the wedding days of Lady L. and Lady G. were as well remembered as if they had been living friends.'[22]

Keyword searches for terms such as 'friend' and its cognates turn up swathes of such material, which can then be carefully contextualized and interpreted.

For many readers, reading is conceptualized as a meeting of minds across time or space. To John Keats, for example, reading Shakespeare was both an act of communion with Shakespeare himself, and a form of imaginative communication with friends across distance: 'I shall read a passage of Shakspeare [*sic*] every Sunday at ten o Clock – you read one [a]t the same time and we shall be as near each other as blind bodies can be in the same room.'[23] Across a very wide time period, metaphors about books recur. They are friends, adversaries and comrades, rooms, lands, whole worlds, meat and drink, addictive drugs and poison, to name just a few ways in which books are repeatedly depicted. The relevance of such metaphors to our knowledge of reading in the past is that they provide an insight into the ways in which historical readers thought about their books. If 'the past is a foreign country', where 'they do things differently', as L. P. Hartley suggested, knowing more about the minds of the inhabitants of that country must surely be the first step to understanding how that country worked.[24] This is precisely the kind of information that cannot be retrieved from any other kind of evidence in the field of the history of reading. If the thousands of 'picturesque anecdotes' now collected in UK RED had remained, as Simon Eliot warned that they might, 'permanently fragmented', it would be almost impossible even to *find* enough reading experiences such as these, let alone to try to start to analyse their similarities and differences in order to recognize the conceptual frameworks that they have in common.

In the best possible way, then, UK RED is opening up avenues for genuinely new kinds of research and new kinds of connections to be made. The most recent developments in the RED project (involving the collaboration of a number of international partners who are each developing their own national databases of reading experiences based on the software and database structure of the original UK RED project) have the potential to extend the possibility for comparative analysis. These developments reflect not only recent trends in book historical scholarship towards the transnational and the global, but also, of course, historical practice: both books and readers move around. Developing a transnational RED, made up of a number of national REDs, is thus an excellent first step in reflecting the fluidity of books and ideas across space, added to RED's existing ability to represent the movement of ideas across time.

There are serious technical challenges to be met, however. The need for each national database to set its own parameters regarding dates that reflect that nation's print history is one. The development of the capacity to include audiofiles and visual images is another. The need for bilingualism – or trilingualism – is yet another. And maintaining interoperability while allowing for these sorts of customizations and flexibility is the greatest of all. All of the members of the international RED project are extremely aware of the dangers involved in such issues, but we should have confidence in the robustness and rigour that is being brought to the business of avoiding these. The increasing internationalization of both book history and reading history suggests that the lessons learned by the international RED project will have wider ramifications for other digital resources in the future.

Conclusions

It is important to make the point that any one method of analysing the sources in RED will often tend to provide a biased or partial historical narrative. Instead, several of the methods of analysis touched on above need to be utilized simultaneously if we are ever to have a full and accurate picture of reading in the past. The same caveat applies to most, if not all, electronic resources. The lessons learned by the RED project team suggest that at all stages of the construction and development of a digitization project, data must be collected and stored in a way that does not limit the data to only one kind of analysis. But the responsibility does not lie only with the creators of such resources. Users of digital resources need to become more aware of the kind of work that goes on behind the front end of an electronic resource if they are to use that resource most effectively, and they need to understand the importance of using a wide range of methods to analyse data in order to avoid reductionism. Computers are useful tools which add to our understanding of the past, but they must be used alongside, and should not replace, more traditional historical methods.

Notes

1 See, for example, J. Raven, H. Small and N. Tadmor (eds), *The Practice and Representation of Reading in England* (Cambridge: Cambridge University Press, 1996), in particular the chapters by J. Fergus (pp. 202–25), J. Brewer (pp. 226–45) and W. H. Sherman (pp. 62–76); A. Grafton and L. Jardine, '"Studied for action": how Gabriel Harvey read his Livy', *Past and Present*, 11: 129 (1990), 3–51; R. Darnton, 'First steps towards a history of reading', in R. Darnton, *The Kiss of Lamourette* (New York: Norton, 1990), pp. 154–87; J. Pearson, *Women's Reading in Britain, 1750–1835* (Cambridge: Cambridge University Press, 1999), pp. 122–51; W. H. Sherman, *John Dee: The Politics of Reading and Writing in the English Renaissance* (Amherst: University of Massachusetts Press, 1995).

2 See Saenger for the shift from reading aloud to reading silently, and Engelsing for the shift from intensive to extensive reading. R. Engelsing, *Der Bürger als Leser. Lesergeschichte in Deutschland 1500–1800* (Stuttgart, 1974), *passim*; P. Saenger, 'Silent reading: its impact on late medieval script and society', *Viator*, 13 (1982), 367–414, and see extended discussion on the theory and potential of RED to challenge or confirm these theories by S. Colcough, 'Recording the revolution: an introduction to the reading experience database', *SPIEL*, 19 (2000), 36–55.

3 W. St Clair, *The Reading Nation in the Romantic Period* (Cambridge: Cambridge University Press, 2004), pp. 1–18, 394–403.

4 See http://www.open.ac.uk/Arts/reading/uk [accessed: 25 March 2012].

5 See http://www.open.ac.uk/Arts/reading [accessed: 25 March 2012].

6 S. Eliot, 'The reading experience database; or, what are we to do about the history of reading?' No p.n. http://www.open.ac.uk/Arts/RED/redback.htm [accessed: 25 March 2012].

7 Eliot, 'The reading experience database'.

8 'What is a reading experience?', http://www.open.ac.uk/Arts/RED/experience.htm [accessed: 25 March 2012].

9 See http://www.open.ac.uk/Arts/RED/volunteers.html and http://www.open.ac.uk/Arts/RED/contribute.htm [accessed: 25 March 2012].

10 See http://www.oldbaileyonline.org [accessed: 25 March 2012].

11 The inclusion of fields to store audio and visual evidence was part of the last phase of technical development but is still (as of July 2011) being tested before being made public.

12 For example, see the *John Johnson Collection*, http://johnjohnson.chadwyck.co.uk/home.do and *Mass Observation Online*, http://www.massobs.org.uk [accessed: 25 March 2012].

13 See R. Pearson, 'Etexts and archives', *Journal of Victorian Culture*, 13 (2008), 88–93.

14 See also J. Mussell's comments in 'Ownership, institutions and methodology', *Journal of Victorian Culture*, 13 (2008), 94–100.

15 We have used the nineteenth century for this example as the bulk of records contained in UK RED come from that period. Assessments of other periods at this time are liable to misinterpretation given the quantity of evidence collected. This is the result of a three-year funded period (2006–9) which was tied to the collection of data for the period 1800 to 1945. The figures discussed in this chapter are accurate as at February 2011.

16 On the rise of the memoirs of the working classes in the nineteenth century, see J. Rose, *The Intellectual Life of the British Working Classes* (New Haven and London: Yale University Press, 2001), *passim*.

17 For a detailed analysis of this, see R. Crone, 'What readers want: criminal intelligence and the fortunes of the metropolitan press during the long eighteenth century', in K. Halsey and W. R. Owens (eds), *The History of Reading, Volume Two: Evidence from the British Isles, c1750–1950* (Basingstoke: Palgrave, 2011), and also R. Crone, K. Halsey and S. Towheed, 'Examining the evidence of reading: three examples from the reading experience database, 1450–1945', in B. Gunzenhauser (ed.), *Reading in History: New Methodologies from the Anglo-American Tradition* (London, 2010).

18 See http://johnjohnson.chadwyck.co.uk/info/about.do#mappCrim [accessed: 25 March 2012].

19 See http://www.connectedhistories.org/ [accessed: 25 March 2012].

20 Hitchcock, 'Towards a new history lab for the digital past'.

21 G. O. Trevelyan (ed.), *The Life and Letters of Lord Macaulay* (Oxford: Oxford University Press, 1978), vol. 2, p. 388.

22 J. E. Austen-Leigh, *A Memoir of Jane Austen by her Nephew*, edited by Fay Weldon (London: Folio Society, 1989), p. 79.

23 H. E. Rollins (ed.), *The Letters of John Keats 1814–1821* (Cambridge, Mass.: Harvard University Press, 1958), vol. 2, p. 5.

24 L. P. Hartley, *The Go-Between*, edited by Douglas Brooks-Davis (London: Penguin Classics, 2000), p. 5.

6 Writing history with the digital image
A cautious celebration

Brian Maidment

Not so many years ago, but far enough in the past to be seen as part of that remote period that might be called 'pre-digital', I had the opportunity to spend a week in the Guildhall Library in London as part of the preparatory research for a book I was writing on the representational and cultural history of London dustmen. It proved to be a productive week. The Library had folders of prints and texts under the heading of 'dustmen', the knowledgeable Library staff brought me other material that they thought might be relevant, and there was time to look through some serendipitous files just in case. I came away well satisfied with my replete notebooks and copious photocopies. Not so long afterwards, the JISC funded *Collage Portal* was established which made available on the internet a vast range of the graphic images held by the Guildhall Library.[1] Ostensibly a collection of material related to London and its history, nonetheless the website showed a mass not just of documentary material but also images belonging to modes as various as caricatures, the urban picturesque and series of street cries. An early exercise in digitizing a major collection, and funded centrally by JISC, the organization of the Guildhall website offered a variety of search terms that stepped beyond obvious categories like 'place' or 'trade', and offered search results in pages of thumb-nail images that could be easily and rapidly viewed on the screen. In a single morning, sat at my computer in Salford, and quickly scanning page after page of assembled thumb-nails, I doubled the number of images from the Guildhall collections that were relevant to my work. Contrary to my expectations, I did not substantially conduct this search of the Library's holdings of images by means of the wide-ranging and helpful categories into which the site was organized, and which seemed to promise an easy and immediate means of finding relevant material. The organization of the search categories in this collection will be discussed in more detail later in this chapter.

Although the available 'artists' category was of relatively little help because many of the kinds of images I was interested in were produced by little-known, unexpected or simply anonymous artists, and the 'print-making method' of similarly limited use because the images I wanted were produced in every medium (including oil painting), the 'publishers' category proved extremely productive. Working through entries for publishers with known specialisms in urban street scenes immediately massed together a wide range of relevant prints.[2] But the basic method I used for working through the Guildhall digital collection was a visual scrutiny of massed thumb-nail images. In this instance, despite the extremely sophisticated tagging of images and a clear and extensive listing of search categories made painstakingly available, the gathering together of relevant dustman images from this digital resource remained rooted in the ability provided by the website to see a lot of images very quickly rather than a consequence of the site's considerable efforts to support the researcher's work through search categories and good metadata. Such a dialogue between traditional empirical research and the modes of identifying, gathering, organizing and classifying information that characterize digital resources for academic research forms a central interest of this chapter.

I narrate the above anecdote of what must have been a commonplace experience for ageing researchers not just to represent the naive wonder of a 'digital immigrant' scholar when confronted with the new-found plenitude of research material offered by the web. Rather, I want to think through some of the implications of this experience for a researcher reared thirty years ago on traditional empirical methods of discovery and analysis, of no great technical computing proficiency (while not quite a Luddite about new technologies), but committed inevitably and not unwillingly to the digital realm as a mechanism for carrying out research in visual culture. My field of interest lies largely in mass circulation, 'middle-' and 'lowbrow' image making and print culture in the first half of the nineteenth century and, while this scholarly field has been massively represented and extended by recent web-based publications, I have no experience that would let me talk of the impact of digitization on the study of fine art images. What follows, then, is entirely derived from attempts to study specialized kinds of image making within a limited range of genres and modes from early nineteenth-century print culture – pictures made for a newly energetic and volatile marketplace where the image was becoming central to commercial success.

It has to be said immediately that such a research interest would have been, and indeed was, extremely difficult to pursue without the advent of the kinds of digital resources made available through the web. The study of visual culture has been extremely well served by the compulsion to digitize. Yet one obvious immediate consequence of the flood of images made available on the web is the danger of mistaking plenitude for comprehensiveness, or even representativeness. Any sense of what might be absent recedes under the press of what is so obviously and overwhelmingly present and the immediate satisfaction to be gained from that presence. Having more than enough images than can be viewed, let alone understood or explained, in a scholarly lifetime is both exhilarating and daunting. In order to manage such plenitude, an immediate scholarly impulse is towards thematic modes of organization – editors of scholarly journals undoubtedly will have already received a glut of articles on 'the representation of' street music, or scavengers, or almost anything under the nineteenth-century sun that bring together the material to be found by thematic searches of web-based resources. The consequences of a scholarly impulse towards such modes of apprehending the visual will be discussed later in this chapter.

The dialogue between plenty and representativeness or comprehensiveness in the availability of digitized visual culture can be immediately approached by listing some of the more obvious resources now available for scholarly purposes. It is important to make an initial distinction between text- or print-based digitization projects and those concerned solely or primarily with images. Most web-based publications of printed material are given shape by the generic, functional or historical coherence of the sources used – court records, for example, or nineteenth-century literature about the city, or newspapers from a particular area. Such material is generally shaped into some form of coherence that bears witness to intended users as well as editorial preoccupations and perceptions. The web-based publication of images tends to be a much more miscellaneous or even incoherent process, sometimes based on visual attractiveness as much as public usefulness. In particular, much of the visual material appearing on the web is present in, but incidental to, its source – I use the term 'incidental to' here deliberately in preference to the more optimistic 'integral within'. The illustrations to periodicals and newspapers provide obvious examples of this process, raising many complexities about how illustrations are to be found and 'read' when they are seldom amenable to word search, and offering immediate issues about how far digitization offers an effective simulacrum of the original image. Clearly there are major differences between the nature of a digitized text and digitized image which will be considered later.

But more important still is the recognition that collections of images have an institutional history fundamentally different from that of archives of printed texts and books. As already suggested, the visual and the graphic often have an archival presence that is largely incidental upon a primarily text-based collection. To give an example, the extraordinary collections of eighteenth- and early nineteenth-century satirical prints in the Lewis Walpole Library in Farmington, Connecticut, were put together largely by a private collector using personal funds as an 'illustrative' resource for the editing of a massive edition of Horace Walpole's *Letters*.[3] Their immediate function was to supply visual information to explain, illustrate or underscore historical understanding centrally derived from traditional text-based resources, although, of course, subsequent curatorial policy and development of the collection has made it one of the outstanding collections of British caricature quite aside from its Walpole connections.

More recent scholars concerned with the presence of the image in historical research have sought to oppose or at least sophisticate a crudely 'evidential' response to visual culture, pointing to the need to acknowledge the history of representation itself as one of the central discourses that constructs historical meaning.[4] They have pointed to the many ways in which images construct their own version of reality built out of particular generic and icononographical traditions, the ideological assumptions of their makers, the assumed interests, beliefs and needs of their consumers, and the modes of production and consumption through which they became available and carried social meanings. Just to take one small but telling symptom of the highly mediated nature of visual culture as evidence, the colouring of prints remains extremely difficult to interpret. To use my own interest in nineteenth-century dustmen as a test case, is it safe to assume that, based on the vast consensus of evidence provided by coloured caricatures, dustmen almost invariably wore red velveteen breeches?[5] There is some confirmatory evidence for this belief to be obtained from printed sources, but nonetheless there remains the possibility that dustmen in red breeches were largely the invention of hard-pressed colourists looking to give their black and white outlines some visual impact – or even the awful possibility that a colourist had a good red easily available and slapped it on, thus forming a precedent taken up by subsequent colourists quite independent of any 'truth' about what dustmen actually wore.

Such issues about the necessary refusal of a predominantly or crudely evidential approach to the interpretation of images is, of course, important whether the image is studied in its original print form, in a book, or on a computer screen. What matters here is whether the digital image is more likely, in its increasingly naturalized and normalized web-based screen presence, to lead the researcher away from the task of filtering the historical information to be gained from pictures through the many representational codes and traditions through which they are constructed. In the case of the Lewis Walpole Library, the publication of a 'Digital Collection' to some extent frees the images in the collection from the circumambient collections of printed materials, manuscripts and artefacts in which they were originally situated and which allocated them to their evidential function. Yet, despite the Library's obvious respect for their autonomous potential as a visual collection, nonetheless the assembled caricatures still show important traces of their original function. The formation of this particular collection depended on the interests, financial resources, collecting ability and immediate scholarly purposes of an individual. It was assembled to serve the purposes of a particular literary historian undertaking the specific task of editing Horace Walpole's extensive correspondence. Thus, while the Lewis Walpole Library's collection of eighteenth-century caricature remains one of the most extensive available anywhere in the world, it is not entirely free (despite an astute recent acquisitions policy) from a belief that caricature provides the most visually effective way of understanding eighteenth-century politics, and that the aesthetics of caricatures are of less interest than their socio-political content. Underlying these assumptions remains the implication that visual culture is a 'supplementary' form of historical understanding.

By a further accident of the Library's collecting history, it has extensive holdings of comic and satirical prints published in the Regency and early Victorian periods, a noticeably difficult area to research, which are also available in the Digital Collection. In this instance, in recognition that the Library's function is primarily to offer resources for the study of eighteenth-century British history, there have been only limited attempts by the Library to fill out gaps or give range and coherence to those collections that stand outside the central research interests of scholars of eighteenth-century British history.[6] Thus, while the Lewis Walpole's collections offer an immensely valuable visual resource, what is available in their Digital Collections remains extensive but incoherent, accessible but accidental. The wealth of what is available in its range and richness has the potential to conceal what is absent and what is incomplete.

The Lewis Walpole Library's decision to digitize its 'flat satires' as a first stage in making its collections widely available in electronic form was driven by a number of motives. The first was a clear recognition of the scholarly importance and uniqueness of its holdings. The second was a realization that digitization is an essential means of preservation for delicate paper-based artefacts – however complex and risky a process digitization might be, it forms a key method of limiting the amount of handling that paper-based artefacts need to endure. The third was amenability of caricatures – largely produced as single sheet images – to the processes of electronic reproduction. The fourth, crucially, was the availability of enough funds, expertise and will to undertake such a large-scale project. Few institutions will have a comparable combination of outstanding but physically coherent collections, available funds and expertise, and a strong sense of responsibility to scholars worldwide. It remains unusual among the sponsors of major digitization projects in its central commitment to visual material. Large-scale digital archives or collections that primarily derive from an impulse to assemble and preserve predominantly visual material are on the whole somewhat rare. Major nationally important institutions do, of course, have a web presence that includes digital material, and sometimes this presence is extensive. The New York Public Library, for instance, has included a large-scale presence of visual material on its website.[7] The Science Museum in London offers a rich sample of images as a means of apprehending its collections.[8] The British Museum website has a considerable number of satirical prints on offer, all with extremely comprehensive catalogue entries.[9] Yet the digital presence in these cases, while recognizing the public responsibilities of such august institutions, is largely that of a 'showcase' for their prodigious holdings, and, as such, a recognition that visual attractiveness and variety form important elements in bringing in and engaging readers and visitors. More complex in its function is the wonderful digitized collection from the *John Johnson Collection* of printed ephemera at the Bodleian Library, Oxford, a collection in which visual culture intersects powerfully with print culture, and which accordingly offers a unique resource for cross- and interdisciplinary research. Here the visuality of print culture is stressed in ways which offer an alternative to the stress shown by historians on the verbal as the primary medium for historical understanding.[10]

Yet the *John Johnson* digital archive, while freely available to scholarly and public libraries in Great Britain, was mounted as a commercial project, and it is expensive for overseas users. While not as inaccessible on grounds of cost as the commercial image libraries like Getty Images or the Bridgeman Library which are directed largely at providing pictures for newspapers, magazines and books, nonetheless the marketing of the *John Johnson* website does acknowledge that dedicated collections of images can be used to generate income. In the case of many libraries, like the Guildhall Library, the income generated by the scholarly use of images drawn from the collection is doubtless of real value in sustaining and augmenting the collections, and in allowing further digitization to take place. But many scholarly authors are finding that the increasing charges made for the republication of images in books and essays, which embrace both fees for republication and charges for the mechanics of the reprographic process, to say nothing of the complexity of obtaining reproductive permissions and the labyrinthine demands of copyright law, paradoxically often put the full exploitation of the newly visible richness of digital resources beyond the reach of the resources available to support publication.[11] While Google Books and Project Gutenberg make full texts (and, of course, their illustrations) freely available, the digitizing of the image has nonetheless derived to a large extent from a strong sense of the commercial potential of the web-based collection.

If few large-scale dedicated collections of graphic images beyond a number of specialist repositories and those collections mounted as an element within the websites of major libraries and museums exist, there remain a mass of other electronic sources whose motives for mounting a digital collection of images on the web extend far beyond the commercial. As already suggested, the appearance of a mass of images is often contingent upon, ancillary to, or an integrated part of collections built round particular thematic concerns. Obvious examples would be the Guildhall Library (ostensibly a collection dedicated to the history and topography of London but inevitably including many images of how people inhabit the urban space in every way) and the Wellcome Institute[12] (dedicated to the history of medicine, which has proved to be a theme highly attractive to caricaturists and genre painters alike). Local thematically organized museum collections, like the People's History Museum in Manchester,[13] are rich in visual resources that are beginning to find their way on to supporting websites. In all these cases, the image is primarily situated in the collections as 'evidence', furthering any tendencies the researcher might have to see visual culture in primarily illustrative terms, and to organize the gathering of material for study by thematic relevance.

Further extensive sources of images available on the web derive from less directly commercial and educational motives or the wish to advertise and celebrate major national resources. Interest groups, collectors and knowledgeable individuals frequently assemble extensively illustrated websites to express and further their interests, and many of these, especially in areas such as the history of the comic strip, step beyond 'hobbyist' limitations to offer important scholarly information and content.[14] While often such sites are less than full in the accounts of the many images they bring on to the web, and metadata is frequently non-existent, they perform an important function in mediating between 'amateur' enthusiasm and scholarly process. Scholars need to show a certain humility in the face of the levels of information and understanding available outside the narrow confines of the academy – it is easy to assume that websites devoted to the enthusiasms of collectors, like *Yesterday's Papers* will not be sufficiently scholarly to support academic study, yet there is much here of use to the researcher. While the digital presence of the uncontextualized or unascribed image is a hazard to which the websites of interest group and enthusiasts and collectors are particularly prone, such a problem is not only an issue for digital publications. Even more valuable than interest group or individual websites are the web-based illustrated catalogues posted by dealers in prints and other visual material.[15] Dealers have a vested interest in making accurate descriptions of their wares, and they also bring to their stock more experience of seeing and handling a mass of prints over many years than is available to the average scholar. Additionally, because their stock is always changing, dealers' websites provide an unpredictable range of images gathered together by their commercial potential rather than their generic compatibility or homogeneity of content. Such accidental contiguity is often the source of some unexpected but valuable connection or possibility.

It is probably the case that the majority of nineteenth-century images drawn from the web that will be used by historians derive from illustrations that form integral elements of text-based publications. The astonishing presence of massed ranks of digitized books, magazines and newspapers on the web offers historians, among much else, unprecedented access to the ways in which the Victorians represented their world to themselves. Resources such as *British Periodicals Online*, Project Gutenberg, and Google Books, which reproduce texts by scanning individual copies of titles, immediately make a vast stock of images available to the historian in digital form. Key sources of illustrations such as *The Illustrated London News*, which has been used over and over again by historians in pursuit of evidence of 'popular opinion' – or just a telling illustration – are now widely, though scarcely freely, available. Despite the occasional (but potentially very serious) issues raised by editorial policy and the technical and formal limitations of the screen versions of such publications, it is an endless delight to be able to work with the illustrated page and to assess illustrations in their printed context within an issue of a magazine. In the future, scholars will be forced to work not just with digitized images drawn from print-based publications, but also to find ways of accommodating into their work images produced primarily, or even exclusively, as digital ones. In these cases, the challenge of a descriptive methodology is one that has scarcely yet been addressed.

The interpretative issues raised by working with such a profusion of graphic images drawn from print-based media are immediately apparent. Some are complexities that historians have long had to address. How does an illustration relate to its circumambient text? How trustworthy is the comic or caricature image as an index of public opinion? Did the illustrators who drew for magazines which, like *The Illustrated London News*, made huge claims for the authenticity and accuracy of their reportage, both verbal and visual, actually ever see the places, events and phenomena that they drew? How could the dominant reprographic method employed by the Victorian book and magazine – the wood engraving – claim to be an authentic way of representing reality when its monochrome and linear form, to say nothing of its visual simplification, seemed totally inadequate to the task?

But beyond these perennial questions, the digital simulacrum of the wood-engraved or lithographed illustration asks new and particular questions of the historian. The first concerns issues that recur in all forms of reproduction – can the reader/viewer be sure that the full text has been made available? In particular, how far have para-textual elements been sought out and included? And who made the decisions about what para-textual material to include – a cataloguer, a librarian, a historian, or even a publisher? Any scholar working with printed copies of periodicals has to recognize the importance of advertisements, covers, and supplements of various kinds, to say nothing of more closely integrated para-textual elements, in assessing the likely editorial policy, readership and social register of a particular journal or magazine. I well recall having worked through all the bound volumes of Richard Oastler's *Fleet Papers* available in the British Library in search of poems by the artisan poet John Critchley Prince and finding no relevant publications, only to have Ruth and Eddie Frow at the Library of the Working Class Movement draw my attention to an important poem printed on the inside cover of an issue of the magazine, a cover that had been discarded in binding up the British Library copy. If such problems exist for scholars working from printed copies in libraries they are even more acute for digital editions, where copies available for reproduction may not be at all 'complete', and where editorial policy may centre on text rather than para-text. Indeed, digital editions, because of their propensity to become the 'definitive' or 'go-to' texts for many scholars geographically or economically unable to visit major libraries on a frequent basis, require very considerable editorial expertise and persistence in order to ensure their accuracy and comprehensiveness.[16] In terms of the available text, digital editions need to be used with at least as much wariness as printed copies as their screen presence serves to conceal lacunae, blemishes or absences in the text that are potentially more visible when physically present to their readers. Attacks on the autonomy of the printed page carried out either by means of the editorial decisions and reprographic processes of digitization, or by the hazards of survival which have resulted in the separating out of images from their printed space and context, form a serious hazard for historical research.

Such issues about what might form a 'complete' digital account of the physical presence of a printed text merge into the wider questions about 'presence' and 'absence'. In particular, how damaging is it for the historian to lose the 'presence' or, to use Walter Benjamin's still relevant term, the 'aura' of the image through the processes of digital reproduction? And is there a difference in kind as well as intensity between the digital presence of the image and the presence of the image in its original physical form? It does seem to me that there is a difference in kind involved here. How an image is made constructs its meanings differently to the ways that printing and typography construct verbal meanings. And it seems obvious that viewing a digital simulacrum of an etched, engraved or lithographed image puts a further barrier, an additional layer of 'reproduction', between the viewer and the image in comparison to working from the original book or print. Often it is difficult enough to establish from the 'original' print or illustration the reprographic medium used in its making,[17] let alone the image's relationship to the empirically observed reality it seeks to represent. But in practice there may be less of a loss of self-referential or self-revelatory 'technical' information in digitally produced images than might be expected. Often, digital images are presented on the web with detailed metadata that offers the viewer clear information about how the print or illustration has been made. While for some scholarly purposes it would be well to confirm this information from close scrutiny of the print itself, for most purposes the information provided by an expert cataloguer is trustworthy enough. Also, through the kinds of manipulation of the image that have become digitally available, closer and more precise scrutiny of the details that reveal how precisely a print was produced can be made. It is an exhilarating experience as a teacher to see a class, in an effort to determine the reprographic medium of a print, turn away from the print itself to study its digital equivalent where magnification can make clear whether the ends of lines show the burr of copper engraving or the smoother entry and exit of etching.

But perhaps the central problem among issues to do with the digital 'presence' or 'aura' of the image concern the extent to which the endless succession of similarly sized pictures that cascade down the computer screen have lost those physical qualities through which they reveal and explain themselves. A representational medium like the wood engraving, which is acutely limited as a representational force by its nature as a monochromatic and linear medium in which complex tonality or the illusion of naturalism is difficult to achieve, widely advertises its own representational mechanics, and serves a useful purpose in reminding the researcher of the highly mediated and artificial nature of the image. Nonetheless, there are a number of ways in which working with digitized images rather than the 'original' page or print helpfully foregrounds the complex of mediations between artist and image which any historian using visual resources needs constantly to acknowledge. The loss of the material presence of the image and its 'aura' and the substitution of a screen-based simulacrum should act as a constant reminder of the need to remain aware of the representational distance between fact and image.

Yet, as everyone who has used projected images as a pedagogic aid will know, it becomes very easy to assume that all pictures are the size of a classroom screen and have a flat picture plane irrespective of the medium used in their making. The imposed confines of the computer screen and the 'unnaturalness' of the presence of images upon the screen should, in theory, prompt the researcher to continually re-inscribe back into his or her work the complex of discourses about materiality and social mediations that surround prints and complicate their evidential potential. The loss of its original material form in the digital reproduction of prints, as suggested above, does increase the difficulty of acknowledging its mode of production. Colour and size are only two of the obvious ways in which digital reproduction 'misrepresents' its subjects. Each reprographic medium, of course, has its own economic and social history, particular set of generic formulations and distinctive mode of consumption defined by audience or readership. While all genres of graphic reproduction to some extent share common iconographical and representational codes drawn from right across the culture that produces them, nonetheless each distinct reprographic medium becomes historically more closely associated with particular purposes and audiences – the etching and metal engraving with single plate caricature in the second half of the nineteenth century, the aquatint with landscape in the same period, the wood engraving with the mid-Victorian novel and literary periodical, the lithograph with, for example, music covers and scraps. The reprographic processes of digitization inevitably inhibit images from being able to use physical presence to impose their particular cultural history on the viewer.

I have already mentioned the excellent Guildhall Library *Collage* site which led the way in publishing online the 20,000 images that formed the Library's Print Collection, and which now forms part of the London Metropolitan Archive.[18] The curious visitor to the site is greeted by a range of carefully thought-out search categories that offer an interesting sequence of choices that were designed to both mimic and facilitate the ways in which a researcher would seek out relevant visual material using printed resources. The entry categories include such broad topics as 'trades' or 'people'. Clicking on these takes you to more specialized groupings – 'people' would take you to 'office/title', for example, and then clicking on 'Lord Chancellor' would bring up images of particular office holders, such as Lord Brougham, for example. Thus the researcher could put together a folder of images of Lord Chancellors – a topic that might just sustain, or at least start a relevant train of thought, that could result in a plausible article or dissertation, perhaps.

The genesis of the *Collage* site was, indeed, prompted by a wish to explore the nature of search categories for images as well as recognition of the significance of the Guildhall's holdings, which spread way beyond a straightforward topographical record of the built environment of London. The introductory information for the site declares, entirely accurately, that the resource can be word searched by using 'artist, subject, date and medium'. Despite the opportunities offered by these listings, it is worth thinking a little about how the site structures the hierarchy of available search categories for more detailed study. The three primary categories – 'Artists', 'People', 'Places' – correspond with the interests of the most likely users of the sites: art historians looking for signed works by major artists, historians researching political and social history and with an interest in the careers or activities of named individuals, and a range of researchers looking for visual evidence of how particular places in London looked at a precise historical moment. They also reflect the major holdings of the collection – signed and 'significant' oil paintings and prints, portraits of individuals whose lives were tied up in some way with the history of London, and topographical representations in various genres and forms. The use of such categories, which requires the researcher to have a single 'name' or 'word' to use as a starting point, is here little different in method or outcome from the kinds of broad-based and speculative word searches that might form some of the first processes in any piece of traditional research whether using printed texts or visual resources. Discussions of this kind point to a central issue concerning the development of search categories for visual material – how far do cataloguers, curators and technical specialists need to develop and build into their websites search patterns for visual material that differ in their construction and approach to those familiar from printed material? Clearly, word searching for catalogued graphic material remains productive to some extent – artists, publishers, engravers, printers and titles can all be accessed by traditional word searches. But it is a much more complex and contentious activity to develop a vocabulary for describing the visual content of images let alone the more abstract elements of a visual image such as colour or tone. Indeed it is entirely possible to misread visual content by failing to recognize what is depicted, and even the most sophisticated cataloguers are prone to misreadings or false identifications of visual content. 'Vocabularies' for the description of visual content are being developed and given wide circulation – the Library of Congress, for example, has produced a specialist vocabulary for curators and cataloguers. But there remains much development work to do, and it is necessary that the different skills belonging to an art history-trained cataloguer, a visually aware social historian and a computer scientist well attuned to the ways in which scholarly research in the Humanities and Social Sciences is undertaken are drawn together in the further development of the metadata needed to structure the online publication of visual collections.

Furthermore, most researchers in pursuit of visual material have broad thematic or topic-based categories in mind, and may well be more interested in the unknown, the unnamed and the obscure rather than the kinds of responses offered by precise word searches. Recognizing such likely need, the Guildhall *Collage* site has introduced a set of 'fuzzier' supplementary search categories which were formulated out of the kinds of broad areas of most interest to historians, including such major fields as 'religion and belief', 'politics', 'leisure', and 'trade and industry'. These categories, even without further refinement, lead on out into pages of thumb-nail images which can be rapidly scanned and assembled to fit the exact purposes of the researcher. One of the Guildhall categories – 'abstract ideas' – is of particular interest as it moves towards offering an *interpretation* rather than a *description* of the available image. The tension between these two modes of reading images is of central importance to the historian, and is immensely problematic. At a primary level the historian needs to know what an image depicts – those aspects of a graphic representation that seek to realize the textures, colours and shapes of the empirically observable world in an accurate and recognizable manner. But of course much of the information about the observable world conveyed by an image will be coded through the representational traditions and iconography of the form used by the artist. To cite one example I used in my research on the cultural history of London dustmen, William Heath's well-known 1829 caricature 'Dusty Bob – The Parish Dustman' has been widely used by costume historians to show the characteristic work garb of that trade, which is shown in remarkable detail. Yet, of course, the caricature appears in a series called 'Parish Characters', a sequence in which Heath satirizes prominent politicians, and 'Dusty Bob' is centrally a caricature of Robert Peel's role as sweeper-up of unresolved governmental problems. But even this tension between the 'real' and the 'caricature' is rendered more complex by the para-textual elements of the print. This is 'Dusty Bob', a well-known stage character made famous and universally recognizable through the cultural babble constructed by Pierce Egan's 1823 novel *Life in London* and its many later manifestations on the stage, in song and in ceramic figurines. So who is present here – a dustman, Robert Peel, or Dusty Bob?

Such issues of interpretation are of course not unique to digital images but adhere in any form of visual representation. But they do centrally affect the ways in which images are 'tagged' and which consequently renders research using visual culture entirely different from text- or word-based sources. The Guildhall site tackles this issue in an extremely creative way. The search categories that lie just beyond 'abstract ideas' move on to 'actions', 'emotions', 'social concepts' and 'states', taking the researcher usefully but contentiously on further into interpretative categories based on a 'reading' of the implicit rather than the informational content of the image. Thus, under 'actions', we reach such places as 'forgiveness', 'honesty' and 'lustfulness'. At an immediate level such categories are immensely helpful to the historian in quest of visual evidence. A researcher working on, for example, prostitution in London could burrow down through the *Collage* site via 'abstract ideas' to 'lustfulness' under 'actions', to 'immorality' under 'social concepts' and to 'temptation' under 'states'.

In the case of the Guildhall *Collage* website the sophisticated categorizing and tagging of the collection is without doubt a model of its kind, and immensely helpful to the researcher, especially as the site allows for other, less focused searches through such headings as 'publishers' and, of course, 'date'. There are other websites which have sought to combine making important visual resources freely available with the development of complex verbal tagging mechanisms that seek to replicate or lead the research needs of its users. *The Database of Mid-Victorian Wood-Engraved Illustration*, developed with AHRC funding at Cardiff University by a team led by Julia Thomas, has been of particular value in publicizing and discussing issues to do with 'describing', 'naming' and 'tagging' illustrations.[19] One activity that the Cardiff team pursued was that of sending copies of illustrations to a range of 'ordinary' respondents and asking them to describe what they believed was depicted in the detail of the image. The discrepancies in their responses bring home the instability of the 'information' offered to the historian by visual sources. The *British Museum Catalogue* has been digitized, and all the verbal detailed descriptions of the holdings are thus amenable to word search, although even the observational powers and contextual knowledge of Dorothy George are sometimes inadequate to the demands of identifying exactly what is present in particular caricatures.[20]

For the vast bulk of images available to researchers on the web, however, these kinds of sophisticated if fallible search mechanisms based on word searches will not be available, and the scholar will be thrown back on the much more haphazard process of trawling through pages of thumb-nail images or digitized editions of periodicals and books. The difficulties of word searching a mass of visual material held within texts when the captions or titles that might identify relevant images, if any, may offer little clue to the nature of the accompanying illustration are acute. Furthermore, deciding what is actually being represented within the image is not easy, and the perils of 'misreading' have been enumerated extensively above. Obviously, the researcher looking for particular events can use dates and word searches to bring him- or herself into contact with a broad spectrum of digitized material that may well include illustrations. But there is still no more reliable mechanism currently available in many instances than the scroll button.

This chapter is subtitled as a 'cautious celebration' of the triumphant presence of the digital image as a pragmatic and easily accessed resource available to support and enhance historical research. The reasons for that somewhat grudging caution have been suggested above. First, the overwhelming screen presence of web-based images, and especially their profusion, their accessibility and their amenability to digital manipulation, tends to lead the historian away from thinking through and questioning their status. The computer screen promises an ever-present simulacrum of the image so intense, so available, so convincing that, combined with the often excellent metadata to be found on responsible scholarly websites, it becomes all too easy to accord such images an autonomous status. Such unjustified (but understandable) awestruck admiration for the flickering screen presence tends to nullify the need to deconstruct the sequence of mediations through which representation becomes available as evidence. Digitization adds yet one more process to the complex of socio-cultural and aesthetic transformations through which empirically gathered understanding of the world is represented in the image. Recognition and acknowledgement of the digital as a transformative process is thus important for any researcher.

Second, the ways in which images have been collected, stored and made available by research repositories has often separated them from their particular history within print culture. There is no equivalent of the British Library or Library of Congress for visual culture. Nearly all major collections have been formed by genre or topic rather than by any attempt at representativeness. Many began as the obsessive interest of an individual, which was then bequeathed to or accidentally fell into public or institutional hands. To take an obvious example, a dedicated collection centred on the history of medicine will have gone out of its way to identify, purchase and assemble images precisely related to this topic. In the process of building the collection, the librarians and archivists will often have dislocated images relevant to their particular interests from their context in other publications. Images will have been cut from magazines, salvaged from scrapbook pages, or floated free from publications of all kinds. In digitizing a collection of this kind, the primary purpose of the institution will not be to reassemble the print history of each image but rather to strive for the bringing together of the greatest number and range of relevant or interesting images. In the boxes of print dealers and second-hand book dealers, in the lengthy list of separate images offered by book dealers who 'break' volumes for their plates, in the minds and with the scissors of scrap-book makers, images are constantly being de-contextualized from their source in ways largely unknown to printed texts, which largely retain evidence of their place of publication, authorship and print history. Despite the mass of visual culture being mounted on to websites, many seemingly informative images immensely attractive to the historian as illustration or evidence have floated free from their historical and cultural context. It is often extremely difficult to restore them to their proper historical place and moment.

Third, the available mechanisms for searching images, despite increasingly sophisticated experiments and projects, still fall way short in effectiveness from the more familiar processes of keyword searching that can be easily undertaken for digitized texts. The titles and other para-textual content of images, particularly illustrations, often contain few or no verbal elements that might link the image to its subject, thus obscuring the link between the subject and the title of a print or illustration. Artists and engravers are often not named or represented only by their initials, which are frequently not catalogued. While highly developed specialist websites, like the *Guildhall Collage* or the *Lewis Walpole Digital Collection*, offer lists of terms derived from the contents of the assembled images that allow for more traditional word searching for 'content', their effectiveness depends on the quality of observation, knowledge and detail available to the cataloguer.

Fourth, the mechanisms available for searching visual culture on the web, even with all the constraints suggested above, tend to encourage the assembling of images by topic rather than genre or mode, thus reinforcing the dangerous tendency still widely visible in historical research to see images as fundamentally 'illustrative'. Editors of scholarly journals must wince at submissions with titles like 'The Representation of [submit any topic – say, street music or ballad sellers] in the [choose a promising source, say, the mid-Victorian Illustrated Periodical Press]'. It is important not to use visual culture as an easy short cut to 'popular opinion', however interesting and available graphic sources may be to any chosen topic.

But even recognizing the complexities and developmental issues which still surround the emergence of visual culture into scholarly consciousness through the mechanisms and mediations of the web, there are many grounds to be excited and optimistic about the kinds of research that have become available through the accumulated digital archive. Not only has a hitherto only glimpsed mass of images risen into relatively accessible visibility, but there is also widespread evidence of a growing eagerness to make these resources available, for whatever reason, in enough mass and variety to make writing a more comprehensive history of representation a feasible, if still daunting, possibility.

Notes

1 See http://collage.cityoflondon.gov.uk/collage/app [accessed: 25 March 2012]. The Guildhall Library Prints Collection, which formed the basis for the *Collage* website, is now part of the London Metropolitan Archive and no longe located in the Guildhall Library.

2 There are many areas of web-based research on print culture where the names of publishers prove an extremely successful search term. Print genres like song books, for example, where titles, authors and editors are unknown to any useful form of printed listing, often reveal themselves to web-based research through using the name of a publisher specializing in this genre. The same holds true for the pursuit of ephemeral illustrated periodicals.

3 The 'digital collection' of The Lewis Walpole Library at Farmington can be found at http://www.library.yale.edu/walpole/collections/digital_collection_images.html

[accessed: 25 March 2012]. One great strength of the *Lewis Walpole Digital Collection* is that full entries can be found on Yale's Orbis library catalogue. The full record for each image uses the descriptive vocabulary evolved by the Library of Congress to 'tag' elements of content and thus provide a searchable keyword listing for each print. There is a more detailed discussion of tagging and word searching later in the chapter. It is worth noting that Lewis's edition of the Walpole *Letters* has also been digitized by the Lewis Walpole Library and is freely available – a wonderfully beneficial example of enlightened digitization.

4 For useful discussions of these issues see R. Porter, 'Prinney, Boney, Boot', *London Review of Books*, 20 March 1986, pp. 19–21; R. Porter, 'Seeing the past', *Past and Present*, 118: 1 (February 1988), 186–205; F. Palmeri, 'The cartoon: image as critique', in S. Barber and C. M. Peniston-Bird (eds), *History Beyond the Text: A Student's Guide to Approaching Alternative Sources* (London: Routledge, 2009), pp. 32–48; B. Maidment, 'Graphic bric-a-brac: comic visual culture and the study of early Victorian lower-class urban culture', *Key Words*, 8 (2010), 76–93.

5 See B. Maidment, '101 Things to do with a fantail hat: dustmen, dirt and dandyism 1820–60', *Textile History*, 33 (2002), 79–96.

6 Although, of course, as the history of collecting becomes established as a major scholarly interest, the way in which the Farmington collections were assembled becomes a subject of study in itself.

7 The Library's website offers access to over 700,000 images, organized into large-scale 'collections' of related material. See http://digitalgallery.nypl.org/nypldigital/ [accessed: 25 March 2012].

8 The Science Museum's website is built round a range of themes and is constructed largely for education purposes. Nonetheless, there is a wealth of visual material available here. See http://www.sciencemuseum.org.uk/onlinestuff.aspx [accessed: 25 March 2012].

9 The mass of material available on this website means that it takes a while to find ways of using the 'advanced search' page to reach relevant material, but it is worth the effort. See http://www.britishmuseum.org/research/search_the_collection_database. aspx [accessed: 25 March 2012].

10 See http://johnjohnson.chadwyck.co.uk [accessed: 25 March 2012].

11 Against this rather gloomy picture, it is important to recognize that the appearance of cheap and effective digital scanners has allowed scholars to exploit personal collections or non-institutional sources in order to include images in their work. The emergence of PowerPoint presentations as a central element in lecture-based teaching and web-based student learning materials has also been effective in increasing awareness of the expository power of the image, although the temptation to included images in pre-sentations to students largely for their diversionary or decorative effect has to be resisted. Additionally, some collections are beginning to introduce a fee-free element in their web-based publications.

12 See the *Wellcome Images* website at http://medphoto.wellcome.ac.uk [accessed: 25 March 2012].

13 See http://www.phm.org.uk/our-collection/ [accessed: 25 March 2012].

14 See, for example, the *Yesterday's Papers* website at http://john-adcock.blogspot.com [accessed: 25 March 2012].

15 The websites for specialist dealers like G. J. Saville and Grosvenor Prints represent an important resource for research, especially as the images available for inspection change regularly.

16 The Nineteenth Century Serials Edition project led by Isabel Armstrong and Laurel Brake at Birkbeck College provided a major forum for scholars thinking about editorial practices in relation to digital publications. See www.ncse.ac.uk [accessed: 25 March 2012], and J. Mussell and S. Paylor, 'Mapping the "mighty maze": the nineteenth-century serials edition', *19: Interdisciplinary Studies in the Long Nineteenth Century*,

1 (2005), at http://19.bbk.ac.uk/index.php/19/article/viewFile/437/299 [accessed: 25 March 2012].

17 The differences between etching and metal engraving are often particularly hard to define, especially when many prints used a combination of several different media.

18 See http://collage.cityoflondon.gov.uk [accessed: 25 March 2012].

19 See www.dmvi.cardiff.ac.uk [accessed: 25 March 2012].

20 F. G. Stephens and M. D. George, *British Museum Catalogue of Political and Personal Satires* (London: British Museum, 1874–1950).

Teaching history in the digital age

7 Studying the past in the digital age

From tourist to explorer

Mark Sandle

Changing approaches to the study of the past have been driven by many things over the past couple of centuries: the use of new sources (statistics, oral history, memoirs), interest in previously unexplored fields (culture, mentalities), or just changing intellectual fashions. A key driver of change in recent times has been the conglomerate of phenomena which come (loosely) under the umbrella of the 'digital age': the post-industrial era in which new technologies and concomitant social practices have combined to bring about a constantly shifting, accelerating transformation in the relationship between human beings, technology, information, knowledge and consciousness.[1] History is inexorably part of this process. Leaving aside the challenges that the digital age will provide for future historians – in terms of the preservation of the historical record, the transience of human communication, and the sheer volume of information and opinion being generated – a number of issues confront contemporary practitioners of historical study. This chapter will focus on some of the pedagogical issues about studying history in the digital age. In particular, this chapter will explore the diverse ways that both established and apprentice historians are using new technologies, and begin to unpack how this is changing the manner in which students encounter, experience, understand, think and write about the past.

Learning in the digital age

One of the dangers in applying a particular label to any era of human history is that it serves to obscure and over-simplify a complex set of interrelated processes. So it is with the 'digital' or 'information' age. Although this is clearly a characteristic of the contemporary era, the temptation to label it as *the* characteristic should perhaps be resisted, and the developments in technology and their associated practices should also be viewed in the wider matrix of social, economic and political change associated with globalization, population expansion, mass human migration, environmental degradation, and the increasing levels of economic inequality and financial uncertainty. The Higher Education (HE) classroom is changing in a number of different ways. More students are taking advantage of the increased opportunities for undergraduate education. Public funding for HE is being squeezed everywhere, providing resource constraints for practitioners.

The make-up of the student body is changing, with students from different cultures, backgrounds, ethnicities and religions all occupying the same learning spaces. The HE classroom is increasingly diverse, bigger and underfunded. It is within this context that we must situate the developments in digital learning.

The question of learning in the digital age is itself a fraught one.[2] How, if at all, has the digital age changed the nature of human learning? How have knowledge production and acquisition been impacted? Those whom one might term 'optimists' or 'determinists' have tended to stress the transformative power of technology, and the ways in which it is changing what, how and where people learn. In particular, as Warschauer has outlined, the rapid diffusion of new technologies and the differential take-up across generations are perceived to be changing the nature of learning and literacy, creating autonomous learners and multiplying the spaces and places in which learning takes place. Others occupy what one might term a more 'instrumentalist' position, seeing technology as part of a wider process in the development of human learning, which helps to lever change, but its role is somewhat circumscribed. Here technology acts as a framework within which humans operate and interact, but is dependent upon the human actor for the extent and depth of the change it creates.[3]

What are the types of learning which characterize the digital age? This shift – encompassed in the move away from learning based around text-paper-book, passive information transmission and linear trajectories all delivered by the 'expert' at the front of the class, to digital learning – can be detailed as follows. John Seely Brown notes the following 'dimension shifts': first, an evolving sense of literacy which includes integrating image, sound and screen, and navigating and processing a massive quantity and diversity of information. Second, learning through discovery, rather than by an authority-based approach, transmitted from 'above'. Third, a move away from deductive and abstract reasoning and towards what Brown terms 'bricolage': the ability to find something that can be used to make something new. Finally, Brown notes the shift towards action: learning by doing, often with others. Digital learning prefers social to individual learning, is inherently collaborative, and is done concretely through exploration and experimentation.[4]

How has this been given particular expression within the disciplinary confines of History? Here once more we run up against the issue of trying to isolate or identify those factors that are specific to the digital age. It is important to be wary of *post hoc, ergo propter hoc*. It is easy to confuse temporal sequence and causality. The discipline of History has changed enormously over the past 30 years: techniques, intellectual trends, themes of study, numbers of faculty and students, funding, curricula have all evolved. The impact of the digital age on the study of the past needs to be woven into this broader story of cultural, social and intellectual change. History is an interesting example of the impact of technology. Often perceived to be a conservative profession, resistant to change and wedded to particular techniques and practices, historians and history students have started to embrace many of the new opportunities and openings afforded by technological developments. In the following sections, some of the many ways in which new technologies have been integrated into the study of the past will be described and then evaluated and assessed to explore how far, and in what ways this has changed the nature of learning about the past. A concluding section will reflect upon the significance of changes in the learning and teaching of History for the discipline as a whole.

The landscape of History has changed quite dramatically in recent years. The range of innovations arising out of technological shifts within the discipline of History on both sides of the Atlantic is substantial. These include everything from the very basic incorporation of web-based materials into the regular curriculum, through to online museum exhibitions, interactive hypertext history, simulations, virtual learning environments (VLEs) and the incorporation of Web 2.0 social media into the learning process.[5] These changes have impacted almost every aspect of the study of the past, ranging from the source material that is available right up to the techniques and working practices of the history profession itself. What does all this activity mean though? Have these changes deepened and improved the quality and nature of student engagement with the past and with the methods and conventions of the discipline? How should we assess the impact of the digital age on the study of the past?

If we accept the idea for a moment of 'the past as a foreign country',[6] then how might we describe the historian: tourist, explorer, pioneer? While there is no physical encounter between the past and the historian in the same way as there is between a foreign country and its visitors, this picture, whilst imperfect, tells us something about the nature of the encounter. Traditional student encounters can be likened to that of the tourist: a fairly passive, guided, predictable, whistle-stop tour which employs an expert tour director to whisk you there and back; participation is minimal; the tourist always returns home. Is it possible to argue that the digital age has fundamentally transformed the nature of the encounter between the student and the past? Are we now describing a relationship more akin to exploration, than tourism? Is this now more autonomous and less guided? More open to the unknown and the unexpected, than fixed and pre-dictable? Is it more immersed and less superficial? It seems evident that the digital age is witnessing the creation of a different scenario for studying the past. Inter-estingly though, what seems to be changing (although we are still at an early stage) is the mindset and outlook of the student. The past of course remains unchanged, but in promoting a sustained encounter with the methods of the historian, the digital age may well be shaping the consciousness of students which will change the ways they encounter and understand the past.

Sources, sources, sources

Any appraisal of the digital age centres on what we view as being essential in terms of 'understanding the past'. The past has gone, but grappling with the traces left behind by the past forms the core of the historian's activity. In this regard the opportunities afforded by increased access to the range and types of sources can be seen as beneficial. Students have been exposed at a far earlier stage in their intellectual development to sources and documents that they would never have been able to read and analyse 20 or 30 years ago. Source material has been painstakingly transcribed, translated, digitized and published. They have also been able, more recently, to engage with a spectacular array of types of primary source material – video, artwork, diaries, cartoons, letters – which in previous times very few students encountered. It is not just primary sources though. Electronic access to scholarly databases, e-journals, blogs and the like has also given students greater and easier access to a whole range of secondary source materials.

It is not certain that the digital age has been the cause of this explosion in exposure. Much of this has been coincidental with the revolution in historical study that has seen, ever since the emergence of the Annales School, a growing interest in using non-conventional source material. The changing appreciation of scholars of the value of different sources has underpinned their desire to expose students to different sources. It has also coincided with the explosion of academic publishing caused by competition for research funding, tenure and the metrics system for measuring research impact amongst scholars. The digital age has facilitated this, broadened it and made it easier, but has not caused it. Over the years, the range, type and quality of material has increased, until we reach the present moment where there is a bewildering array that can be accessed (assuming that you have either the physical resources in your home/school/ neighbourhood/college/university to do this, or that you live in a country which allows unfettered access to the internet). If we break down what is available by category then we can identify the following types of material.

Access to primary sources

One of the ways in which the digital age has dramatically expanded what students of the past can examine has been through the digitization of primary source material. The breadth of primary sources available now almost defies description, but upon almost any topic now you can access high-quality copies of documents, papers, images, letters, diaries, newspapers, street plans, poems and so on. A few examples will suffice, but each historian working in their own field will be able to provide their own list of the greatest sites around. Not all sites are available free of charge, and some now include a fee to gain access.

- The *National Archives* UK have put the full records of the 1901 and 1911 censuses online. These are fully searchable and include images of the original documents.[7]
- The *National Archives* UK have also provided access to the Domesday Book. You can search it and download colour images from the text.
- The *Avalon Project* at Yale Law School aims to bring together an enormous number of primary source documents on law, politics, government and diplomacy.[8]

- The *Times Digital Archive* gives online access to *The Times* newspaper from 1785–1985.[9]
- *British Pathe*: it is described as the world's first digital news archive, and offers a huge database of over 3,500 hours of the *British Pathe* Film archive.[10]

The list could go on forever, although an exceptionally useful site which has categorized and classified many of the resources available on the internet is the *intute.ac.uk* site. This was a project, funded by JISC in the UK, which grew out of a grass-roots community of information specialists who wanted to provide a portal for researchers and students, a 'best of the web' as it were. It was taken over by a consortium of seven UK universities and expanded to become a superb gateway, constantly updated and checked. Unfortunately, funding expired in July 2011 and at the time of writing its future was unclear.

This last example points up a potential problem: transience. Sites come and go. Links get broken or removed. Funding disappears. Access is, it appears, contingent and constantly vulnerable. The issue of transience is mitigated in part by the Internet Archive, which has archived over 150 billion web pages from 1996.[11] This is of course by no means exhaustive or total, but it is the start of an attempt to archive digital content, and so preserve material which might otherwise have been lost. In many ways, it mirrors some of the problems of getting to primary sources in 'real' archives, as only a selection of material is ever preserved, funding for archives is constantly under threat, and there can be cultural and political obstacles which prevent researchers from getting access to primary source materials.[12] Historians have always had to address logistical problems in doing historical research. The digital age has solved some problems of access, but created others.

Creation of archives

Alongside the digitization of primary sources has also come the emergence of thematic collections of sources, a type of online archive. Many of these are free to access. Others have to be purchased, through private companies who have digitized them and made them available through subscription. Such collections include the *Atlantic Canada Virtual Archive*,[13] *Mass Observation Online*,[14] *Empire Online*,[15] *Valley of the Shadow*,[16] *Cold War International History Project*,[17] *Moving Here*[18] and so on. Clearly those archival collections that are accessed via subscription raise questions about selective digitization for company or institutional agendas, or the imperatives imposed by the profit motive. This is in part a funding issue, as private firms seek to defray the costs of digitization and public bodies do not have the resources to do this. Once again, this is a new expression of an old problem: unequal access to research materials has always existed.

These issues reflect a more general concern with the increasing commercialization of historical content on the web, with the linking of content to the selling of commodities, or as a means of advertising a TV channel or a magazine. But so far, the vast majority of web content remains free to users. What is perhaps more worthy of note is the predominance of content that relates to modern history and to warfare in particular. This is, clearly, a reflection of popular demand, of the availability of sources and of the priorities of the publishing world. But grounds for optimism lie in the fact that those who are advocates or enthusiasts for less 'mainstream' history are able to create, produce and publish their materials now.

A more interesting development is the creation of new archives, rather than digitizing documents, images, or film from existing collections. A good example is the BBC's *A People's War* archive.[19] This is a collection of personal memories and reminiscences covering a whole variety of aspects of the Second World War, including the Home Front, internment, work, women and entertainment. Local historical groups have also used the opportunities afforded by the internet to create local oral history collections of life in particular districts or towns. A burgeoning example of this is the site *www.iremember.ru* which deals with collections of oral testimony from the Second World War in Russia (and in Russian). The lines of cause and effect are somewhat blurred here. The interest in the Second World War era in Russia (and elsewhere) is enormous. The growing interest in oral history, memory and memoir testimony has fuelled more projects to try and capture these stories before the participants die and their story is lost. The availability of the technology to disseminate these stories to a much wider audience creates an impetus for people to both record and to participate in these projects, although the nature and content of these archives is shaped by other, broader socio-cultural factors.

The significant issue here is that the technology appears to be driving the type of archive being created. In much the same way that archives in previous generations have reflected the technology available (textual cultures preserve texts, and these texts overwhelmingly reflect the activities of the educated, literate and wealthy), so the digital archives that are emerging are reflections of contemporary society: diverse forms, varied content, multiple producers. However, within this complex patchwork of new archives two things stand out. In particular the burgeoning interest in popular remembering or oral testimony, and the current obsession with war, has tended to dominate the new landscape. Whether or not this new material has been generated and produced with the requisite amount of care and critical appraisal is open to question, but this of course is a perennial problem for any researcher.

Museums, libraries and archives

Internet access to museums, libraries and archives and their cataloguing systems has given scholars access to millions of records (although not the actual sources), and obviously can be a huge boon for researchers who wish to consult the holdings and order sources online. This can save researchers an enormous amount of time and money, but also enables them to sift through what might be available, devise new paths to take or find new sources to underpin the scholarship which is being undertaken. Archives such as *A2A* (a database which outlines all the archives held locally in England and Wales, and which is searchable) help scholars do a lot of the early sifting-type research quickly and cheaply, saving time and also ensuring that fewer things are missed.[20] Another advantage of holding this information electronically is that it prevents obsolescence, can be updated quickly and easily, and so is a constantly useful reference work. Museums are another resource which people can now visit online, although the nature of the online experience needs to be contrasted with the physical experience of being in the museum itself. However, it does give people the opportunity, albeit remotely and electronically, to examine artefacts and exhibitions that may well have been impossible to visit before the advent of the World Wide Web.

So, there are a number of ways in which the digital age has contributed to increased access to and availability of a range of materials and sources for history students to use in their study of the past. But this explosion in the quality, quantity and variety of primary source material has raised two concerns about the study of the past. The first is that the study of source material is mediated through the technology, which changes the relationship and the nature of the process of inquiry and analysis. The second is that the acquisition of multi-media literacy is being acquired at the expense of the traditional 'historical' literacy of the text. In essence, both posit a disjuncture between 'history in the digital age' and 'traditional history', and that something crucial is being lost in this shift.

Undoubtedly, the use of technology mediates the relationship between historians and their sources. The physical sensation of touching the documents, searching the catalogues, opening a folder in an archive, or gazing upon a piece of artwork is lost when staring at the computer screen. Although the trace-of-the-past is present, it is also removed. Although its content should be faithful to the original (if everyone has done their job properly), it is usually cleaned up, typed up, nicely laid out. The computer version is unlikely to perish through age; instead it is more likely to disappear through connectivity or hosting issues. The digital forms of primary sources though are only as useful and as good as the amount of work and effort that goes into preparing and publishing them. The researcher, because he or she has not actually handled the original, is somewhat at the mercy of those people providing the digital version, to ensure it is authentic. The work of verification and corroboration still needs to be done.

The digital experience of research is different from physically turning the pages of the newspaper, seeing the cartoon in context, holding the diary in one's hands. The proximate presence of the trace, so the critique goes, is beguiling but misleading. A tangible connection, the physical, tactile one, is absent and this subtly alters the relationship between the inquirer and their object. This is particularly the case for physical artefacts: tapestries, buildings, vases, jewellery and weapons. Viewing an image of the artefact is very different from handling it or viewing it in person, or seeing its scale, colour and texture.[21] The difference between the actual and the virtual with a textual source is somewhat less, but the point still holds.

Clearly, the form matters. But we need to be careful about this distinction, for a number of reasons. First, undergraduates in previous years had limited experience in working directly with unprocessed primary sources. Archival work was limited. Primary sources were often printed or published and also edited down. For accessing primary sources via the web we can easily substitute using printed primary sources. Second, technology has always mediated our interactions with the traces of the past, be it via microfilm, book, paper and pen. We now have new and different forms of mediation, but mediated it still is. Third, it is important not to create this reified idea of 'authentic historical research' (which is done in archives) and somewhat 'lesser' historical research. This is not to undermine the significance of archival work at all. But it is important to recognize the limitations of this type of work too. We need to be wary of this idea that there is an inherent authenticity that comes with handling directly the traces of the past. Archivists select, sift and discard. We need to remember that all of our encounters with the lingering remnants of the past have to be appraised critically, carefully and appropriately. A recognition of the difference involved in appraising the sources remotely should not diminish the value of this, but nor should we see it as a substitute for going out to explore the sources for yourself. The digital age is changing the way that students access the remnants of the past, but this process is always constantly changing as a result of new fashions, new approaches and new sources.

A second issue is the question of the diminution of traditional forms of literacy, what Jacques Ellul has termed 'the humiliation of the word'.[22] Neil Postman, writing about the relationship between society and technology, describes

> one of the more distressing consequences of what Ellul calls the technological society … [is] that the power, prestige and utility of the word have been significantly diminished. … Indeed for forty years a conversation has taken place among our most prescient social critics about the alarming decline of both the spoken and written word as instruments of civilized discourse.[23]

If we transpose this general concern about the impact of the shift from the printed word to the digital age on 'civilized discourse' to discussions about a retreat from 'traditional history's' concern with text and document to multi-media literacy, is there any cause for concern? At present the increasing emphasis upon visual sources is proving to be something of a corrective to the somewhat visual illiteracy of most 'traditional' historians, rather than undermining the sanctity of the text. Most historians working in universities work with texts, communicate through the spoken and written word, and are aware of the importance of conveying the centrality of textual analysis and communication in their work. However, as the wider shifts in practices around communication evolve through Web 2.0, it is by no means clear what impact this will have upon the practices of historians. At present though it is a force for augmenting and enhancing traditional history.

The chimera of 'total' research

Another idea raised by source proliferation is that it is now possible to do 'complete' research. This is an illusion. This illusion has been generated not just by increased access to primary sources, but by the availability and breadth of secondary sources/reference works. The amount of scholarship now available is immense. The increased volume of scholarship is almost entirely down to the pressures for research and publication which now are at work. This pressure to publish has created a discipline marked by over-specialization, fragmentation and Soviet-style increases in output each year. Technology is providing a solution of sorts to this increased volume of material, but is also contributing to it as well.

Gaining an awareness of new scholarship that emerges is a time-consuming task. Obviously the large research libraries in the big universities always had access to a wealth of scholarship – either in books or journals – for its patrons. But the difference is that the publishing houses – through systems like JSTOR or EBSCO – now make available a huge repository of articles, reviews, research notes and discussion forums. These can be accessed directly, grouped, stored or emailed in order to access at a later time. Article alerts can also be created in order to keep up-to-date with the latest things to be published. The sheer volume of material produced by scholars now means that the electronic availability and search functions make it far easier to sort, sift and manage the information that continues to emerge. It is also possible to access material at an earlier stage in the research process. Many scholarly research centres have started to publish their work in progress, giving students and peers access to research at an earlier stage in its gestation, allowing for more collaborative work and also access to the very latest scholarship.

The danger here is the way in which all this material appears, beguilingly, to be a solution to one of the problems historians often confront in researching the past: incompleteness. The availability of so much material – both primary and secondary – in Jordanova's words, 'encourages fantasies of being able to do truly exhaustive research, of access to 100% of the relevant bibliography, of controlling vast data-sets'.[24] This is a state of mind common to most historical researchers: the nagging feeling that there are yet more documents out there to be found and included. The internet, with its massive availability of sources, and the ease of access to it, can feed this neurosis and provide a sense of being able to master the field. But this is a chimera. The field will never be mastered because there are always more things to know, more things to discover, more things to read or just new ways of looking at it. The search is continuous and endless, Sisyphean in many ways. Although one might argue that the scale, connectedness and availability of materials on the internet might actually hinder the completion of research projects, or produce an unwillingness to begin (given the sheer scale of material out there), this would be to blame the technology for what is essentially a problem of human psychology: an unwillingness to live with the contingent, unfinished outcomes of one's painstakingly crafted project.

Transforming the learner

Perhaps the arena in which the digital age has had the most impact in terms of change is not so much in regard to the availability and access to primary source material, but in the steps it has made in transforming the learner. The innovations that have burst into the study of the past have started to change the habits of mind and practices of history students, helping them to develop and refine their skills and techniques and also to create pathways into the scholarly community of historians. In other words, although the past remains as elusive as ever, the digital age is changing the people who are seeking to understand and write about the past, and in so doing the nature of the search itself is beginning to evolve.

The deployment of interactivity in history courses and classrooms has been one of the greatest areas of innovation in the study of the past. The nature of the classroom has been transformed, and as a result the interactions between students, between students and tutors, and between students and the source materials (primary and secondary) have themselves been transformed. This is a result primarily of the evolution to Web 2.0. Web 2.0 refers to the shift towards a more interactive, participative, flexible, dynamic, collaborative approach that uses multi-media. It is user-defined and user-created. Let us look at a few examples.

One of the central features of the classroom in the digital age is the increased opportunities for students and tutors to interact, and to deploy technology to assist in the process of learning. The usual method for this is through the use of a virtual learning environment or VLE (such as Blackboard, WebCT or Moodle). The use of such learning platforms within university and college history courses on both sides of the Atlantic is now commonplace, although what uses are made of it vary quite substantially, as you would expect, between tutors, departments and institutions. At one end there is the use of the VLE as a repository for course information such as handbooks or links to key websites. At the other end though is the integration of interactivity, reflection, discussion, simulation, role-play and journaling. The exploitation of the possibilities for a greater range and depth of interactions between students, tutors and specified course materials has been a key lever in assisting students to develop the key skills associated with the study of the past, and has also been instrumental in facilitating student understanding of what it means to be an historian. The practices that have emerged through the use of Web 2.0 have provided some early inklings for students about what it means to work in a community of scholars.

Some of the examples which have been highlighted in the literature emphasize the ability of the VLEs to help develop core skills, to enhance student participation and discussion, to improve student writing, create more opportunities for reflection, and develop more interactivity.[25] One of the most popular uses of VLEs in teaching and learning has been through the incorporation of online discussion boards. These have been used in a variety of different ways, but essentially they have been used as a form of blended learning: mixing more traditional modes of learning (lecture and seminar) with newer forms (using the VLE to create a virtual learning space). Online discussion boards can take many forms. Sometimes they are used alongside the existing teaching programme, as a way of preparing students for the discussion that is to come and then to continue the conversation after the face-to-face session has ended. At other times they replace face-to-face sessions, and the discussion takes place online before returning to the face-to-face session later on. Discussion boards have also been used in 'real time' as a means of replicating the face-to-face discussion, except this time mediated through the VLE.[26]

One example of an assessed online discussion board that was used in a History course is an interesting case study of the ways in which the online platform is able to change the nature of student interaction and discussion of historical issues.[27] Students in a class of 40 were divided into five smaller groups. Some non-assessed discussion boards had been run previously to give students experience of using them before the assessed exercise. The class as a whole decided the criteria for assessment (and interestingly all students insisted it should be written in a conventionally academic style, not in textspeak or colloquially, abbreviated, etc.). Students were given a question or topic on which to write 1,000 words and then to post on a thread in the discussion forum. All the students in the group had to read each other's writings and then comment and critique it in the week leading up to the 'real-time' discussions. On the day, students met in a computer lab and had two hours to advance their critique of each other and defend their own position. In the week after the discussion, students had to reflect upon the exercise and how their thinking had changed as a result of the discussions. Student feedback reflected a sense that *all* students had taken part in the discussion (something that clearly had not occurred in the face-to-face seminar) and also that the discussion felt, in the words of one participant, 'like a real academic discussion'. Students had a platform to put forward their own views, time to think critically about the views of others, read criticisms of their own ideas, defend their own opinions and reflect upon criticisms of their own work. In other words, it was something like the process of peer review.

Blogs, journals and wikis have also been used in teaching.[28] Wikis – collaborative sites that allow for the creation of a multi-user resource on a particular topic that is editable but can incorporate different types of material (textual, visual, video, audio) – have helped students to develop a sense of shared learning and also to test the viability and validity of the views of others. The process of creation, editing, discussing, writing and rewriting helps students to experience how to weigh the views of others. Blogs and journals have most often been used as a means of getting students to write more, and also to reflect more on their learning, on the material that they have been exploring. Blogs have been incorporated into many undergraduate courses with a number of different aims in mind. For some the express aim was to counter the tendency towards more 'strategic' learning. Some students were required to do a short blog on their reading or after a seminar discussion. This meant that they were required to read more widely across the course, and not just focus on a particular essay or on topics they were revising for their final exams. In other courses students were required to reflect upon how their skills had developed. This act of conscious self-reflection aimed to get students to address how they went about analysing primary sources, or handling images, the problems encountered and strategies for improvement. The act of writing the blog itself became a discipline to allow students to find their voice, refine their writing and learn how to express their ideas about history.

Technology has also facilitated new approaches to old(er) practices too. VLEs have been used to provide quizzes and tests for students as a tool of self-learning and checking.[29] Students can review their answers, go back and complete the quizzes a number of times and do it at their own pace. This was used, for example, by tutors who wanted to teach students key skills around footnoting, understanding essay questions and constructing bibliographies. Simulations, role-play and gaming have also proven to be popular within courses. Technology can be used creatively and effectively here to enhance the sense of participation in the events, and develop a learning track based on experience or 'learning by doing'.[30] Finally, other courses have made use of voting technology, texting, and the social media tool Twitter as a way of incorporating student active participation in the more traditional teaching settings of a lecture.[31] Voting and texting has been used to gain instant responses or check student understanding of particular topics. Twitter has been used, a little like the discussion forums, to continue conversations and discussions outside of the classroom and so deepen student engagement with both the materials and each other. A recent use of Twitter – subscribing to a real-time feed which replicates the events of the Second World War – has proven to be extremely popular in conveying the sense of unfolding events, as experienced by ordinary people.[32] The UK National Archives have also pioneered a similar approach, using information from the War Cabinet archives.[33] One of the great advantages of this use of Twitter over a textual 'timeline' is precisely the kinetic dimension of movement through time which Twitter allows and which is absent from the flat, static timeline. This is, of course, by no means an exhaustive or representative list of all the activities around Web 2.0 and the study of the past in universities and colleges, but it does give us something of a snapshot.

The spread and penetration of the digital age varies across countries, states and cultures. Having experienced the HE systems in both North America and the UK, there are some interesting differences of approach in terms of the use of Web 2.0 and VLEs, although much, as ever, is dependent upon the tutor, rather than the geography. The use of Web 2.0 and the VLEs is well integrated into courses on both sides of the Atlantic, albeit the focus is a little different. Although a generalization, there is a far greater use of the VLE for quizzes and tests in North America than there is in the UK. This is probably a reflection of the differing philosophies of learning which underpin the curricula. In the UK there is a much greater emphasis upon specialization, depth, understanding and analysis within the history curriculum. In North America there is greater emphasis, especially within the liberal arts curriculum, upon breadth, knowledge and context. This explains the different emphases in terms of the use of technology. In addition, the institutional architecture supporting innovation and experimentation is somewhat different. The role of the HEA and the Subject Centre (History, Classics and Archaeology) in funding pilot projects, disseminating best practice and running workshops and conferences to support this has been formative. The American Historical Association (AHA) has run a similar scheme in the USA, including the project *Teaching and Learning in the Digital Age: Reconceptualizing the Introductory Survey Course.*[34] Overall, though, the approach has been less coordinated in North America and has been driven by the excellent work done by scholars in particular universities and colleges. However, North American publishers have been much more active and creative in combining 'textuality' and 'virtuality' in their course texts: maps, documents and quizzes are all integrated into a single package to help students learn, test themselves, review and explore the multiple dimensions of historical study.

One of the features of recent undergraduate study has been the self-conscious attempt to develop the skills and practices of being an historian and integrate them into the curriculum. This is in part a process of training: developing and refining the proper techniques and ways of thinking when dealing with the past. This process has been likened to joining a secret society or a closed community: in order to gain entrance and to thrive inside a scholarly community, you need to know the language, the words, the essential practices of the discipline. Becoming aware of the conventions that govern the operation of any scholarly community is crucial if you are to master its techniques and produce work which will be accepted and read by the community. A critical part of the way that scholarly communities work (or should work) is the sense of a collective search for knowledge, insight, even, dare I say it, truth.

One of the great advances produced by Web 2.0 is fostering precisely this sense of a communal search, of working with others, learning from others, having your work scrutinized by others. The use of online discussion boards, forums, wikis, blogs, texting, tweeting has enabled students both to experience scrutiny of their own opinions, but also compelled them to scrutinize the views of others. By showing the importance of referencing and citing one's work, the academic conventions are taught and explained, not just dictated. It is precisely the connectedness of social media, the greater opportunities afforded by forums and discussion threads both to continue and deepen conversations begun in class that helps to create both a broader and a deeper social context for learning. This was most notable from student reflections on these activities. The time and space created for the development of an opinion, to defending it, and to developing a critique of others' opinions was able to create this sense of 'feeling like an academic debate'.[35] It is also the case that the medium – computer-based discussions – also helps to level the playing field in comparison with face-to-face discussions. Students have remarked how the use of the VLE has given them more confidence to respond and debate, and more time to give a considered response than might have happened in class, where often the more confident will speak up, leaving others a little on the periphery. In sum, the development of a more social context for learning fosters in students an appreciation of the benefits and importance of the opinions of peers in the process of studying the past.

The impact of the digital age can also be seen not just in the development of the social context in which the learner works, but also in developing the personal skills and habits of mind associated with becoming an 'historian'. The social context has a role to play here: peer interactions and discussions help to develop some of the core skills that are essential to the discipline: analysis, critique, reflection, the use of evidence, the development of an argument, and the importance of testing your ideas with others. But there are two further developments which stand out in this regard. First, the availability of huge amounts of primary source material may, given the right circumstances, produce the opportunities for students to explore and develop their own research projects more readily than might have happened previously. This is clearly an area where the guidance of more experienced practitioners is essential, but for those students who are more independently minded, the web of connectedness and the ever-growing volume of materials can create pathways for more autonomous learning, as the history student begins to explore the past for themselves, rather than being guided along the way by someone who has already travelled there. Second, the opportunity – usually exploited through weblogs and journaling – for a very self-conscious reflection on the practices and techniques of historical study has become a springboard for students to think about the ways in which their skills have developed, and the areas in which they still need to develop. This fostering of reflective learning is nothing new. But the availability of the technology has made this much easier to do, and more central to student learning about how to study the past, rather than studying the past in itself.

Producing knowledge

Finally, the digital age (and in particular Web 2.0) has made it much easier and quicker to write, publish, disseminate and discuss. This democratization of knowledge production – broadening the basis of production outside of the academy – has brought with it challenges to the 'traditionalists'. But the digital age has also broadened the type of material being created. There are some interesting examples of the marriage of the old and the new, as when the Academy banded together to create the *Oxford Dictionary of National Biography* (DNB). The *Oxford DNB* describes itself as:

> A collection of more than 57,000 specially written biographies, which describe the lives of people who shaped the history of the British Isles and beyond from the fourth century BC to the twenty-first century. It is the first point of reference for anyone interested in the people who left their mark on the history of the British Isles.[36]

The print version came out in 60 volumes in 2004. The online version is updated three times a year to add new entries and update existing ones. The *DNB* (like its US counterpart the *American National Biography*,[37] which contains more than 19,000 entries) is available to subscribers only. It does contain a wealth of information provided by scholars and experts from a range of fields, and is an indispensable tool for researchers. The easily updatable format of online publishing helps to guard against obsolescence (but can also be commercially exploited to maintain subscription levels).

However, the Academy has lost its privileged position as the sole or dominant creator of content. One of the most popular types of material which has emerged in more recent times is the online reference work, most notoriously *Wikipedia*.[38] *Wikipedia* describes itself as a 'multilingual, web-based, free-content encyclopaedia based on an openly editable model'. It is written anonymously, for free and anyone can contribute. At the time of writing the English language version had over 3 million articles. It is supposed to be written in a neutral, balanced, impartial way using cited, verified information.[39] Wikipedia is part of the WikiMedia Foundation which also includes Wiktionary, Wikiquote, Wikisource, Wikiversity, Wikibooks, Wikispecies, Wikinews, Wikimedia Commons and MediaWiki. All content is constantly updated and checked, and includes media, audio, text and image files. It is distributed using the Creative Commons licence.[40]

Between the peer-reviewed online databases and journal and the online reference works stand a variety of sources of information, opinion and discussion. Scholars have begun to discuss and debate, seek help and assistance, and review each other's works through online discussion forums such as those provided by H-Net[41] and the Institute for Historical Research.[42] These discussion forums – which are freely available via email subscription – provide access into the discussions and deliberations of communities of scholars working in discrete areas. This can be as mundane as seeking accommodation for an archival visit, advice on visas, etc., but also includes discussions over recent revelations, new documents or new publications. This creates insights into the language, ideas and working conventions of scholars which previously would not have been available to undergraduate or postgraduate students. Historians have also been able to take the opportunity for advocacy (such as the History and Public Policy group).[43] Numerous historical blogs have emerged, some as opinion pieces, some as first drafts of ideas, some with a commercial objective. Podcasts – of talks, interviews, presentations – are available to listen to and download. So much material, which might once have been only available to those attending a conference or a keynote talk, can now be accessed, and often for free.

Blogs, magazines and websites are now able to produce, host, advocate, share and connect different stories, viewpoints and opinions. The solo enthusiast, the local history group and organizations with an interest in telling their story are all now able to create and disseminate their research. The edifice of historical output now has a much broader base. Concerns, as ever, are rightly raised about the proliferation of unverified content, and the seeming willingness on the part of some to accept the authority and reliability of internet-hosted material. But this just requires the application of those critical thinking skills that are needed when appraising any source material properly. It also requires those with the knowledge, the passion, the time and the expertise to verify, check and amend where necessary. Such was the case when a US History professor used a class assignment to 'clean up' some of the entries on Wikipedia.[44] In this way students learned the importance of accuracy, evidence and debate, whilst at the same time becoming producers of public content for themselves, and so had to consider questions of accountability and verifiability. The use of the web for conveying damaging historical material that has the appearance of authenticity, such as the 'holocaust denial' material, is also an unfortunate side-effect of this democratization, but this is really a free speech question rather than something specifically relevant to history. This in turn requires us all to be actively engaged to ensure that the damaging, false and misleading material is contested. Some questions may remain about the quality of material that is being produced, but overall this should be a development to be welcomed and embraced. The increased production and creation of historical content from an ever-expanding number of producers and creators testifies to the vibrancy of the discipline and gives a voice and a platform for those areas of history that are less fashionable, less popular and which previously may have been denied any real exposure.[45] It also helps to counter the problems of unequal access through paid subscriptions.

Overall, then, the digital age has created a vast web of new opportunities. The technological innovations and dynamism of Web 2.0 have begun to change the landscape of the study of the past. Web 2.0 allows for a more interactive, participative, shared, social form of learning. It has exponentially increased the sheer volume and variety of materials available to students of the past. It has created a broader matrix of literacies within which students can operate. It has opened ways for students to refine and practise some of the essential skills necessary to try to understand the past. It provides a kinetic sense of experiencing the past. There are now far greater opportunities for students to be creators and composers of content, rather than just consumers. In this respect we can see that the idea of history students moving, over time and under guidance, from being a tourist to becoming an explorer, starts to develop some traction.

In sum, what seems clear from the above discussion is that fundamentally studying the past in the digital age still demands most of the core attributes of historical study.

- A painstaking attention to detail.
- A critical, sceptical attitude to sources and their provenance.
- The need for corroboration, verification and authentication.
- A creative and imaginative approach to the gaps, omissions and problems in the historical record.
- A willingness to accept the contingency and limitations of our viewpoints.
- An acceptance of the importance of the work and views of others in this journey.

Herein lies the crucial issue. The shift outlined here is from tourist to explorer, not tourist to pioneer. It is unrealistic to expect students – at high school, as undergraduates – to become pioneers, exploring uncharted territory, without maps, limits or borders. The 'tourist' model – structured, passive, dependent upon the wisdom and knowledge of the guide –seems at odds with the prevailing climate. Yet the idea of the explorer – someone going off the beaten tracks or well-worn paths, but with guides or basic maps or relying on local knowledge – seems an appropriate one. Many of the studies of the use of Web 2.0 within history courses stress the importance of creating a framework or structure within which students can operate, or of the importance of guidance and prompts from tutors at key moments, whilst at the same time developing a mind-set of autonomy, exploration, searching, creativity. In the end, however, successful exploration requires talented, resourceful, resourced explorers, hence the importance of students developing the core attributes for studying the past.

Conclusion

In an ideal world, the digital age would be diffused and deployed for reasons of pedagogic enhancement. Yet the world is not ideal or equal. Resource pressures and unequal access to technology reduce its potential and undermine its transformative impact. Technology used solely or primarily for 'efficiency savings' for delivery of large courses will rarely produce the beneficial outcomes we have seen above, because the 'student as explorer' needs the input and guidance of those who have gone before at certain points along the way. The opportunities and potential within the technology of the digital age must be integrated into a broader approach to learning which is about augmenting and enhancing its human essence. Not replacing it.

More broadly and more speculatively, the future of historical scholarship and the study of the past may well be substantially impacted by the digital age. In particular, the web of connectedness and the increasingly deep penetration of social media into our everyday lives may produce some interesting transformations into historical scholarship in two ways. The first is the deepening of public historical consciousness. Popular enthusiasm for historical content – novels, films, genealogy sites, cable channels – has never been higher. The causes of this surge in popularity are multiple and complex, but at its root lies the essential curiosity within all of us about the human condition. We want to know more about ourselves, and about others. We want to know why the world is as it is, where our forebears came from, why societies and people did things differently at other times and in other places. While this can be dangerous in some respects – we have to be wary of falling into the trap of romanticizing the past, or wallowing in nostalgia as a way of escaping the travails of the present – it is also likely to nurture a broader interest in the past, decrease the gap between 'popular' and 'academic' history, and perhaps provide an outlet for history to have a more prominent place in public life. This is not to say that increased historical consciousness will make societies better, or provide solutions to present-day problems necessarily. More history in the public sphere will almost inevitably bring more conflict, debate and contention. But it may help to counteract the short-sightedness of certain political groups and media organizations, and help to puncture some of the dangerous and damaging myths about the past upon which many oppressive ideologies rest.[46]

The second is the linkage between personal identity, history, globalization and this web of connectedness. One of the themes that has dominated historical research in recent times has been the nation-state. The writing and researching of history tends to organize itself around national boundaries.[47] But today's classrooms are themselves truly global affairs. Our physical and virtual webs of connectedness with people from all over the globe are sparking increasing interest in global history, in the history of migrations, and in the stories of other people. This may well create a shift in historical scholarship, as we begin to explore the interconnections and patterns of human history without the artificial divisions of nationhood as ways of driving what we study. The digital age may yet mark the onset of a truly global, human history.

Notes

1 For some historical context on the field of information and its place in human history, see T. Weller (ed.), *Information History in the Modern World* (Basingstoke: Palgrave Macmillan, 2010).

2 Some of the issues relating to this field are addressed in texts such as T. J. Veak (ed.), *Democratizing Technology: Andrew Feenberg's Critical Theory of Technology* (Albany: State University of New York Press, 2006).

3 See M. Warschauer, 'The paradoxical future of digital learning', in *Learn Inq*, 1 (March 2007), 41–49. See also C. Greenhaon, B. Roberlia and J. E. Hughes, 'Learning, teaching and scholarship in a digital age', in *Educational Researcher*, 38: 4 (2009), 246–59.

4 J. S. Brown, 'Learning in the digital age', http://net.educause.edu/ir/library/pdf/FFPIU015.pdf [accessed: 25 March 2012].

5 A great example of the range of material out there (and also tips and techniques for finding it and handling it) probably can be found in the course designed by Kevin Linch at the University of Leeds entitled 'Web research for historians'. This can be accessed at http://www2.warwick.ac.uk/fac/cross_fac/heahistory/elibrary/internal/co_linch_webresearchforhistorians_20090928/ [accessed: 25 March 2012].

6 The quote is from L. P. Hartley's 1953 novel *The Go-Between*. It became the title of David Lowenthal's book published in 1985 by Cambridge University Press.

7 See http://www.nationalarchives.gov.uk/ [accessed: 25 March 2012].

8 See http://avalon.law.yale.edu/ [accessed: 25 March 2012].

9 See http://archive.timesonline.co.uk/tol/archive/ (Subscription required).

10 See http://www.britishpathe.com/ [accessed: 25 March 2012].

11 See http://www.archive.org/web/web.php. The website outlines that its purpose is: 'The Internet Archive is a 501(c)(3) non-profit that was founded to build an Internet library. Its purposes include offering permanent access for researchers, historians, scholars, people with disabilities, and the general public to historical collections that exist in digital format' [accessed: 25 March 2012].

12 In my own research I was prevented from accessing an archive in Eastern Europe because of an alleged 'fungal deposit' problem in the archive. The archive was closed for six months, funnily enough the same time period for a national election. Once the election was over, the fungal problem was solved, and the archive was reopened.

13 See http://atlanticportal.hil.unb.ca/acva/ [accessed: 25 March 2012].

14 See http://www.massobs.org.uk/index.htm [accessed: 25 March 2012].

15 See http://www.amdigital.co.uk/collections/Empire-Online.aspx (Subscription required) [accessed: 25 March 2012].

16 See http://valley.lib.virginia.edu/ [accessed: 25 March 2012].

17 See http://www.wilsoncenter.org/program/cold-war-international-history-project [accessed: 25 March 2012].

18 See http://www.movinghere.org.uk/ [accessed: 25 March 2012].

19 See http://www.bbc.co.uk/ww2peopleswar/ [accessed: 25 March 2012].

20 See http://www.nationalarchives.gov.uk/a2a/ [accessed: 25 March 2012].

21 L. Jordanova, *History in Practice* (London: Hodder Arnold, 2006), p. 189.

22 The phrase comes from the title of a book by the same name: J. Ellul, *The Humiliation of the Word* (Grand Rapids: W. B. Eerdmans, 1985).

23 N. Postman, *Conscientious Objections* (New York: Vintage Books, 1988) p. xiii.

24 Jordanova, *History in Practice*, p. 188.

25 There have been a number of interesting case studies published which give some insights and feedback into the sorts of innovations which have been taking place. See, for example, a number of studies which have been published by the History Subject Centre in the UK by the Higher Education Academy (HEA). The elibrary has a back catalogue of interesting reports. These can be accessed at http://www.heacademy.ac.uk/disciplines/history [accessed: 25 March 2012].

26 See, for example, K. Navickas, 'Using a VLE discussion board with final year History undergraduates', http://www.heacademy.ac.uk/assets/hca/documents/case_Studies/using_a_vle_discussion_board.pdf [accessed: 25 March 2012].

27 An example from the author's own teaching. More details available on request to mark.sandle@kingsu.ca

28 See, for example, the HEA Briefing paper from July 2007, 'Using weblogs to encourage reflective learning', which can be found at http://www.heacademy.ac.uk/assets/hca/documents/Briefing_Papers/Using_weblogs_to_encourage_Reflective_Learning.pdf. See also weblogs and module journals in History, which was part of the publication, 'Building inclusive academic communities', which can be accessed at http://www2.warwick.ac.uk/fac/cross_fac/heahistory/publications/briefingreports/cetl/ [accessed: 25 March 2012].

29 See 'Teaching core skills in History via WebCT: 1. Quizzes', in the 'Building inclusive academic communities' report, http://www2.warwick.ac.uk/fac/cross_fac/heahistory/publications/briefingreports/cetl/ [accessed: 25 March 2012].

30 An excellent example which worked extremely well was the use of the Cuban Missile Crisis in a course on International Security which was developed at De Montfort University by David Sadler. The details on this can be found at http://citation.allacademic.com/meta/p_mla_apa_research_citation/1/0/1/3/7/pages101370/p101370–71.php [accessed: 25 March 2012]. The outbreak of the First World War has also lent itself to simulation-type activities, http://www.activehistory.co.uk/WW1_CAUSES/index.htm [accessed: 25 March 2012].

31 See K. Linch, 'Using texting technology in teaching History', http://www2.warwick.ac.uk/fac/cross_fac/heahistory/elibrary/internal/cs_linch_texting_2006xxxxxx/ [accessed: 25 March 2012].

32 For a review and appraisal see http://thenextweb.com/twitter/2011/09/25/how-an-ex-history-student-is-using-twitter-to-bring-world-war-2-to-life/ [accessed: 25 March 2012].

33 See http://twitter.com/ukwarcabinet [accessed: 25 March 2012].

34 See http://www.historians.org/tl/ [accessed: 25 March 2012].

35 Anonymous student feedback on online assessed discussion board project.

36 See http://www.oup.com/oxforddnb/info/quickguide/ (Subscription required).

37 See http://www.anb.org/login.html?url=%2Farticles%2Fhome.html&ip=50.65.25.234&nocookie=0 (Subscription required).

38 See http://www.wikipedia.org/ [accessed: 25 March 2012].

39 Wikipedia does attempt to create a working environment whereby its own contributors police its own content, and to highlight any potentially contentious assertions, ideas or information. For example, where there are facts or information supplied it will highlight 'citation needed'. Contentious incidents or figures often include a disclaimer which highlights that: '*This section needs additional citations for verification. Please help improve this article by adding citations to reliable sources. Unsourced material may be challenged and removed. (October 2011).*' This particular example was from

a Wikipedia entry on David Irving (http://en.wikipedia.org/wiki/David_Irving) [accessed: 25 March 2012].

40 The Creative Commons Licence is an attempt to provide open, universal access to research and information. It describes itself thus: 'The idea of universal access to research, education, and culture is made possible by the Internet, but our legal and social systems don't always allow that idea to be realized. Copyright was created long before the emergence of the Internet, and can make it hard to legally perform actions we take for granted on the network: copy, paste, edit source, and post to the Web. The default setting of copyright law requires all of these actions to have explicit permission, granted in advance, whether you're an artist, teacher, scientist, librarian, policymaker, or just a regular user. To achieve the vision of universal access, someone needed to provide a free, public, and standardized infrastructure that creates a balance between the reality of the Internet and the reality of copyright laws. That someone is Creative Commons.' From: http://creativecommons.org/about [accessed: 25 March 2012].

41 See http://www.h-net.org/ [accessed: 25 March 2012].

42 See http://www.history.ac.uk/ [accessed: 25 March 2012].

43 See http://www.historyandpolicy.org/ [accessed: 25 March 2012]. See also C. A. Bayly, V. Rao, S. Szreter and M. Woolcock, *History, Historians and Development Policy: A Necessary Dialogue* (Manchester: Manchester University Press, 2011).

44 This was begun by Marshall Poe. For details see http://en.wikipedia.org/wiki/Wikipedia_talk:WikiProject_Russia/Archive_1#Russian_History_Project [accessed: 25 March 2012].

45 Jordanova, *History in Practice*, pp. 187–92, has some interesting thoughts on some of these issues.

46 Jordanova, *History in Practice*, p. 190–91.

47 Jordanova, *History in Practice*, p. 193.

8 Beyond ctrl-c, ctrl-v

Teaching and learning history in the digital age

Charlotte Lydia Riley

This chapter will examine the challenges and opportunities involved in teaching history to a 'digital generation'. This chapter will first examine some of the general issues around digital and online technology in academic teaching. The middle section is based around a series of questionnaires and interviews conducted with undergraduate students and postgraduate teaching assistants (TAs) from the History department of University College London, UK, in the academic year 2011–12. Finally, the chapter will present an 'ABC' of digital issues specific to teaching history to undergraduates in a digital world.

Generation Y: a digital generation?

The 'digital generation', also sometimes described as the 'net generation' or 'generation Y/Z', needs to be carefully defined in order to be a working tool for analysis. John Palfrey and Urs Gasser, in their book *Born Digital*, describe the 'digital natives' who 'study, work, write and interact with each other' in ways that are fundamentally different to the 'digital immigrants' who are forced to utilize digital and online resources in their work but who did not grow up immersed in this technology.[1] Palfrey and Gasser do not define this group exactly by age, but refer generally throughout the text to mid-teens, who would have been born in the early 1990s. Freestone and Mitchell, in their work on online ethics, refer to 'Generation Y' as a digitally aware generation that was born between 1977 and 1993.[2]

It can be assumed that the vast majority of new undergraduate students grew up with digital technology. An 18-year-old student starting university in the 2011–12 academic year was born in 1992 or 1993, a couple of years after Tim Berners-Lee invented the World Wide Web; they have never lived in a world without online technology. Both Google and Wikipedia were founded before these students turned ten years old. The iPod was invented and retailed, alongside the iTunes store, before they started secondary school. Members of this digital generation find it difficult to conceive of a society in which digital and online resources are not a fundamental part of everyday life.

The digital and online experiences of university students, both undergraduate and postgraduate, are shaping their approach to learning about the past. Equally, postgraduate teaching assistants (TAs) and early career academics are increasingly themselves part of the digital generation, and their approach to preparing subjects and delivering lesson content is rooted more and more in digital and online resources.[3]

Readily available access to the internet is now the norm for young people in the United Kingdom. An ESRC-funded study into access to digital and online resources among British children and teenagers in 2003 found that 75 per cent of 9- to 19-year-olds had accessed the internet from a domestic computer; 92 per cent had used the internet at school.[4] According to British Office for National Statistics (ONS) reports in 2011, 99 per cent of 16- to 25-year-olds had accessed the internet at some point in their lives, compared to 89 per cent of 45- to 54-year-olds and 78 per cent of 55- to 64-year-olds.[5]

In addition, a report prepared for OFCOM (the independent regulator and competition authority for the UK communications industry) estimated in 2009 that 44 per cent of young people between the ages of seven and sixteen have access to the internet on their mobile phones; portable access to online resources is therefore common even before teenagers start their A level exams.[6] Smart-phones and other mobile internet devices (such as netbooks, tablets, MP3 players and e-readers) have facilitated a more casual use of internet resources, which is integrated into students' daily lives rather than confined to specific periods of computer access. Social networking sites, such as Facebook, Twitter, FourSquare and LinkedIn, rely for content on their interaction with 'real life' and they have become intrinsic to the daily routine of most students.

However, it is important to remember that access to digital and online technology is still governed to a large extent by social class, an inequality that has been characterized as creating a 'digital divide'.[7] In 2008, only 63 per cent of children in the C2DE socio-economic group in Britain had access to the internet at home; these students are thus significantly more reliant on out-of-home access in schools and libraries, and are disproportionately affected by funding cuts to these services.[8] Charities warn that the digital divide in Britain severely disadvantages young people who cannot access the internet at home educationally, as they are excluded from many useful digital educational resources, especially pertaining to revision for their GCSE and A-level exams.[9]

Even if disadvantaged students are able to progress to university study, they are likely to probably have poorly developed digital and online skills compared to students from more affluent backgrounds, and this might continue to disadvantage them in higher education. Lisa Servon has argued that the debate about the digital divide needs to be widened to encompass training on and the content of digital and online resources, beyond simply ensuring access.[10] Digital and online skills should be a key tenet of the 'access agreements' of British universities, which aim to ensure that students from disadvantaged backgrounds are not excluded from higher education.

The inequality created by the digital divide is only increased when the question of digital access is considered internationally. Palfrey and Gasser are careful in their work to avoid characterizing 'digital natives' as a generation, as this experience is not a global phenomenon; only one-sixth of the world's population has access to digital technologies.[11] It is true that digital technology can be harnessed globally to reduce inequality, by allowing access to educational resources in remote areas or by empowering community organization; however, in the developing world, access to digital and online technologies is even more stratified by social class and income than it is in the United Kingdom or the United States.[12]

Let me Google that for you

It is a truism to say that the rapid advances in digital and online technology over the past decade have changed how we obtain information. Cultural and media studies theorists have long argued that the form taken by any piece of media is fundamental to the interpretation of the information contained therein. Marshall McLuhan's declaration that 'the medium is the message' and that the 'message' of any technology or medium is 'the change of scale or pace or pattern that it introduces into human affairs' is arguably more applicable to twenty-first-century digital and online technologies than to the advances in television media in the twentieth century.[13] Stuart Hall's related observations that messages in media must be 'decoded' by the receiver, who negotiates their reception of the message via the dominant hegemonic codes of society, also indicate that the interpretation of information is dependent on the environment in which information is accessed.[14] Members of the so-called 'digital generation' are conditioned to receive information in an on-screen format; they respond to digital and online information in a more natural manner than previous generations.

Perhaps, though, talking about the 'reception' of information is in itself anachronistic. The young people who make up the intake of British universities in the twenty-first century do not passively receive information in the way of previous generations. Digital and online technologies can be extremely interactive in scope. Members of the digital generation are used to their media interaction being active, rather than passive. On television, in books or in newspapers, the reader or viewer is constrained by the format to receive only what information has been selected by the producer of the media, and has a limited right to reply.

In contrast, Palfrey and Gasser have outlined the many 'feedback loops' through which young people can interact with information that they encounter digitally. Websites for news outlets including newspapers and television broadcasters encourage interaction by enabling comments on the articles they present (a position which might feasibly be extended to online academic journals). However, a digitally literate young person might extend their feedback loop by writing a response piece on their own blog or on a discussion board, or creating a podcast or v-log (a short video) to express their views on the subject.[15]

It is important not to overestimate the ability or inclination of the digital generation to produce internet content. Many young people do demonstrate an impressive capacity for producing prolific blogposts, or creating videos to post on YouTube, but most students do not engage with the internet to this extent, not least because to maintain a popular blog or stream of video content is extremely time-consuming. Nonetheless, having the potential capability to cheaply and easily produce content is a major difference between the internet and traditional media such as newspapers, television or publishing.

Students from the digital generation do not view information or content as organized through hierarchy, or as protected by money and establishment. Freestone and Mitchell argue that Generation Y consumers are generally more permissive than older groups when it comes to software, music and film piracy online, arguing that the 'inflated' cost of buying these items legally justifies their actions; only 6 per cent of the young people surveyed agreed that downloading music files illegally was morally wrong.[16]

The digital generation expects access to information to be swift, cheap and simple; this must be remembered when producing academic resources. The speed and simplicity of basic internet searching means that students in the twenty-first century conduct research in a profoundly different manner to their equivalents ten or twenty years ago. The first thought of a member of the digital generation, when faced with a query, is not to pull out an encyclopaedia or a textbook or a dictionary. They go online – almost invariably, they Google it.[17] This is as true of teaching assistants as it is of first-year undergraduate students.

For most Generation Y members, the internet is the first portal for information, even when hard copy books are available. This is not always seen as a positive development among university lecturers. In her book *The University of Google,* Tara Brabazon recounts with despair the story of a student who did not realize that the further reading material for a course was available only in hard copy in the library, rather than online; the student expressed exasperation that she would have to physically 'go into the library and get [the books]'.[18] Brabazon is unhappy that her students are increasingly resistant to traditional, text-based research, and believes that this is directly linked to the fact that a growing section of her students are 'reading less, referencing less and writing with less clarity and boldness'.[19]

It is easy to see why online resources prove so seductive to Generation Y scholars. For young people raised with twenty-four-hour access to information, with the internet and television both providing constant updates on current affairs, brick-and-mortar libraries with opening hours and borrowing limits seem curiously restrictive. However, this does not mean that the students have entirely abandoned traditional literary research. The digital generation interact with libraries themselves through the filter of the internet, using it to check catalogues and to compare holdings across libraries using resources such as WorldCat or Copac. Academic libraries themselves now devote a large proportion of their resources to the provision of online and digital resources in recognition of their importance in higher education.

Being a member of the digital 'generation' is not purely a generational matter. It is, in fact, largely determined by self-perception. There are many people who were born outside Generation Y, before the use of computers and the internet were common workplace occurrences, who nevertheless have embraced these technological changes. Journalists, for example, have had to adapt to a world in which online participation is a fundamental part of their professional lives; their articles are published online, usually with space for reader comments, and many journalists also blog or have active Twitter accounts that they use to promote their writing.

Academia, particularly the humanities, might often feel insulated from the modern world, but in fact there are many people within the historical profession who are comfortable with social networking, online research and digital techno-logy, who use computers and smart-phones and the internet as second nature. For example, Katrina Gulliver, an early career historical research scholar and avid user of the social network site Twitter, compiled a group of 'twitterstorians' from her list of contacts, primarily to 'discuss research and history profession issues'.[20] The list has grown to encompass historical institutions (@brooklynmuseum), jour-nals (*History Workshop Journal* @historywj) and organizations (American History Association @AHAhistorians), as well as many historians at every stage in their career from undergraduate to professor; interested users can use the hashtag #twitterstorians to search for on-topic tweets, and history researchers can use the tag to address questions to colleagues at other institutions. This is a great example of how the internet can be used as a democratic force for communication in academia.

Students, teachers and digital technology

This section is based on the testimony of a selection of undergraduate students and doctoral student teaching assistants (TAs) at University College London, UK. It aims to facilitate an understanding of the level of digital engagement typical among the students and early career staff members in the History Department of an academically competitive British university.

The analysis within this chapter is based on online qualitative questionnaire surveys, supported by in-depth interviews with a smaller sample of under-graduate students and postgraduate teaching assistants. The questionnaires were a mixture of set, multiple-choice questions about digital usage, and open discussion about attitudes to digital resources and history teaching and learn-ing. University College London is a Russell Group university based in the centre of London; as such, a high proportion of the student body is drawn from AB NRS social grade backgrounds, with c. 35 per cent of students having been privately educated and only 3.2 per cent of students having received free school meals.[21] This clearly has implications for the results of this analysis; this group of students is presumably highly digital literate, having been exposed to a large number of digital and online resources both at school and at home throughout their early lives. This might mean that these students display a familiarity with and capability for digital resources that is not yet seen in other cohorts from less privileged social backgrounds, although it can be expected that, as digital and online materials continue to become cheaper and even more ubiquitous, this gap in experience will narrow.[22] There are also a high proportion of international students within the department, mainly from the United States and Europe, but their survey responses were indistinguishable from those of the British students; the quintessentially globalized nature of the online world has in many ways homogenized the digital experience of Western teenagers.

The undergraduate students were first asked whether they considered themselves to be a member of the 'digital generation'. Every student respondent agreed that they did. Responses ranged from simply stating that they frequently used online resources, to hyperbolic declarations that they 'could not live without' the internet or that their lives 'revolve around technology'. Every student surveyed had their own laptop or desktop computer in their home or halls, with access to the internet. A majority of the students also owned a smart-phone, with the most popular brand being Blackberry.[23]

Student respondents especially highlighted their heavy usage of social media sites such as Facebook. They frequently stated a strong psychological dependency on digital and online technology, with many repeating the idea that they felt 'lost' without access to the internet or their phones, and this was often linked to the desire to connect to their friends via social networking sites. Students also focused on their aptitude for using digital and online tools effectively, making statements focusing on their ability to 'keep up with new technology' and comparing this ability to their parents, who were described by one student as being 'boggled by the latest technology'. However, students drew distinctions between different types of online material; whilst every student surveyed had a Facebook account, blogs were variously described as 'pretentious' and 'attention-seeking' and none of the students surveyed admitted to writing one themselves.

Most of the postgraduate teaching assistants surveyed also considered themselves part of a digital generation. These respondents were born in the early to mid-1980s and generally felt comfortable using online and digital resources, which had been commonly available to most of them since secondary school. Some respondents considered themselves proficient members of the digital generation who expected to be able to 'access information and resources at any time, from whatever location'.

A minority of TAs did not consider themselves to be part of the digital generation, saying that the technology had only been available in their late teens and so they had not 'grown up' with digital and online resources. Some of these respondents commented that they had so far rejected new technology such as e-books in favour of more traditional resources, often saying that they did not 'trust' online resources or that they did not enjoy using them as much as their analogue counterparts. Many of the TAs overtly compared themselves to undergraduate students, concluding in most cases that younger students were likely to 'pick up new technology a lot more quickly' and that this made them 'feel old' in comparison; digital and online literacy is therefore still associated with youth. However, all of the TAs surveyed were comfortable with their ability to use the internet to support their research effectively.

Every TA surveyed had a laptop or desktop computer and access to the internet in their homes. However, they were less likely to own a smart-phone than the undergraduate students, and were, anecdotally, also less likely to own this type of technology than their peers working outside academia, supporting the idea that academics are fundamentally more resistant to new technology than other members of society. One TA described smart-phones as 'magic internet-phones';

among several of the postgraduates, there was some pride expressed maintaining a neo-Luddite approach to new digital and online technology. However, all of the surveyed TAs used Facebook, with different levels of immersion in the system ranging from checking the site at least daily, to having an account but rarely using it. Most highlighted the importance of privacy on social networking sites and the necessity of hiding their activity from undergraduate students, with some using these websites only under disguised names or with hidden profiles.

Undergraduate students were next asked about their usage of digital and online technology throughout their undergraduate studies. Students listed a range of different reasons that they used internet resources, including supporting essay writing and seminar preparation; reading about or discussing subjects that they did not understand; accessing articles and books; checking factual information and references; and for revision. Students emphasized that they rely heavily on their computers to complete coursework, which must be word processed and submitted online as well as in hard copy.

Students also highlighted the university email service, which is the primary method of communication between History Department staff and students. In addition, UCL History Department, like most other British universities, utilizes a virtual learning environment (VLE), in this case Moodle; the students emphasized the importance of this service during term time for accessing reading lists, checking class discussion topics, and sometimes for obtaining scanned or PDF copies of journal articles or book chapters. Online library catalogues, including aggregators such as Copac, were also often cited as 'indispensable'. Reference tools were also frequently mentioned by undergraduates; the *Oxford English Dictionary* and the *Oxford Dictionary of Biography* are now fully searchable online.

Students also identified other online and digital resources that they used frequently in their undergraduate study. E-journals were popular, and were generally accessed using aggregator sites such as JSTOR or Ingenta Connect. Students pointed to the search function on these sites as particularly useful, both for identifying articles and for locating specific terms within the articles themselves. It seems it is difficult for members of the digital generation to conceive of a system where journals had to be accessed in hard copy within a library, and where articles could be located only after lengthy perusal of an index. This is demonstrated by the fact that several students identified journals themselves as digital or online resources, apparently forgetting, or unaware, that the vast majority exist firstly in paper form. Many of the TAs, who were all undertaking doctoral research, expressed relief that online journals are now so prevalent in most fields of history; although they were all aware of the existence of paper journals, several expressed resentment at having occasionally to access articles in hard copy because the journal had not been digitized.

Students also mentioned online resources that were specific to their area of study, although these were not as commonly cited as other resources and were much more popular with the postgraduate teaching assistants, who were understandably more familiar with their subject matter. However, third-year dissertation students in particular had experience of using primary source databases such as the

Gale Digital Collections *Eighteenth Century Collections Online* (ECCO), the *Old Bailey Proceedings 1674–1913*, and the University of Wisconsin Digital Collections *Foreign Relations of the United States* (FRUS) archive.

Undergraduates also mentioned some online resources that are not designed for academic research. Google Books and Amazon's 'search inside' function were highlighted by several students as an easy way to check references or read short sections of chapters, often to assess whether the content was relevant to an essay and if the book was therefore worth reading in full in hard copy; in this sense the short 'previews' serve the same purpose as article abstracts. One wonders how many students might have been unwilling to admit the extent to which they use these resources as a replacement for detailed historical research, rather than a supplement.

The responses of the undergraduates can be compared with that of the postgraduate teaching assistants. Even the TAs who did not consider themselves to be part of a digital generation conceded that they had used email and online library catalogues and had word-processed their coursework essays when they were undergraduate students, although many had not been expected to submit work online. They had also used online reference tools such as the *OED*, although resources like Google Books had not been available to many of them.

Some TAs remembered their lecturers making information such as primary source extracts available online (such as through personal websites), although VLEs had not been used at all. JSTOR had also been popular, although several TAs commented that the site now offers better provision of journals and that some features (such as being able to search within PDF articles) had been improved since they were undergraduates; many students also commented that they had often had to use hard-copy journals to read articles. There was a feeling overall that online resources had become a lot more ubiquitous in the years since the TAs were undergraduates, and that the Department would have to continue to modernize its approach to teaching as online and digital resources developed.

In their doctoral research, TAs utilized digital resources in a number of ways: for access to primary sources through resources such as *FRUS*, *Hansard*, the British Library *Digitized Manuscripts* collection or the *Thesaurus Linguae Graecae*; for databases such as the UCL *English Monastic Archives* religious houses, properties and archives databases, the *Montevideo-Oxford Latin American Economic History Database*, or the University of Essex *Great Britain Historical Database Online*; to utilize bibliographies such as the *RHS Bibliography of British and Irish History*, the *International Medieval Bibliography* or the *Dizionario Bibliografico degli Italiani*; and to access scholarly literature through WorldCat, Copac, Google Books and Google Scholar. The doctoral students generally cited more websites related to specific historical content than undergraduate students, which probably indicates more efficient research skills utilizing specialist websites rather than random Google searches, combined with a greater need to work with primary sources and a wide range of literature not easily accessed through university libraries.

TAs also used digital and online technology when preparing to teach undergraduate lessons. They utilized VLEs to disseminate reading, and to answer student queries in message board forums. They used email to keep in touch with their students and to highlight pieces of interesting content around the web, such as contemporary news stories with relevance to seminar topics.

Some TAs used very little digital or online content in their lessons, whereas others relied quite heavily on internet resources to plan and teach seminars. Handouts and presentations were prepared using pictures and photographs found online, using resources such as the University of Kent *British Cartoon Archive* (www.cartoons.ac.uk), the National Gallery and National Portrait Gallery online galleries, and the *Perseus Digital Library Project* art and archaeology artefact browser. Many TAs also obtained online primary source 'gobbets' for use as teaching tools, from sites such as the Fordham University *Internet Medieval and Ancient History Sourcebooks*, the University of Michigan/Cornell University *Making of America* resource, and online newspaper repositories such as the *Times Digital Archive 1785–1985*. Some TAs also used YouTube videos in their teaching, either to show clips from secondary analysis of historical events, such as an extract from a documentary, or to show material for historical analysis, such as newsreel footage or clips from films or plays.

Several TAs mentioned that they had used Facebook and Twitter to source interesting teaching material from members of staff in other departments or at other universities; some respondents had been shown interesting videos or cartoons, or had participated in the email exchange of handouts or presentation slides. Many TAs sourced teaching materials in their field from colleagues whom they had met at specialist conferences and with whom they had kept in touch through social networking websites.

All of the TAs and undergraduate students surveyed mentioned Wikipedia somewhere in their responses. Undergraduates often cited the website as a resource that they had used during their A-levels for essay or exam preparation, but which they felt was seen as inappropriate for undergraduate study. However, most students admitted to using the website at some point in their degree, often as a way to find out information about a new subject or to briefly check facts such as names of protagonists or dates of events. No students admitted to using Wikipedia as a main source for essays, and indeed many explicitly cited this behaviour as unacceptable. However, anecdotal evidence from the TAs surveyed suggested that many undergraduates were utilizing the website to some extent, sometimes to an inappropriate degree. This disparity is almost certainly because of the prevailing academic attitude towards the reliability of the website; students described the website as having a 'stigma' among academics, with one student saying that Wikipedia was 'always condemned' by their lecturers. Most TAs criticized the use of Wikipedia in undergraduate essays, with one respondent saying that it was 'always inappropriate' for undergraduate students to use the website during their degree.

However, all of the TAs surveyed admitted to using Wikipedia themselves when preparing for seminars, particularly when teaching subjects outside their main area of specialization. TAs often expressed sentiments indicating that their usage of the site was more 'acceptable' than that of the undergraduates; one TA said that she 'always' used Wikipedia for lesson planning but would immediately 'mark a student down' if she suspected that an essay had been researched on the site.

TAs mainly justified their use of Wikipedia by saying that they used it to establish facts as background for teaching topics with which they were unfamiliar, rather than to create a piece of written work. TAs also felt validated in their use of the website because they had more existing knowledge about topics and were more efficient at checking information gleaned from Wikipedia for factual accuracy and historical validity than their undergraduate students. However, several TAs acknowledged the hypocrisy in this attitude, with one TA stating that since postgraduate students and lecturers use the site 'all the time', it should 'get a bit more credit' for being a useful academic resource. The general attitude among TAs was that resources such as Wikipedia could only be used effectively if students were willing to interrogate the source thoroughly, a skill which should in any case be integral to undergraduate history study. Wikipedia has itself produced a useful guide for students using the website for research, which addresses issues such as bias and incomplete information. It summarizes this advice as: 'You should not use Wikipedia by itself for primary research (unless you are writing a paper about Wikipedia)'.[24]

Students and TAs were also surveyed on their attitudes to digital resources compared to traditional primary and secondary sources for studying history. Undergraduate students were split on their attitude to digital sources, despite their reliance on online primary and secondary resources. Many students felt that digital and online resources were less useful to historians than traditional secondary sources because they were 'less reliable', 'riskier' or 'less factually accurate' than traditional secondary publications. Some students expanded their answers to explain that this attitude was based on questions of bias or disputed authorship in online texts; many students cited Wikipedia as an example of an 'unreliable' online secondary source.

In contrast, some students said that online sources were more useful to historians because of ease-of-access, and pointed out that digital secondary sources can be searched for keywords, allowing students to find specific references quickly. Finally, some students demonstrated a more balanced attitude to online secondary sources, pointing out that both digital and analogue publications can be subject to bias and errors, although the relative ease of producing online resources and frequent lack of editing or peer review might mean that some online resources are less accurate than published monographs on topics. However, digital versions of published secondary sources, such as journal articles or e-books, are clearly as accurate as their hard-copy equivalents.

TAs generally had a fairly nuanced understanding of the relative benefits of online and digital resources compared to printed secondary sources. All secondary resources that had undergone the vigorous process of academic publishing were considered acceptable, whether online or hard copies. TAs also highlighted the possibility that blogs or online articles might be produced by academic historians; these resources would be just as accurate as attending a lecture or seminar by the author, but might be more accessible to undergraduate students, and several TAs expressed regret that more academic historians did not post the text of their lectures online to increase the dissemination of their ideas.

Many TAs were worried about the lack of formal peer review on the internet, with one comparing secondary historical websites to 'self-published books'. However, most TAs agreed that using these resources could be effective if they were properly interrogated and cited; one person described an 'inbuilt distrust' of online secondary resources, but described this as 'irrational' given the likelihood that printed historical material might also be inaccurate. However, it was agreed by most TAs that the majority of a bibliography should come from traditional secondary sources such as books and articles (whether accessed online or in hard copy), and that a student who relied heavily on non-traditional online secondary sources would probably receive a comparatively low mark for an essay.

The main complaint of TAs when teaching undergraduates was that students became too reliant on online resources, and were often too 'lazy' to go to the library and use texts that were not available digitally.[25] This was a complaint that was particularly relevant when the course had relied heavily on a VLE. One undergraduate student felt that lecturers appreciate, on the whole, that 'students are more likely to do the reading [for a seminar] if they can do so from the comfort of their own beds on a Sunday morning'. Encouraging students to complete the required reading was a central concern of the TAs, who tended to be fairly inexperienced and thus lacked confidence in their own authority over students. However, this method of teaching made it far less likely that the undergraduates would do any extra reading or locate relevant books themselves that were not on the reading list.

Some TAs expressed concern that the use of VLEs was eroding undergraduate research abilities, which are a key transferable skill gained from studying history. Students often seemed unable or unwilling to locate more obscure texts which were not available online and could only be accessed, for example, in the British Library. They were also less likely to make accidental discoveries of useful material on library shelves, although this was offset by the ease of searching by subject in databases such as Jstor and thus finding a huge number of scholarly articles on any topic.

Students and TAs were also asked about the reliability of digital and online primary sources compared to traditional sources. Online source collections were regarded as not just acceptable but absolutely essential for studying and teaching many areas of history; the role of archives in digitizing holdings has been vital in increasing access to primary documents. Both undergraduate students and TAs were clear that it would be difficult to do primary research on many subjects without online provision of sources, particularly when sources are very fragile, precious or relating to areas outside the holdings of the National Archives or the British Library (especially in the fields of international and ancient history). There were some concerns about the practical issues arising from the usage of online primary sources, with one student, for example, talking about finding scanned newspaper cartoons, which could not be used for an essay because they had been posted on a blog without proper citation.

Students and TAs were also questioned about using new primary sources produced on the internet, such as blog entries written by participants in historic events, or leaked documents accessed through Wikileaks. For many of the respondents this was not a relevant concern; however, some students and TAs working on very modern or contemporary history had engaged with this issue.

It was felt by both students and TAs that online primary sources could be useful as long as students were aware of the problems of bias and account- ability relevant to all primary source analysis; one student summarized this by saying, 'as [a webpage] is a source, it should be used the same as any other source'. However, online primary sources might have specific issues arising from the fact that internet pages can be edited after publication, and are there- fore less permanent – and less accountable – than printed ephemera. However, there were many forms of primary document produced directly online that were considered to be as accurate and reliable as their print counterparts. For example, British government departments produce a wealth of online informa- tion that can be considered an accurate reflection of their strategic position, such as the Foreign and Commonwealth Office's series of web pages on 'Global Issues' including the war in Afghanistan, the Commonwealth and NATO, which might be of interest to students and TAs working on twentieth- and twenty-first-century foreign policy.[26]

Finally, students and TAs were asked about their experience of academic his- torians' attitude to online and digital resources, and whether they felt the History department effectively utilized online resources. Students felt that they were strongly encouraged or required to use certain online resources, such as VLEs, email and JSTOR, but were either left without guidance or were actively dis- couraged from using other online resources. Undergraduates were often unsure how to reference online resources, so had to cross-check information found on the internet with hard-copy texts for their bibliography. Many students avoided using online resources because they felt that the presence of online citations would diminish their work, with several students concerned that lecturers 'do not like' website references. However, students highlighted some key instances of digital technology being used to effectively support learning, such as the use of philosophy podcasts on a political thought course, and the use of the British Museum and Petrie Museum online artefact catalogues in ancient history and archaeology courses.

All TAs were aware that undergraduate students expected to be able to do the majority of their work online. Most of the respondents felt that there should be clearer guidance provided to students about the acceptability of online and digital resources, and that where these were available they should be more strongly promoted to students. Several TAs highlighted that digital and online resources are not necessarily more accessible than analogue texts; many primary source e-databases are only available through expensive subscriptions, which effectively means that they are impenetrable to undergraduate students unless the university is willing to subscribe as an institution. It also became clear that many of the 'acceptable' digital and online resources were those that were created by universities and made available to students in other institutions. It was felt that it would be beneficial for more universities to take part in projects like this, which could then become shared resources for teaching and learning History around the world. One undergraduate student supported this idea with the suggestion that an online database of 'reliable academic sources' should be created to advise students of best practice.

The TAs interviewed were divided on whether they had been encouraged to use digital resources in their teaching; around half felt that this had been strongly encouraged, whereas the rest felt that either they had been discouraged from this or that there were not enough digital resources available to support their subject. It was acknowledged by many that most undergraduate students would pursue jobs outside academia, and that as online research skills were vital to many careers, this should be something that is demonstrably strengthened through pursuing a History degree.

These undergraduate students and PhD student teaching assistants form only a small proportion of the students and TAs currently involved in British academic history. However, their attitudes and experiences can be seen as a microcosm of the digital generation. The conceptual issues arising from this analysis, and the opportunities which are presented by digital and online technology, will be discussed in the next section.

The 'ABC' of digital issues

Accessibility

Digital and online resources have already created a more accessible culture within academia. Digitization projects in archives have enabled scholars to study primary documents stored thousands of miles away at a low cost and with great ease. This does much to enable undergraduates to work with online sources, as most will not have the resources to make trips around the world to research coursework essays. It also helps to protect the condition of the documents, and enables large numbers of students to access primary sources at the same time, which is ideal when teaching a seminar or lecture around a specific document.

Digital and online resources can also help to make academic study more accessible to students who have obstacles preventing them from partaking in a typical university lifestyle. As mentioned above, podcasts can be useful teaching resources, particularly for students who have impaired sight or who find it difficult to read large amounts of material because of conditions like dyslexia or ADHD (Attention Deficit Hyperactivity Disorder). Students who find it difficult to attend classes and lectures on campus because of illness, disability or difficult personal circumstances can be kept up-to-date with lectures and seminars through online resources, and can interact with their lecturers and fellow students through web-conferencing resources such as Skype. This can also be a useful method for academics who are on sabbatical leave or research trips to keep in touch with their research students. Lecturers should be available to their students via email, although they can stipulate a 'virtual office hour' in which they will respond to all non-urgent queries, to avoid being swamped with constant requests.

Digital and online resources could still be used more effectively to make academia more accessible for all. Online journals are still subject to heavy subscription charges, which are more difficult to justify than the same fee for the production and postage of paper copies. Historians working in universities could also utilize digital and online resources to make their own work more accessible outside the bubble of academia. With 'impact' at the forefront of the Research Excellence Framework (REF) undertaken by the British government to assess the quality of research conducted in higher education institutions in Great Britain, writing for an online audience is an ideal way for historians to communicate with the wider public. The *History Blogging Project* was funded by the Arts and Humanities Research Council (AHRC) and aimed to develop training resources for postgraduate historical researchers, to enable them 'to create, maintain, and publicize a blog on their research'; the project is an effective blueprint for sustained and coherent online engagement by academic historians.[27]

Assessment

Exams have long been criticized by some people for being an unrealistic way to assess student ability; most teachers would agree that a written exam is to a large extent an assessment of how well a student performs in an exam, rather than how well they know the subject matter of the course. This is even more applicable for the digital generation. As one student said when interviewed for this chapter:

> For better or worse, students of my generation are so used to having information at their fingertips and, more pertinently, to being able to review and rewrite their analysis, that a three hour handwritten test is never again, in my opinion, going to be a conduit through which their ability can be accurately tested.

It is difficult to conceive of another situation where a person would need to sit and write for three hours, on a subject that they have been expected to memorize, without being able to check their facts or easily rewrite their ideas. University education is supposed to prepare students for their professional lives, and exams have become anachronistic in a digital age, where a skilled researcher is expected to utilize the internet to easily and quickly access factual information. In any case, history degrees are supposed to educate students in the understanding and application of theory and conceptual arguments, rather than create a class full of automatons blindly reciting names and dates. The University of Southern Denmark has already moved to eliminate traditional exams, instead allowing students to complete online tests with access to the internet throughout their assessment;

the standard rules against plagiarism have been kept in place, and students are given enough time to draft and rewrite their work to abide by strict word limits, so that they cannot simply regurgitate pages of notes but must instead think carefully about the question posed.[28] This system is arguably much more suited to assessing the new digital generation of students than traditional written exams.

Anonymity

One of the major concerns cited by students and TAs about web-based resources was the vast number of sources that are produced by anonymous contributors. This was a particular concern when thinking about secondary sources, such as blogposts and Wikipedia entries; traditional analogue primary sources are more frequently anonymous than traditional secondary texts, and students are more vigilant about partiality when reading primary documents. Clearly, using anonymous documents to glean factual evidence is a dangerous pursuit. However, sometimes anonymity can be a positive force, allowing authors to write more freely than if their real identity was known; this was seen in Iran's Green Revolution in 2009, when Iranian revolutionaries were able to use blogposts and Twitter to reveal what was happening in the riots and unrest.[29] These sources would be an interesting teaching tool for historians of the Middle East or of popular protest. Generally it can be seen that it is better not to use anonymous sources for factual information, which could be accessed elsewhere. However, as undergraduate students are expected to question the veracity of the sources that they use, the concept of anonymity on the internet can be used when teaching about the provenance and reliability of historical material. A teaching handbook on Wikipedia suggests that the website should be used with a 'degree of caution'; this is advice which should be passed on to students working with any source.[30]

Bias

This issue is sometimes linked to that of anonymity in online resources, but can also be a problem with documents that have been attributed to a named author. Undergraduate students should understand the concept of bias in historical sources and should be educated about the dangers of accepting the ideas contained in any source, primary or secondary, online or analogue, without questioning the perspective from which it is written. Online secondary sources might be especially prone to bias because they are often produced by non-academic authors who are working without payment and who are instead motivated by an ideological or emotional commitment to portraying their version of events.

Bias can therefore be particularly problematic for subjects of current political controversy. Wikipedia strives for a 'neutral point of view' to be reflected in its subject pages, but often finds this difficult to maintain on a website that can be edited by anybody with an internet connection. The website lists among its most controversial and therefore most edited topics many historical subjects, including the Crusades, the Berlin Wall, Bloody Sunday, the Jim Crow Laws, the

Confederacy, the Holocaust, Israel, the Irish Potato Famine, the Spanish Civil War and Tiananmen Square; this controversy also affects concepts of interest to historians, including ethnicity, women's rights, slavery, radicalism and, perhaps rather unexpectedly, the Middle Ages.[31] Wikipedia makes this information freely available, and so the controversy around these subjects can be used to underline how they remain relevant to a contemporary audience. By highlighting the fact that many subjects studied in History classes remain contentious, the question of bias and controversy in online sources can be used as a valid tool for teaching. Indeed, the concept of a 'neutral point of view' could itself be an interesting topic for debate in a historiography seminar.[32]

Breadth

The internet is enormous. It is difficult to conceive of the amount of information that can be stored on the World Wide Web. For example, the British Library, one of the largest libraries in the world, holds around 150 million items, which requires 635km of shelving for storage.[33] In comparison, Google claimed in 2011 that there were at least one trillion unique URLs on their index of the internet; the capacity for growth is theoretically limitless.[34] On one hand, this is undoubtedly exciting for anybody who is interested in research, communication and the accumulation of information; on the other hand, it can be incredibly daunting.

The sheer size of the internet can be problematic for teaching and learning history. Any internet search for subjects of sufficient general interest will reveal far more information than can ever realistically be assessed. For example, if a student Googles 'the British Empire', there will be more than 15 million results returned. Much of this information will be useless – either because it duplicates other websites, or because it is of insufficient quality, or because it is not relevant to the specific topic being studied. Students in the digital generation should be comfortable with sifting through information they find on the internet, and they should even be fairly proficient at distinguishing useful websites from those which are irrelevant or unhelpful. However, problems may occur if academic websites are produced that do not utilize search engine optimization (SEO) efficiently, or which are poorly designed in terms of access or aesthetics; these websites may attract little attention from students who are used to dealing with polished web content, which is presented high in the search engine rankings.

The sheer size of the internet can prove an unwelcome distraction to students and lecturers alike; in practice, quickly checking a date or fact can often result in a large chunk of wasted time, as attention is diverted across millions of online results. However, the ability to make connections between different subjects, whilst frustrating or distracting, can also be a useful research tool. This is particularly true for students or early career researchers, who do not have a large background of general knowledge to support their studies in any one subject as might more experienced academics.[35]

Cheating

Cyber-plagiarism and other forms of online cheating are possibly the biggest worry for academics when teaching undergraduates from the digital generation. The *New York Times*, for example, reported that students rarely bothered citing from online sources and that only 29 per cent of undergraduate students surveyed believed that copying work from the internet constituted 'serious cheating'.[36] The idea that members of the digital generation are not respectful of intellectual property (or academic honesty), and that they are therefore likely to plagiarize their work, is endemic among some university faculties.

However, it could be argued that digital and online technology actually makes it easier to detect plagiarism by undergraduate students. Most universities now require students to submit coursework electronically, and this can then be run through anti-plagiarism software, such as Turnitin. This type of program can evaluate work against archived student essays, as well as journals, periodicals and books; the ability to search work against previously submitted coursework guards against peer-to-peer plagiarism, even when the two essays have been submitted months apart or when the course has been taught by several different instructors. In addition, the ability to scan work against published content is particularly useful for early-career lecturers, who might not have as exhaustive a knowledge of the secondary literature around the subject as their more experienced colleagues, and so might miss work plagiarized from obscure texts. It is actually easier to detect work that is copied from a webpage than any other form of plagiarism; a TA marking essays can type a suspicious phrase into a search engine and quickly check whether the student has taken it from somebody else's work.

Collaboration

For many academics, 'collaboration' between undergraduate students might sound like a thinly disguised euphemism for cheating. However, one of the most exciting opportunities afforded by digital and online technology is the ability for students and lecturers to collaborate on projects right across the world. Discussion forums, websites, web-conferences and email lists can be set up to connect students with similar interests, to allow a wider perspective into the interpretation of historical subjects. For example, a lecturer teaching Anglo-American relations in a British university might establish a connection with a politics class in the USA, thus allowing a transatlantic perspective on the 'special relationship'. In the same way, students studying Greek archaeology in London might benefit hugely from communicating with students studying the same subject in Athens, particularly when considering debates like the present-day ownership of ancient artefacts.

Digital technologies can also be utilized to further interdisciplinary study of historical subjects. In her article on e-learning, Suzanne Guerlac cites the example of Emory University's *Samothrace: Framing the Mysteries in the Sanctuary of the Great Gods* as a digital project which brings together art historians, archaeologists, statisticians, computer scientists and geospatial information to explore ideas about 'architecture, landscape and religious ritual' in the ancient world.[37] Using a digital interface can help to bridge the gap between different disciplines, downplaying different approaches and creating a common ground from which to approach a subject.

Collaboration can also be enacted effectively on a smaller scale. Students can share work more easily for group projects using cloud computing, where data is stored on a 'cloud system' online and can be accessed from a number of different locations. Digital technology can also provide an effective way for lecturers to work with students on their coursework or larger projects; digital editing allows a large number of comments to be made on a document, whilst it remains legible. Marking essays and returning them online can save time and paper.

Collaboration is also linked to accessibility. If academic historians despair at the quality of existing online resources about their subject, they can collaborate with more experienced web designers to produce their own digital content. If lecturers in British universities are concerned that students are writing poor essays because of their reliance on Wikipedia as a source, then those lecturers can join the website as contributors and update the relevant pages to an acceptable level of accuracy and detail.[38] The Wikimedia Foundation, the organization which oversees Wikipedia, began conducting research in 2011 to understand why academics do not often get involved with editing Wikipedia pages and to develop some ideas about how to improve academic participation in the project.[39] Digital and online technologies have created exciting opportunities for academic historians to collaborate across borders to make their work more accessible to all, and this should be embraced.

Conclusions

The digital generation, whether undergraduate students or postgraduate teaching assistants, brings a new perspective to teaching and learning History in British universities. This should be embraced and encouraged. Ultimately, there should be no distinction for students or teachers between online and traditional historical sources; there should always be a distinction between reliable and unreliable historical sources. Students and teachers should approach all sources, whether textbooks or primary documents or articles or blogs, with a critical eye, and this ability to analyse and evaluate the veracity of information is one of the greatest skills imparted through a History degree. Students should be encouraged to utilize digital resources but there must always be a strong focus on academic rigour. Most History undergraduates are not planning to pursue a career in academic history and are liable to underestimate the importance of professional standards of historical research, but these need to be constantly reiterated to ensure that their learning is meaningful and effective. Lecturers should acknowledge that there are limitations to digital and online resources, whilst at the same time using the knowledge of these limitations to improve the interaction between academic history and the online portrayal of the subject.

The digital era is not accompanied by harbingers of doom. Digital and online materials can revitalize History teaching to make it more relevant to the next generation of undergraduate students. Used well, they are a gateway to a more global study of history with a more significant public impact. Digital resources can protect historical documents from careless handling; they can bring obscure journal articles to the attention of undergraduate students; and they can create an international community of scholars working on the same project in many different cities, countries and time zones. Digital and online resources are the future of history; rather than eclipsing good historical practice, they can only complement it.

Notes

1 J. Palfrey and U. Gasser, *Born Digital: Understanding the First Generation of Digital Natives* (New York: Basic Books, 2008), pp. 2–4.

2 Presumably those born after 1993 are now forming Generation Z; O. Freestone and V. W. Mitchell, 'Generation Y attitudes towards e-ethics and internet-related misbehaviours', *Journal of Business Ethics,* 54: 2 (October 2004), p. 123.

3 This chapter is shaped by the personal experiences of the author, who grew up as a member of the digital generation in Britain and who attended university in London to undertake undergraduate and postgraduate study of History. Some of the experiences or attitudes of students or early career teachers contained within this chapter will be specific to the United Kingdom; however, an important aspect of the growth in digital and online resources is the ease of internationalization in studying and research, an idea that will be explored later in this chapter.

4 S. Livingstone and M. Bober, *UK Children Go Online: Listening to Young People's Experiences*, October 2003, p. 5, http://www.lse.ac.uk/collections/children-go-online/reports.htm [accessed: 25 March 2012].

5 ONS, *Statistical Bulletin: Internet Access 2010*, 27 August 2010, p. 12, http://www.ons.gov.uk/ons/rel/rdit2/internet-access–households-and-individuals/2010/index.html [accessed: 25 March 2012].

6 I. Mori, *Children's and Young People's Access to Online Content on Mobile Devices, Games Consoles and Portable Media Players*, September 2009, p. 2, http://stakeholders.ofcom.org.uk/market-data-research/media-literacy-pubs/ [accessed: 25 March 2012].

7 For a summary of the debates around this issue, see S. Dewan and F. J. Riggins, 'The digital divide: current and future research directions', *Journal of Association for Information Systems*, 6: 2 (2005), 298–337.

8 OFCOM, *Media Literacy Audit: Report on UK Children's Media Literacy*, 16 May 2008, pp. 14–16, http://stakeholders.ofcom.org.uk/market-data-research/media-literacy-pubs/ [accessed: 25 March 2012].

9 J. Cooper, *Digital Divide Grows*, 20 April 2010, http://www.e-learningfoundation.com/digital-divide-grows [accessed: 25 March 2012].

10 L. Servon, *Bridging the Digital Divide: Technology, Community and Public Policy* (Malden: Blackwell, 2002), p. 8.

11 Palfrey and Gasser, *Born Digital*, p. 14.

12 Servon, *Bridging the Digital Divide*, pp. 1, 43.

13 M. McLuhan, *Understanding Media: The Extensions of Man* (London: Routledge, 2001) (first published 1964), pp. 7–8.

14 S. Hall, 'Encoding, decoding', in Simon During (ed.), *The Cultural Studies Reader* (London: Routledge, 1993), pp. 93, 101–3.

15 Palfrey & Gasser, *Born Digital*, p. 243.

16 O. Freestone and V. W. Mitchell, 'Generation Y attitudes', pp. 123, 126.

17 The verb 'to Google' was added to the *Oxford English Dictionary* on 15 June 2006; OED, *July 2006 Update*, http://www.oed.com/public/update0606/june-2006-update#oos [accessed: 25 March 2012].

18 T. Brabazon, *The University of Google: Education in the (Post) Information Age* (Aldershot: Ashgate, 2007), pp. 15–16.

19 Brabazon, *The University of Google*, p. 15.

20 Interview conducted with the author via email, 25 January 2012.

21 The Sutton Trust, 'Responding to the new landscape for university access', December 2010, www.suttontrust.com/research/responding-to-the-new-landscape-for-university-access/access-proposals-report-final.pdf [accessed: 25 March 2012].

22 The cohort comprised students in their first, second and final years at UCL, in the 2010–11 academic year. The questionnaire was sent to all undergraduate students in the department, of which there are *circa* 300. Of those, 104 students responded to the survey, and twenty were then engaged in face-to-face or email interviews. The students were an equal mix of male and female, and were all born between 1988 and 1992. There were fifteen postgraduate TAs comprising five men and ten women in the department 2010–11, and these were all interviewed by questionnaire and face-to-face.

23 Despite its business image, the Blackberry is popular among secondary school students because of its 'BBM' messaging service, which enables free messages to other Blackberry users. It is also slightly cheaper than an iPhone, which may also account for its popularity.

24 Wikipedia, *Wikipedia: Researching with Wikipedia*, http://en.wikipedia.org/wiki/Wikipedia:Researching_with_Wikipedia [accessed: 25 March 2012].

25 This reflects the concerns raised by Tara Brabazon, above.

26 Foreign and Commonwealth Office, *Global Issues*, http://www.fco.gov.uk/en/global-issues/ [accessed: 25 March 2012].

27 The History Blogging Project, *About*, http://www.historybloggingproject.org/about/ [accessed: 25 March 2012].

28 S. Cunane, 'The Danish gambit: online access, even during exams', *Times Higher Education*, 12 May 2011, http://www.timeshighereducation.co.uk/story.asp?storyCode=416090&sectioncode=26 [accessed: 25 March 2012].

29 R. Schoenman and N. Mansoori, 'Iran's internet-savvy youth sidestep the regime', *Comment Is Free: Guardian.co.uk*, Tuesday, 16 June 2009, http://www.guardian.co.uk./commentisfree/2009/jun/16/iran-election-protests-internet-mousavi [accessed: 25 March 2012].

30 P. Ayers, C. Matthews and B. Yates, *How Wikipedia Works: And How You Can Be a Part of It* (San Francisco: No Starch Press, 2008), p. 117.

31 Wikipedia, *List of Controversial Issues*, http://en.wikipedia.org/wiki/Wikipedia:List_of_controversial_issues#History [accessed: 25 March 2012].

32 Ayers et al., *How Wikipedia Works*, p. 464.

33 British Library, *About Us: Facts and Figures*, http://www.bl.uk/aboutus/quickinfo/facts/index.html [accessed: 25 March 2012].

34 J. Alpert and N. Hajaj, 'We knew the web was big', *The Official Google Blog*, http://googleblog.blogspot.com/2008/07/we-knew-web-was-big.html [accessed: 25 March 2012].

35 These connections can be facilitated through unlikely media; a Facebook status referencing Marshall McLuhan, for example, can yield a suggestion that the user also 'like' Edward Said, a Palestinian-American literary theorist and advocate for Palestinian rights.

36 T. Gabriel, 'Plagiarism lines blur for students in digital age', *New York Times*, 1 August 2010, http://www.nytimes.com/2010/08/02/education/02cheat.html?_r=4&emc= eta1 [accessed: 25 March 2012].

37 S. Guerlac, 'Humanities 2.0: e-learning in the digital world', *Representations*, 116:1 (Fall 2011, *The Humanities and the Crisis of the Public University*), 111–12.
38 The issue of academic historians contributing to Wikipedia is examined more fully in R. Rosenzweig, 'Can history be open source? Wikipedia and the future of the past', *Journal of American History*, 93: 1 (June 2006), 117–46.
39 Z. Corbyn, 'Wikipedia wants more contributions from academics', *Guardian*, 29 March 2011, http://www.guardian.co.uk/education/2011/mar/29/wikipedia-survey-academic-contributions [accessed: 25 March 2012].

The future of history in the digital age

9 New universes or black holes?

Does digital change anything?

David Thomas and Valerie Johnson

Introduction: digital Doomsday?

In 1995, Jeff Rothenberg of the Rand Corporation published an article describing how, in 2045, his grandchildren will find a letter and a CD-ROM in the attic of his house. The letter explains that the CD-ROM contains a document which provides the key to Rothenberg's fortune. But the children have never seen a CD-ROM before and there is doubt as to whether they can find the right hardware or software to read it. Rothenberg's view of the fragility of digital documents, best expressed in his mantra that 'digital information lasts forever – or five years, whichever comes first', motivated a generation of digital preservation experts and is the current orthodoxy.[1] The Rothenberg view of the world is neatly summarized on the website of the British Library:

> Without the right computer, disk drive, operating system and software, the information on a computer disk cannot be seen or understood.
>
> The storage media for digital materials can also be short-lived. Magnetic materials such as floppy disks and magnetic tape deteriorate in a very short time compared to paper.
>
> The greatest challenge, however, is the speed at which the technology is developing and changing and the rate at which hardware and software become obsolete, with little or no backward compatibility. Even if a CD-ROM were to last for 100 years, there may no longer be a computer or software to read it.[2]

The Library of Congress takes an even more apocalyptic view:

> How does our nation ensure that the knowledge and wisdom endowed to us by generations of Americans, continuously collected and preserved since the founding of the Library of Congress (the Library) in 1800, will continue to grow?
>
> What is at stake is the loss of data representing billions of dollars of investment in new information technology, new scientific discoveries, and new information upon which our economic prosperity and national security

depend. Also at stake is the transmission of ideas, knowledge, and the American people's legacy of creativity to future generations.[3]

The clear implication is that historical information and records – the future evidence base of historians to come – is at risk of massive and irretrievable loss. As a result of this line of thinking, the US National Archives (NARA) developed its *Electronic Records Archive* (ERA) system which is intended to resolve all these issues. It is hugely sophisticated and is designed to handle both semi-current and older electronic records, and to ensure their long-term survival. It cost the US taxpayer some $567 million to build, with an estimated life-cycle cost of $1.3 billion. The current volumes of records held by the system are quite small – just over 100 terabytes – but are expected to grow by about 40 terabytes a year. There will be some big acquisitions along the way, including the US military command system in Iraq, and the 2010 US census which is about 500TB.[4]

Rothenberg's original article was published in a very different world. In 1994, there were a range of competing architectures and operating systems and a fragmented range of applications, while document formats were controlled by software manufacturers. Recently, his ideas have come under attack. In 2009, David Rosenthal discussed Rothenberg's main ideas, pointing out the importance of open standards and the development of the web, as well as the impact of an anti-trust investigation into Microsoft. He said that in the current world, significant documents survive online, while the problem of unstable storage media had been resolved because systems automatically migrate documents to new media when needed. Because formats are standard and independent of applications, format obsolescence rarely happens. He cited the example of the Unix operating system which is 30 years old and is still capable of reading every file produced in that period.[5]

The problem of scale

For a long time the National Archives in the UK took the same view as NARA – that it would be facing a large inflow of digital document created in government departments and that this would pose huge technical problems because of the fragility of digital material. While the National Archives believes that, in the long term, Rothenberg may be right and radical changes in technology might pose huge difficulties for librarians, archivists and historians, in the short term it believes that the major threats are around poor capture, the inability to achieve safe storage and, increasingly, the sheer volume of material to be preserved. The National Archives' experience is that it has not acquired a large quantity of records on fragile media. Digital records are acquired either by crawling websites or are sent by government departments on removable media such as memory sticks, or transferred digitally. Once at Kew they are stored on disk or tape and are regularly backed up and migrated to new media when necessary. Nor are these records difficult to read. The growth of the use of computers in government departments has coincided with the widespread implementation of Windows-based computers. The vast majority of modern government records are standard file types that can easily be read on modern software, though there remain some oddities. The 1986 BBC Domesday Disks, for example, required a major piece of work to make them readable.[6]

The National Archives acquires the vast bulk of its digital records from crawling websites; it archives a copy of every government website every few months. Up to the end of 2011, the volume of records other than websites it had taken in was quite small – largely restricted to the records of public inquiries.

For contemporary historians, the years from 1997 onwards mark a watershed. Up to that date, sources for government history are largely paper-based. This is partly because, until the early 2000s (with the exception of a few early adopters such as the Treasury and Foreign Office), British government departments had a policy of printing out significant documents. They were slow to realize the potential long-term value of digital archives. The same was true of the internet. Until Brewster Kahle began his one-man campaign to archive the World Wide Web in late 1996, few websites had been preserved.[7]

The next few years will see a radical increase in the volume of digital sources being created. In the UK, the National Archives is beginning to take in huge volumes of digital material, including websites, the records of the 2012 London Olympic Games, as well as large volumes of electronic copies of paper documents, notably ones recording military service.

These born-digital records will be very different in character from the current generation of paper-based ones because they will not be subject to a complex selection process. Paper records are currently selected by departments, advised by National Archives staff before they are transferred. Some material, such as Cabinet papers, are transferred more or less intact, but files from less significant ministries, or more complex ones such as the Ministry of Defence, are carefully reviewed. In the digital age, such selection is not really practicable. How could an archivist review individual files within an Electronic Document Management System or data within a database?

So in future, born-digital records will come in larger volumes than traditional paper records and they will be less coherent. As Rosenthal pointed out, this poses a huge problem of scale and of cost. Archives will have to deal with unimaginably large volumes of material. Portico, the not-for-profit organization which preserves digital books, articles and digitized historical collections, houses 19 million archival units (books, articles, etc.). The Internet Archive, which is attempting to archive the World Wide Web and to create a digital copy of every book ever published, has over 3 million texts and 150 billion web pages in its collections. The cost of caring for these mammoth libraries is determined largely by the extent to which they provide a full digital preservation service. The Internet Archive has a simple model which involves capturing and storing material which costs about 5 cents a gigabyte per year. Portico has a detailed preservation plan for each item and may take a number of preservation steps, for example, converting digital copies of books to a standard format. Consequently it costs Portico much more.[8]

The scale of the digital preservation challenge is a long-term issue for archives and libraries. Can individual institutions afford to preserve ever-growing volumes of material? Will they have to consider more cooperative preservation ventures such as Portico, and is more attention going to have to be paid to selecting material of long-term research value? Indeed, can historians make use of this growing volume of material?

One particular problem which has been identified by the Mellon Foundation is how, in the digital world, can libraries acquire and preserve the papers of political, literary and other significant figures? The problem is that the archives of a prominent author may contain paper manuscripts, digital text files, emails, online postings on blogs, Flickr, MySpace and Facebook, and a variety of analogue and digital audiovisual material. Stanford University holds the papers of Stephen Jay Gould, the scientific writer. These comprise 850 boxes of textual material, approximately 450 audiovisual items, and 1,180 computer media files. How can these be preserved and made accessible? Mellon has funded projects to help with the Gould archive and other similar collections.[9]

Where is the current coherent vision?

There are similarly complex problems when paper records are digitized. Motives for digitizing records are quite diverse. The largest sources of digitized records are those created by the for-profit family history publishing companies – Origins, Ancestry, Find My Past and others – who digitize records for use by family historians, and who make money from selling subscriptions. Other records are digitized either to present the results of scholarly endeavour or to provide resources for future research. These are the motivations behind the funding bodies, the Research Councils and JISC, as well as the specialist academic publishing companies, such as Gale, Adam Matthew, Proquest and others. Finally, some archives and libraries digitize records for preservation purposes. The UK National Archives, for example,are digitizing some First World War War diaries to ensure their long-term survival.

As Table 9.1 shows, there has been a huge level of public expenditure on digitization over the past 10 years.[10]

Table 9.1 UK expenditure on academic digitization project

Funding source	Investment (£million)
New Opportunities Fund Digitization Programme (NOF Digi) (1999–2003)	50
Joint Information Systems Committee (JISC) (2004–2011)	27.5
Arts & Humanities Research Council (AHRC) (2000–2007)	10
The National Archives, UK	5
National Library of Scotland	0.7
British Library	n/a
Total	93.2

It is worth comparing the scale of investment in scholarly digitization with that undertaken by the family history companies. Family historians use resources such as census records, wills and parish registers, which are also used by academic historians. The largest player in this space is the Utah-based *Ancestry.com*, which has a market capitalization of nearly a billion dollars. The company has about 1.7 million subscribers, who are able to access the billions of pages of digitized material that *Ancestry* makes available online; and the number of subscribers is growing. Up to the end of 2010, Ancestry had spent about $110 million acquiring digital content, either by digitizing records or through business acquisitions.[11] The Dundee-based BrightSolid operates family history websites in the UK, Ireland and Australia. Its UK site provides access to over 750 million records while its Australian business has over 55 million records relating to Australasia.[12] Both companies are able to digitize records at an industrial scale. For example, BrightSolid digitized the 1911 census for England and Wales, which occupied two kilometres of shelving and contained the details of 36 million people.[13]

The consequence of this multi-streamed approach to digitization of resources for humanities has been a lack of coherence in the resulting corpus of digital material. The family history companies have been the most coherent, painstakingly digitizing all the relevant records. The academic funding bodies have been more eclectic. In the UK, JISC has spent a fortune digitizing everything from photographs of watermills to pictures of polar expeditions, not to mention creating a 3D replica of a model of the court of Pompeii originally made for the 1854 Crystal Palace Exhibition.[14]

It is easy to find excuses and partly the funding bodies are to blame. They have preferred to support relatively small digitization projects to answer specific research questions, but have failed to engage with a large-scale vision. However, the historical community must share some of the criticism. Unlike historians, classicists have a clear image of what they need to support their research. They have a vision of an *apographeme* – an online database of all written material from the classical era. Every stone, papyrus, paper or parchment that contained Latin or Greek would be made available to scholars. The images of the documents would be linked to translations and metadata. This is only achievable because the amount of written material from the period is finite and small, but its breadth of vision should inspire scholars of later periods.[15]

In 2010 two Harvard scientists, Erez Lieberman-Aiden and Jean-Baptiste Michel, suggested that the written record of the human race should be digitized over a ten-year period. The incoming leader of the historical profession in America responded that it was a wonderful plan, but that it could not be achieved in the proposed time. This response perhaps exemplifies the lack of a powerful drive towards large-scale humanities digitization.[16]

Implications: are we witnessing a revolutionary break with the past?

Eclectic or not, there now exists a large corpus of material online for use by historians and other researchers. This raises a number of issues. What are these digital objects, and are they just records like paper records? Does search change in a digital world, and with what consequences? How about research? Or are these changes simply flutter, whilst the deeper waters remain unruffled? Underlying all these is the fundamental question of whether digital represents a genuine break with the past or a continuum.

On the face of it, this question seems foolish. It seems a truism that the digital represents a paradigm shift in records and research, a revolution that has transformed records, recordkeeping and the research that is based on them. First, there is the loss of the physical record and its implications. Then, there are radically new types of records such as audiostream and websites, which have no analogue equivalent in the paper world. Third, there are new problems of authenticity, provenance and originality, as well as issues around the concept of records as unchanging versus the continually shifting nature of new 'records' such as websites and databases. Where is the 'real' 'original' record when 15 people file the same Word document? How can one say it is authentic when numerous people have editing privileges?

Many would argue that this means the end of the record as we know it. And if the concept of the record collapses, does the idea of the archive collapse with it, knocked flat as in a cascade of dominoes, each collapsing concept having a knock-on effect? Is this the end of the archive as we know it, as all collapses into raw data?

... Or simply a calm continuum?

So far, so much an indication of a break, a revolution, or a new paradigm. Yet on further consideration, all is not so clear.

Though the digital has indeed added complexity, it has not wiped away the analogue world. The idea of overlapping technologies, where old does not replace new, but simply co-exists with it, can be seen in the writing of commentators such as David Edgerton in his highly influential book, *The Shock of the Old*.[17] Edgerton points out the lack in various cases of a clear break, stating, 'time was always jumbled up ... We worked with old and new things.' Edgerton describes how 'technologies do not only appear, they also disappear and reappear, and mix and match across the centuries'.[18] A good example is that of the telephone, which was rejuvenated initially by its adaptation as a mobile phone, then by subsequent technologies and mixtures of technologies, such as the camera phone, up to and including the i-phone.[19] The same can be said for the radio, widely predicted to be heading for obsolescence on the advent of the television, but now revitalized and with growing audiences. The book versus the e-reader is only the latest of a series of examples, all rehearsing and proving the same thesis: many technologies adapt and survive; they do not die.

Conversely, new technologies often mimic either the presentation or aspects of old technologies. Car power is still measured in horsepower; oil in barrels; cycle lamps in candlepower. The Save button on all laptops and PCs still consists of a tiny picture of a floppy disk, years after the disappearance of that technology;

and e-readers have been designed as far as possible to mimic the book, from size and shape, through to functions such as page-turning. The recent revelation that the shutter sound from a digital camera had nothing to do with taking a picture but had been added to please users stunned many people, who were convinced that the noise issued from a genuine source.[20]

Returning to our theme, the same can be seen in the domain of digital records and archives. In the same way as the floppy disk icon, new emails are indicated on the toolbar by a small envelope, a meaningless symbol in electronic terms. And yet, the email *can* simply be viewed as a letter. Although in the previous section of this chapter the authors have highlighted issues about what is a record, it could be argued that this does not matter, and that arcane definitions aside, most people can easily cope with the concept of an email as a digital 'letter'. So is there really a problem here? Is it that the medium of the record has changed, but not the concept? Though the medium of a digital agreement might have changed, the concept of it as the record as a transaction being preserved for future evidence has not.

Michael Axe, in a recent online article on *JDSupra.com*, described how in October 2010, new court rules came into effect in England and Wales which reinforced the importance courts are placing on electronic evidence. To quote Axe:

> When the Civil Procedure Rules were first introduced in 1998, the relevance of Electronically Stored Information (ESI) was not at the forefront of anyone's minds. But as the way in which businesses operate has fundamentally changed over the course of the last decade, the Courts have had to develop new rules to deal with the avalanche of new technology that has become not only available, but commonplace.

And importantly, from the point of view of this chapter, he continues:

> The Courts have confirmed that electronic 'documents' include not only the obvious examples of word-processing documents, spreadsheets and emails, but also SMS text messages, digital voicemails, instant messages, web-based applications, peer-to-peer files, electronic calendars and webpages, as well as 'deleted' files and hidden metadata.[21]

Here, we see something truly interesting: not simply the absorption of the old into the new, as exampled above, but the reverse, the absorption of the new into the old.

In other aspects too, the paper world has seen and dealt with issues that, on first sight, appear to have sprung from the digital, for example, the idea of fluid-state records mentioned earlier. Some records have always been dynamic, even in paper form. Indeed, it is often the *same* sets of records, for example, datasets, records of shareholdings, medical records. The archivist and archive has always had to deal with the record as a shifting entity. The paper file can change: papers can be added, removed, scribbled on, redacted, torn, and so on. This is nothing new.

And here it is also important to mention the 'archival turn'. Authenticity, originality and provenance, and objectivity present problems whatever the medium. In a postmodern and postcolonial academic world, it is now an archival commonplace that archives and information are not objective and impartial, but a contested ground of politics, privilege, power or powerlessness. From what is kept, to how it is described, to who controls it, and who uses it for what purpose, the claims of archives and archivists to impartiality are now openly challenged.[22]

Digitization: implications

So are we simply looking at the same thing in a new medium? Certainly, with digitized records, there is a direct translation: what was paper is now rendered electronic. One result has been the opening up of large swathes of material for worldwide access via the internet. This is all good, and professional and amateur researchers alike have flocked to consult and download these newly accessible sources.

But there is what might be termed a dark side to digitization. There are challenging issues about what is digitized. The process of digitization privileges particular types of records. In some cases, large collections of genealogical sources have been digitized; in others, highly specialized and arcane academic texts. As mentioned earlier, this has resulted in an eclectic mix of online material, skewed in the main towards one or other of these extremes.

This situation begs the question of the fate of the invisible mass of undigitized material. Will these collections become forgotten, languishing in record offices unconsulted; or conversely, will they become the hunting ground of the professional academic historian? In time, will the researcher's quest for new and original material mean that digitized primary sources will pick up a secondary status: not counting as a 'real' primary source, or viewed mainly as aimed towards family historians? Conversely, will the paper become doubly precious: the preserve of the 'real' historian?

Digitization also has other serious implications. What does it mean for non-paper records such as seals, medals, artwork and artefacts, where digitization results in the loss of the material and visual aspects of the item?[23] And the question of questions for researchers remains: what are digitized records? We have discussed how the idea of the digital has challenged the concept of the record. How much more so the digitized? Neither original paper nor born-digital, in many ways the digitized document is the orphan of records.

Many of the questions about the nature and impact of digitization can be explored through the example of The National Archives' *Home Guard* project. *Home Guard* records dating from 1940 to 1945 are the first in the series of Second World War armed forces service records set to come to The National Archives. The organization has struggled with the cost of storing and cataloguing large volumes of individual records in the past. Yet it has made the decision to preserve this series due to its unique importance to family and other historians. However, the full series requires much more storage space than The National Archives can possibly make available. The organization is therefore undertaking a pilot to digitize a proportion of the *Home Guard* series to trial new ways of making large record collections available to the public. The pilot will test whether digital records created from the original paper files can become the authentic public record and be kept available for future generations. The pilot project will therefore allow The National Achives to test a new concept: to retain volumes that would have been inconceivable in the paper world, the result of which is that the digitized material replaces the 'original' paper as the true record.

In other words, though discussion of these issues might at first glance seem merely metaphysical and arcane, opportunities opened up by new technologies mean that issues such as the nature of the record, authenticity and trust suddenly become very real with huge practical consequences for archivists, historians, and the material that might be made available now and in the future.

Search and research: glass half full?

One of the implications of this is that more material will be kept. As mentioned earlier, selection is impracticable on a micro-scale in the digital world, and projects such as that just described to take digital surrogates as the 'original' will increase by multiples the amount of records retained. And as archivists are able to keep more, pressure to do just that will increase. There have already been calls to 'keep everything'.

So where does this leave search and research? It leaves it in a new focal position. As more material is kept, effective search and discovery systems will be central, the key to finding the needle in the haystack of digital material.

For the same reasons, the outcome of search – the presentation of search results – is also increasing in importance, and the object of exciting and innovative research. New types of presentation have been developed, such as geospatial visualization, seen, for example, in the *Vision of Britain* project, a digital collection of information from a number of sources such as census reports, travel writing and maps, that aims to present history graphically and cartographically.[24] A very different sort of presentation – emulation – displays digital files in the original format rather than via migration. Emulation technologies aim to offer 'the full digital paratext – the native digital environment and context – ... enabling research not only into the content but also the technological medium itself'.[25] They can be particularly meaningful in relation to the digital records of individuals. Elsewhere, libraries and other institutions are rapidly developing ways of making access to digital collections more accessible via mobile devices,[26] which present their own unique challenges.

Not just in terms of search and presentation but more fundamentally, there is evidence that research questions, indeed the very nature of research, is changing under the influence of the digital. For example, the rapid interrogation of large-scale data is possible for the first time: the analysis of *trends* across large-scale data, rather than the deep drilling-down into the individual piece and item of the paper world. For example, electronic versions of the records of more than 197,000 trials from 1674–1913 have been put online as part of the *Old Bailey Online* project, and a recent article reports how 'among other insights into the history of crime and punishment, digital searches of Old Bailey court records offer a glimpse of the rapid rise of plea bargaining and of a growing tendency within the legal system to treat marriages as partnerships of love, not convenience'.[27] Professor Tim Hitchcock of the University of Hertfordshire, one of the project leaders, described how 'finding a revolution in legal practice at that time came as a complete surprise'.[28] Another of the project's historians showed via bigamy trials how Victorian-era women were becoming increasingly independent.[29]

As well as clear evidence of use to show innovation in interrogation and application, yielding new findings that would have been impossible in the analogue era, innovative uses of digital resources have started to emerge in teaching. For example, academics can now tailor student textbooks to course content, picking and choosing content to create their own customized course books.[30] One author has even suggested that 'it's time to go much further: to actually ban non-electronic books on campus. That would be a symbolic step toward a much better way of teaching and learning, in which all materials are fully integrated', and 'because it makes a bold statement about the importance of moving education into the future'.[31]

... or glass half-empty?

However, as before, there is an alternative narrative here. The digital has meant some losses. Where editors once spent decades producing scholarly editions of texts, building up expertise and making intelligent connections between different variants of place and personal names, now computers do this. And though new semantic technologies are making gains in this area, they cannot yet reproduce the experience, knowledge and expertise of a human.

There has also been a failure to join up resources, as has been mentioned earlier. There are notable exceptions, and some institutions and projects have been both pioneering and exemplary in their work at the forefront of these efforts, for example, the Institute of Historical Research project, *Connected Histories*.[32] However, there still exist too many projects with proprietary software and customized search tools sitting in isolation, with no funding either for sustainability or transfer.

And there is the consequence of the earlier assertion that digital information is not being lost: if it is surviving, is there simply too much information? In a debate in the English House of Lords in January 2012, Lord Black raised the issue of digital overload, commenting that 'although digital technology may assist in making government more open, it has the paradoxical effect of making a permanent archival record far more difficult to establish, because documents disappear into digital landfill'.[33]

Welcomed with open arms?

So have academics embraced the digital? Many have, but many have not. In all fairness, there do exist genuine problems to resolve, for example, around online publication. Here, issues such as peer review and the role of digital publications in academic career development need real resolution.[34] Even basic questions of citation are problematic.[35] Adam Crymble wrote recently about trying to cite the *Old Bailey Online* project and his struggle with whom to credit. The project team had decided not to include any names when citing the project to avoid leaving people out and focusing credit in the hands of only some of the team members. Though Crymble admired this noble approach, he disagreed with it, believing that academics risked producing research outputs with no named work for them to cite in support of their CV and career.[36]

There is also some evidence that research using digital resources is less valued by some scholars. For an example, taking again the *Old Bailey Online* project, one article describes how 'Cohen and his colleagues know that many humanities scholars hold digital humanists in as low esteem as Old Bailey prosecutors once held women accused of bigamy'. In Professor Tim Hitchcock's view, that is certainly true of historians. He wrote: 'In their world, data-crunching makes rude noises with no apparent historical meaning.'[37]

Attitudes to the digital have also had an influence in changing attitudes to the 'original'. There have been issues in the past around what has been called 'the fetish of the original', where researchers attach emotional iconic status to the 'real' or unique document or artefact, a status that bears little relation to its information value.[38] Interestingly, that too now seems to be changing. Many users at The National Archives now want – and expect – every item to come as a digital download, and express irritation if they are told that they have to come into the record office to look at the documents.[39] Richard Ovenden has described how users are bifurcating into two: those using archives as material culture, and those using archives as data.[40]

Learning from the failures – and successes – of the past

With this powerful impact, has the enormous investment of public and private funds into digitization been a good investment? To an extent, humanities scholars are unusual in that their main means of discourse remains the monograph and article, while their main research materials remain obstinately physical. This is a big contrast with the world of computational sciences – astronomy, computer science, mathematics, quantitative biology and statistics – whose entire means of working and of scholarly discourse is now online.[41]

One serious problem facing historians who wish to move to a more digital way of working and to exploit the possibilities of digital resources is that some of the material which was digitized at public expense has been allowed to disappear. Between 1998 and 2003, the New Opportunities Fund in the UK spent £55 million on 155 digitization projects. It has been reported that of these,

25 cannot now be found, while there have been no changes to another 83; a loss rate of 16 per cent.[42] Our own unpublished research indicates that there is about a 10 per cent attrition rate from resources funded by AHRC. Clearly such a loss of resource cannot represent good value.

More serious, however, is the sheer confusion and lack of direction about what is available digitally. It is very hard to know what resources are available online and how to find those which are relevant to one's personal research. In some cases the only thing to do seems to be to trawl through the lists of digitization projects funded by the research councils and other bodies.

In 2005, the Arts and Humanities Research Council conducted a review of its Resource Enhancement Scheme. The review was refreshingly honest and identified many serious failings. It discovered that:

> while resources supported by the scheme have been valued by individual researchers and project teams, their use amongst the wider community is less clear. It considered the scheme to be ineffective in identifying and addressing gaps in resource provision and meeting the resource needs of the arts and humanities research community. There was an insufficient evidence of research into user needs, both at the application stage and during the lifetime of awards. Although it is too soon to assess the wider impact of projects, awareness and usage of some resources was found to be low. This was coupled with weak promotion and dissemination to potential users. The review also raised concerns about the sustainability of digital resources, noting the absence of clear strategies for sustaining and updating resources beyond the period of AHRC support. In light of the evaluation, the Research Council has discontinued the scheme.[43]

While not being as self-critical as the Arts and Humanities Research Council, other funding bodies have begun to take a hard look at the way in which they have funded the creation of online digital resources. In 2008, the Mellon Foundation set out the priorities for its Scholarly Communications Programme. In the past it had supported the creation of online collections of primary resources in the fields of classics, Near Eastern studies, medieval studies, musicology, archaeology, art and architectural history, and visual studies. Although Mellon expected to fund modest additions to these collections, it announced that given the depth and coherence of most digital collections, funding priority in the Scholarly Communications Programme would shift from building the resources to activities that demonstrated and enhanced their scholarly value and that fostered the aggregation of collections and the development of shared technology platforms in order to enhance sustainability.[44]

Similarly, in the UK, JISC recognized in 2009 that there now existed a critical mass of digital information resources that could be used to support researchers, learners, teachers and administrators in their work and study. It saw the crucial need as being to help provide convenient access to resources for research and learning through the use of resource discovery and resource management tools, and the creation of better services and practices.[45]

It is worth comparing progress in the academic world with that in the family history community. The latter has a small number of very large websites, each of which allows access to a range of family history resources. The sites also provide guidance to users as well as software to facilitate research. The largest player in the market and the oldest is *Ancestry*. This site's real success is that it has managed to engage with its users on a huge scale: in some senses it is closer to a social networking site than to a pure family history one. Over the past four years, its users have created over 30 million family trees containing over three billion profiles of individuals; they have also uploaded photographs, scanned documents and written stories.[46]

It is unlikely that the scholarly community and the funding bodies could have ever created anything like *Ancestry*, and it is fair to say that *Ancestry* serves hobbyists, rather than scholars. However, *Ancestry* and its fellow family history sites have three huge strengths which academic digitization projects currently lack: superb search tools to help their users; industrial scale digitization; and a real focus on the needs of their customers.

Looking to the future – looking to the stars

There is evidence that academic sites are gradually learning these lessons. While it seems unlikely that historians will develop the bold and overarching vision for digitization which their colleagues in classics have done, there does seem to be one ray of hope which comes from the development of what can best be described as planetary systems of digitization. These digitization projects have been developed around a single theme or closely connected themes, and are beginning to develop a critical mass that will create the possibility of new approaches to scholarship being developed, and allow new connections between sources to be made. These sites offer centralized research tools which make it possible to use a single search site to find scattered research resources. By a mixture of accident and design a number of such systems are beginning to emerge.

A good example has already been mentioned: the *Connected Histories* project, a joint venture between the Universities of Hertfordshire and Sheffield, hosted by the Institute of Historical Research. The website allows searches across 15 major historical sources for early modern and nineteenth-century British history, including records of the Old Bailey, British newspapers and pamphlets, Parliamentary Papers and Convict Transportation Registers. Unusually, it provides a search of both free and subscription-based content. The project's search facility adapts to each resource to allow searching across the full range of chosen sources for names, places and dates, as well as keywords and phrases. One very useful feature is that, as well as a facility to save and export search results for further analysis, it also has a collaborative workspace which allows users to document connections between sources.[47]

Anyone interested in intellectual activity in the seventeenth and eighteenth centuries – the Republic of Letters, the establishment of the Royal Society, and the Enlightenment – is equally well served with digital resources. At the heart of these is the Oxford-based *Electronic Enlightenment* project, which has digitized 59,489 letters and documents, and is the most wide-ranging online collection of edited correspondence of the early modern period, linking people across Europe, the Americas and Asia from the early seventeenth to the mid-nineteenth century.[48] This huge resource has been the basis of the Stanford-based *Mapping the Republic of Letters* project which seeks to develop tools to enable the data in Electronic Enlightenment to be visualized, an innovative form of results presentation mentioned earlier.[49]

The Republic of Letters was essentially about correspondence, which by its nature links two places and thus makes it eminently suitable for mapping. The *Mapping* project is linked to the Oxford-based Cultures of Knowledge project, a suite of seven research projects, one of which 'is working to produce an online catalogue of 48,000 manuscript letters deposited in the Bodleian Library; others are working to produce digital calendars and archives of the papers of leading thinkers of the period. The project is international and is working with scholars in Prague, Cracow, and Budapest.'[50]

Over in the Netherlands, a group of Dutch universities is building a corpus of 20,000 letters of scholars who lived in the Dutch United Provinces during the seventeenth century. Their aim is to develop what they call a *Collaboratory*, a complex of networked IT services and applications which researchers can use to add, edit, transcribe and annotate letters, analyse the corpus and visualize the results.[51]

Equally significant in English history is the circle centred round the study of crime and poverty in eighteenth-century England. This started with the digitization of the records of the Old Bailey, and was then joined by the *London Lives* project, which makes available, in a fully digitized and searchable form, a wide range of primary sources about eighteenth-century London, with a particular focus on plebeian Londoners. This resource includes over 240,000 manuscript and printed pages from eight London archives, and is supplemented by 15 datasets created by other projects. It provides access to historical records containing over 3.35 million named instances. Facilities are provided to allow users to link together records relating to the same individual, and to compile biographies of the best documented individuals.[52] Even more recent is *Locating London's Past*, which allows researchers to search through a wide range of digital resources relating to early modern and eighteenth-century London and to plot the results on a GIS (Geographic Information System) compliant version of John Rocque's 1746 map of the city.[53]

Other galaxies seem to be in the process of formation. Anglo-Saxon history has the benefit of having a relatively small evidence base, enthusiastic scholars and generous funders, who have worked actively to produce editions – mostly printed – of charters and stone sculpture. From quite an early date in internet history, there have been attempts to publish key documents online. Sean Miller's *Anglo-Saxons.net* included some charters and texts of *The Wanderer* and *The Seafarer*, while there are a number of modern translations of the *Anglo-Saxon*

Chronicle. The Centre for Computing in the Humanities at King's College London has been involved in a number of projects concerning charters, and is now working on developing a new web-based digital resource articulated around the Anglo-Saxon charters as core material through which the data and the corresponding metadata embodied in each of the component projects is made available together in a thematic cluster.[54]

Finally, a major planetary system is being developed around the papers of the Founding Fathers of the United States. The Virginia Foundation for the Humanities has received funding to make 68,000 historical papers of John Adams, Benjamin Franklin, Thomas Jefferson, James Madison and George Washington available online to supplement the more than 120,000 historical documents which had been available in printed editions and which are now being made available online by the University of Virginia Press.[55] In addition, Mellon has funded work on a scholarly resource to create a biographical glossary combined with a group study (prosopography) of Americans born between 1713 and 1815.[56] There are a number of other portal sites, including *American History Online* which provides access to 362 collections.[57]

In the long term the development of improved search tools, industrial scale digitization and planetary systems of digital scholarly resources have the potential to transform the practice of history.

Conclusion: brave new world

So what can the historian in the digital age expect in the way of digital resources? The authors believe they face a mixed economy. To quote from a recent report by the Research Information Network which looked at researchers and new technologies, 'none of the participants in our study is yet ready to abandon print and manuscript resources in favour of digital ones. Rather, they engage with a range of resources and technologies, moving seamlessly between them. Such behaviours are likely to persist for some time.'[58] In other words, we return full circle to Edgerton and his overlapping technologies. Researchers and historians will continue to use a smorgasbord of sources, selecting what suits their needs.

Digital sources will certainly be guided by new definitions and standards. Indeed, these are already appearing. For example, scholars grappling with new definitions of what is a record have tackled the idea of fluidity in the newly defined concept of 'bounded variability', where some change is permitted in line with certain rules.[59] There has also been a shift to seeing archives less as individual objects and more as systems within a wider socio-economic and socio-technical context. The hugely influential continuum theory of recordkeeping put forward by Australian archivists in the mid-1990s is part of this movement.[60] This theory embraces fluidity, and does not feature fixed records as 'end products'. Exponents argue that 'historical recordkeeping tasks, for example, create the record anew or ... recontextualize the document'.[61] Records are 'always in a process of becoming', definable 'only in terms of their multiple and dynamic documentary and contextual relationships, configured and reconfigured by their use in and through space and time'. Australian archivists Frank Upward, Sue McKemmish and Barbara Reed argue that 'this is a better way of thinking about documents in a digital era than one that imagines that archival documents only endure in fixed forms'.[62] Other archivists too have explored how the digital world, with its new ambiguous and multiple provenances, can be seen more accurately to reflect new ideas of archives as socially constructed, changeable and fluid.[63]

On a less conceptual level, new file formats and open source software are enabling better and greater sharing. Here too, new standards are appearing. For example, the Reference Model for an Open Archival Information System (OIAS) adopted as an international standard in 2003; outputs from the *Inter PARES* research projects; the 2000 Australian metadata schema; and the 2007 American Electronic Records Management Software Applications Design Criteria Standard DOD 5015.02 – STD.[64] In January 2012, a new international standard on electronic document management was approved.[65] Funded research projects aiming to tackle digital archiving have started to report and share research results.[66]

As time passes, reassurance about persistence will grow. As in the paper world, no one can give guaranteed assurance as to survival, but it is likely that need, coupled with technology and money will provide solutions. The move towards uniformity, through the dominance of Microsoft office, means that as long as Word, Excel and PowerPoint can still be read, a huge proportion of the world's digital documents will remain readable.

It may be that these issues usher in a new era of partnership between archivists and historians, as digital challenges bring both disciplines together in a shared concern for the selection, presentation and use of these novel resources, and it is hoped, a shared sense of a new need to work together to address them.[67] With the onset of the digital world, what has come to be seen almost as a separate discipline, Digital History, has sprung up, building a wall between scholars who are highly engaged with digital resources, and those who are less so. This wall must come down. A recent report by the Research Information Network notes that in all their case studies: 'we found researchers working with new tools and technologies, in increasingly collaborative environments, and both producing and using information resources in diverse ways'.[68] Initiatives like Harvard University's *Academic Room*, an online resource 'to facilitate multidisciplinary engagements among scholars and researchers around the world', and a mission 'to democratize access to scholarly resources, which are organized in over 10,000 academic sub-disciplines' will continue the pressure to mainstream the digital.[69]

As for a coherent vision of joined-up resources, here too there are some green shoots of new growth in this area. For example, at the end of January 2012, the UK-based Collections Trust announced a new three-year initiative named *Enumerate*, the primary aim of which 'is to create a reliable baseline of statistical data about digitization, digital preservation and online access to cultural heritage in Europe'.[70] Funded by the European Commission, it will 'assess the extent to which European Member States are digitising their cultural heritage and making it available online ... [and] provide strategic intelligence about digitisation to inform future policy and funding priorities across Europe'.[71] Elsewhere, *Europeana* is working to provide 'a single access point to millions of books, paintings, films, museum objects and archival records that have been digitised throughout Europe'.[72]

As the authors have outlined, the best hope is to develop more of what we have called these planetary systems – projects grouped around a theme, be it content or geographic area. With the building of more planetary systems – to stretch the metaphor – perhaps we will eventually spawn a digital galaxy.

Notes

1 J. Rothenberg, *Ensuring the Longevity of Digital Information* (Santa Monica: Rand, 1999), p. 2, http://www.clir.org/pubs/archives/ensuring.pdf [accessed: 25 March 2012].

2 See http://www.bl.uk/aboutus/stratpolprog/ccare/introduction/digital/digpreschal/digpreschal.html [accessed: 25 March 2012].

3 *Preserving our Digital Heritage, National Digital Infrastructure and Preservation Program 2010 Report* (Washington: Library of Congress, 2010), p. 1, http://www.digitalpreservation.gov/multimedia/documents/NDIIPP2010Report_Post.pdf [accessed: 25 March 2012].

4 See *Current Status of the ERA Project*, April 2011, http://www.archives.gov/era/status.html [accessed: 25 March 2012]; J. Miller, 'NARA to suspend development of ERA starting in 2012', *Federal News Radio*, 17 December 2010, http://www.federalnewsradio.com/?nid=697&sid=2204570 [accessed: 25 March 2012].

5 D. S. H. Rosenthal, *How are we 'Ensuring the Longevity of Digital Documents'?* LOCKSS Program (Stanford University Libraries, 2009), http://lib.stanford.edu/files/rosenthal_pasig_lockss.pdf [accessed: 25 March 2012].

6 T. Gollins, 'Parsimonious preservation: preventing pointless processes!', *Online Information 2009 Proceedings*, pp. 75–78, http://www.nationalarchives.gov.uk/documents/parsimonious-preservation.pdf [accessed: 25 March 2012].

7 'About the internet archive', http://www.archive.org/about/about.php [accessed: 25 March 2012].

8 Rosenthal, *'Ensuring the Longevity of Digital Documents'*, slide 22.

9 H. Cullyer and D. J. Waters, *Priorities for the Scholarly Communications Program*, Andrew W Mellon Foundation, Annual Report 2008, http://www.mellon.org/news_publications/annual-reports-essays/presidents-essays/priorities-for-the-scholarly-communications-program#note1 http://lib.stanford.edu/special-collections-university-archives-blog/stephen-jay-gould-papers-project-update [accessed: 25 March 2012].

10 For the New Opportunities Fund, NOFDIGI, see *New Opportunities Fund (NOF) Digitisation Programme 1999–2004*, http://web.me.com/xcia0069/nof.html [accessed: 25 March 2012]. For JISC, see *JISC, Aims of the Content and Digitisation Programme*, http://www.jisc.ac.uk/whatwedo/programmes/digitisation.aspx [accessed: 25 March 2012]. For AHRC see *AHRC Projects with a Digital Component, 1996 Onwards*, http://web.me.com/xcia0069/ahrc.html [accessed: 25 March 2012]. The British Library does not use core funding to digitize materials and relies on external sources; the National Library of Wales spent less than £100,000 in this period. Cambridge University Library refused a Freedom of Information request for information and the Bodleian Library in Oxford did not respond.

11 See Ancestry.com Inc, *Form 10K Annual Report* for the period ending 31 December 2010, http://files.shareholder.com/downloads/ABEA-3SYR2V/1569836196x0x449154/7584A9D3–14A8–41E7–857D-DB32ADC817F3/ACOM_10-K.pdf [accessed: 25 March 2012].

12 See brightsolid, *Find My Past UK – Online Publishing*, http://www.brightsolid.com/online-publishing/about-us/findmypast.co.uk.html and brightsolid, *Find My Past Australia – Online Publishing*, http://www.brightsolid.com/online-publishing/about-us/findmypast.com.au.html [both accessed: 25 March 2012].

13 brightsolid, *Case Study, The National Archives*, http://www.brightsolid.com/Case_studies_TNA.pdf [accessed: 25 March 2012].

14 A list of JISC-funded digitization projects is available at JISC Content, *Find a Collection*, http://www.jisc-content.ac.uk/find-a-collection/term?tavail=224 [accessed: 25 March 2012].

15 G. Crane, A. Babeu et al., 'Classics in the million book library', *Digital Humanities Quarterly*, 3:1 (Winter 2009), paragraph 10, http://digitalhumanities.org/dhq/vol/3/1/000034/000034.html [accessed: 25 March 2012].

16 A. Grafton, *Loneliness and Freedom, Perspectives on History* (American Historical Association, March 2011), http://www.historians.org/Perspectives/issues/2011/1103/1103pre1.cfm [accessed: 25 March 2012].

17 D. Edgerton, *The Shock of the Old: Technology and Global History Since 1900* (London: Profile Books, 2006).

18 Edgerton, *The Shock of the Old*, p.xii. Quoted and discussed in V. Johnson, 'Plus ca change … ? The salutary tale of the telephone and its implications for archival thinking about the digital revolution', *Journal of the Society of Archivists*, 32:1 (April 2011), 79–92.

19 Johnson, 'Plus ca change … ?'.

20 See 'How engineers create artificial sounds to fool us', BBC News website, 8 July 2011, http://news.bbc.co.uk/1/hi/programmes/click_online/9533769.stm [accessed: 25 March 2012].

21 M. Axe, 'Brave new world – English court rules emphasise the need for early cooperation on electronic evidence', JDSupra.com, 12 March 2010, http://www.jdsupra.com/post/documentViewer.aspx?fid=ea456582–85c29–41f4-bd1c-adee0bcf7cf9 [accessed: 25 March 2012].

22 Among a burgeoning literature on postmodernism, see, for example, T. Cook, 'Fashionable nonsense or professional rebirth?: Postmodernism and the practice of archives', *Archivaria*, 51 (2001), 14–35; T. Nesmith, 'Seeing archives: postmodernism and the changing intellectual place of archives', *American Archivist*, 65 (Spring–Summer 2002), 24–41. On objectivity specifically, see V. Johnson, 'Creating history? Confronting the myth of objectivity in the archive', *Archives*, 23:117 (October 2007), 28–143.

23 Although new technologies that can either scan in 3-D, or enable digital touch, are emerging. For example, see 'Safeguarding skeletons using 3D digitisation', 29 November 2011, http://www.pasthorizonspr.com/index.php/archives/11/2011/safeguarding-skeletons-using-3d-digitisation [accessed: 25 March 2012]; S. Tennant, C. Koch, M. Palakal, J. Rogers and M. P. Baker, 'Negotiating virtual and physical museum space', http://vis.iu.edu/Publications/Tennant_VSMM.pdf [accessed: 25 March 2012].

24 See http://www.visionofbritain.org.uk/ [accessed: 25 March 2012].

25 L. Carroll, E. Farr, P. Hornsby and B. Ranker, 'A comprehensive approach to born-digital archives', *Archivaria*, 72 (Fall 2011), 61–92. This quotation p. 86.

26 C. Mitchell and D. Suchy, 'Developing mobile access to digital collections', *D-Lib*, 18:1/2 (January–February 2012), http://www.dlib.org/dlib/january12/mitchell/01mitchell.html [accessed: 25 March 2012].

27 B. Bower, 'Crime's digital past', *Science News*, 180: 3 (30 July 2011), http://www.sciencenews.org/view/feature/id/332393/description/Crime%E2%80%99s_digital_past [accessed: 25 March 2012], p. 20.

28 Bower, 'Crime's digital past'.

29 Bower, 'Crime's digital past'.

30 For example, see http://www.pearsoned.co.uk/custompublishing/ [accessed: 25 March 2012].

31 M. Prensky, 'In the twenty-first century university, let's ban (paper) books', *The Chronicle of Higher Education*, 13 November 2011, http://chronicle.com/article/In-the-21st-Century/129744/ [accessed: 25 March 2012].

32 See, for example, the Institute of Historical Research *Connected Histories* project, a federated search facility for distributed digital resources relating to early modern and nineteenth-century British history. See http://www.history.ac.uk/projects/connected-histories [accessed: 25 March 2012].

33 See 'Freedom of Information Act 2000, question for short debate', *Hansard*, Lords Daily, 17 January 2012, col. 539.
http://www.publications.parliament.uk/pa/ld201212/ldhansrd/text/120117–0002.htm# 12011759000121 [accessed: 25 March 2012].

34 Although some scholars are taking things forward themselves. For example, the University of Michigan Press recently opened one of its born-digital publications to open peer review. After this process, the book was to be published both in print and open-access digital versions. See D. Daniel, 'Open peer review of the digital book "Writing history in the digital age"', email to Jiscmail list, H-Histbibl@H-Net.msu.edu, 4 November 2011.

35 See, for example, the discussion in S. Sukovic, 'References to e-texts in academic publications', *Journal of Documentation*, 65:6 (2009), 997–1015.

36 A. Crymble, 'Citation in digital humanities: is the Old Bailey online a film, or a science paper?', 13 January 2012, http://adamcrymble.blogspot.com/2012/01/is-old-bailey-online-film-or-science.html [accessed: 25 March 2012].

37 Bower, 'Crime's digital past'.

38 For a good discussion of this, see H. Wood, 'The fetish of the document: an exploration of attitudes towards archives', in M Procter and C. P. Lewis (eds), *New Directions in Archival Research* (Liverpool: LUCAS, 2000), pp. 20–48.

39 Personal communication to authors.

40 R. Ovenden, 'The impact of digitisation and its implications for the future direction of archives and special collections', unpublished paper to Archives and Society seminar, Institute of Historical Research, London, 24 January 2012. Available as a podcast at http://historyspot.org.uk/podcasts/archives-and-society/ impact-digitisation-and-its-implications-future-direction-archives-and [accessed: 25 March 2012].

41 A. Grafton, 'Apocalypse in the stacks? The research library in the age of Google', *Daedalus* (Winter 2009), 93.

42 New Opportunities Fund (NOF) *Digitisation Programme 1999–2004*, http://web.me.com/xcia0069/nof.html [accessed: 25 March 2012].

43 Arts and Humanities Research Council, *Resource Enhancement Scheme Review*, http://www.ahrc.ac.uk/FundedResearch/Pages/ResourceEnhancementSchemeReview.aspx [accessed: 25 March 2012].

44 Cullyer and Waters, *Priorities for the Scholarly Communications*, section 2.

45 JISC, *Information Environment Programme, 2009–2011*, http://www.jisc.ac.uk/what wedo/programmes/inf11.aspx [accessed: 25 March 2012].

46 Ancestry.com, *About Ancestry.com*, http://corporate.ancestry.com/about-ancestry/ [accessed: 25 March 2012].

47 See http://www.connectedhistories.org/ [accessed: 25 March 2012].

48 'Electronic enlightenment, overview', http://www.e-enlightenment.com/info/about/ [accessed: 25 March 2012].

49 'Mapping the republic of letters', https://republicofletters.stanford.edu/ [accessed: 25 March 2012].

50 'Cultures of knowledge: an intellectual geography of the seventeenth-century republic of letters', http://www.history.ox.ac.uk/cofk/ [accessed: 25 March 2012].

51 'CKCC: circulation of knowledge and learned practices in the seventeenth century Dutch republic', http://ckcc.huygens.knaw.nl/the_project/targets.html [accessed: 25 March 2012].

52 'London lives, 1690 to 1800, crime, poverty and social policy in the metropolis', http://www.londonlives.org/ [accessed: 25 March 2012].

53 'Locating London's past', http://www.locatinglondon.org/ [accessed: 25 March 2012].

54 'Anglo-Saxon cluster', http://www.ascluster.org/index.html [accessed: 25 March 2012]; 'Durham University, corpus of Anglo-Saxon stone sculpture', http://www.dur.ac.uk/corpus/ [accessed: 25 March 2012]; Anglo-Saxons.net, http://www.anglo-saxons.net/hwaet/ [accessed: 25 March 2012].

55 *Online Access to the Founding Fathers Papers*, National Archives, press release, 29 September 2011, http://www.archives.gov/press/press-releases/2011/nr11–190.html [accessed: 25 March 2012].

56 'Documents compass, people of the Founding era', http://documentscompass.org/projects/pfe/ [accessed: 25 March 2012].

57 American History Online, http://www.americanhistoryonline.org/ [accessed: 25 March 2012].

58 Research Information Network, *Reinventing Research? Information Practices in the Humanities* (London: Research Information Network, 2011), p. 7.

59 See on issues of trust, P. Conway, 'Archival quality and long-term preservation: a research framework for validating the usefulness of digital surrogates', pp. 293–309; and L. Duranti and C. Rogers, 'Educating for trust', pp. 373–90, both in the Special Issue on 'Archives, records and identities – questions of trust', *Archival Science*, 11:3–4 (November 2011).

60 See for the continuum theory, F. Upward, 'Structuring the records continuum Part One: Post-custodial principles and properties', *Archives and Manuscripts*, 24:2 (November 1996), 265–85; S. McKemmish, 'Placing records continuum theory and practice', *Archival Science*, 1: 4 (2001), 333–59.

61 F. Upward, S. McKemmish and B. Reed, 'Archivists and changing social and information spaces: a continuum approach to recordkeeping and archiving in online cultures', *Archivaria*, 72 (Fall 2011), 197–237. This quotation p. 199.

62 Upward, McKemmish and Reed, 'Archivists and changing social and information spaces', p. 203.

63 For example, E. Monks-Leeson, 'Archives on the internet: representing contexts and provenance from repository to website', *American Archivist*, 74 (Spring/Summer 2011), 38–57, particularly the concluding discussion.

64 C. A. Lee and H. Tibbo, 'Where's the archivist in digital curation? Exploring the possibilities through a matrix of knowledge and skills', *Archivaria*, 72 (Fall 2011), 123–68, in particular, pp. 132, 137–38.

65 'Electronic document management – design and operation of an information system for the preservation of electronic documents', ISO 14641–1, Message to JISC-Mail list Records-Management-UK, Paula J Smith, 'ISO14641–1 approved', 19 January 2012.

66 See the result of the Mellon-funded AIMS project, which reported in January 2012. The project's White Paper can be found on the project website 'AIMS born-digital collections: an inter-institutional model for stewardship', http://www2.lib.virginia.edu/aims/whitepaper/ [accessed: 25 March 2012].

67 See, for example, in T. Cook, 'The archive(s) is a foreign country: historians, archivist, and the changing archival landscape', *American Archivist*, 74 (Fall/Winter 2011), 600–32, and in particular in F. X. Blouin Jr. and W. G. Rosenberg, *Processing the Past: Contesting Authority in History and the Archives* (New York: Oxford University Press, 2011). Blouin and Rosenberg's book is discussed by R. B. Townsend, 'Processing the past: a conversation with Francis Blouin and William Rosenberg', *Perspectives on History* (November 2011), available at: http://www.historians.org/

perspectives/issues/2011/1111/1111con1.cfm [accessed: 25 March 2012]. For a discussion on the 2012 AHA Conference panel on 'Archivists, historians, and the future of authority in the archives', see K. Theimer, 'Some observations on the "archival divide," or what I said at AHA [American Historical Association] about historians and archivists', 7 January 2012, http://www.archives next.com/?p=2448 [accessed: 25 March 2012].

68 Research Information Network, *Reinventing Research? Information Practices in the Humanities* (London: Research Information Network, 2011), p. 6.
69 Email, 'Next generation platform for academics', from Academic Room Editors, 22 December 2011. See also http://www.academicroom.com [accessed: 25 March 2012].
70 See the project website at: http://www.enumerate.eu [accessed: 25 March 2012].
71 G. McKenna, 'Opportunity to inform European policy for digitisation', email press release to Jiscmail list, Archives-NRA, 25 January 2012.
72 See http://www.europeana-libraries.eu/ [accessed: 25 March 2012].

10 Conclusion

A changing field

Toni Weller

This book has suggested that the digital present, as much as the past, is a significantly undiscovered country for most historians. The digital age will (and is) affecting *all* who practise and study history professionally, but historians do not necessarily need to learn new technologies or computer code; they do not need to become computer scientists. As noted in the *Introduction*, much of the existing literature about history in the digital age is directed towards self-proclaimed digital historians and can be alienating to the historian who does not necessarily value or wish to embrace digital resources. I, and the contributing authors to this book, have argued that part of the 'them and us' problem thus far has been too much emphasis on historians becoming something they are not, to the detriment of the fundamental skills and expertise that is the craft of the historian. Consequently, the traditional historian has tended to be overlooked as digital history has become the buzz-word for avant-garde historical scholarship in the digital age.

Undoubtedly, history in the digital age faces many very real and significant questions on the logistics and practicality of data migration, the cost to provide and access digital resources, issues of control, dissemination and accuracy, to name but a few. Whilst the historian should certainly be aware of such questions, and engage with them where possible, the primary focus of this book deliberately has not been on digital practicalities for the historian. Instead, it has centred itself around the premise that the digital age is creating a new set of conceptual and methodological challenges, of which the traditional historian is already a part, something which not all historians have hitherto acknowledged. As Luke Tredinnick (2) points out, 'the digital age is itself a situated moment in the making of history'. Historians, as citizens of that situated moment, also form part of the digital age and are contributing to changes in the way in which we understand and engage with the past every day, through our everyday actions. It is these issues with which the authors of this book engage. Although each of the chapters in this volume can be read independently of one another, there are some points of commonality which emerge across the whole collection that should be considered collectively.

Historiography

In 1912, James Harvey Robinson wrote that

> history is bound to alter its ideals and aims with the general progress of society
> and of the social sciences, and that it should ultimately play an infinitely more
> important role in our intellectual life than it has hitherto done.[1]

A century on, Robinson's point is as relevant as ever. Social and political interaction in the digital age is occurring in ways manifestly different to ever before and yet so commonplace as to be almost unnoticed. There are some very real and pertinent questions that need to be asked of historical study of the future – and some would argue that we should have been asking these questions a decade ago.[2] As many of the chapters here note, source material will look (does already look) very different to that which we have traditionally used in research. Of course the printed word and image will survive – the digital age certainly does not mean an end to all books – but there will be new types of source material which will require a different way of thinking. How many people, for example, are now writing diaries directly into word-processing packages on computers and how will the historian be able to access them, if they are even preserved at all? Are the important decisions of the day, and indeed, social interaction generally, being recorded by written letter anymore or instead is email and text message becoming more dominant? It is much easier for a physical artefact to survive serendipitously than it is for a digital document on a personal computer. As Mussell (4) argues, as such research tools 'continue to change, so too does the practice of history'. The 'great and the good' may donate material to digital collections but what about Joe Public, the voice of the everyman, or the person who becomes significant to the historian only after their death? How will historians of the future, looking back at the period from the 1990s onwards, understand and access such historical material? Will they even be able to do so, or will much of it have been lost through casual use of the delete key or passwords that die with their owners? One Cambridge College library told me anecdotally that in trying to put together an exhibition of first drafts from its famous literary alumni, it was presented with the problem that the majority of contemporary alumni no longer write with pen and paper but instead write directly onto a word-processing package with a keyboard. Thus, 'first drafts' were often reworked many times without any tangible offering that could be sent to include within an exhibition.[3] Whilst 'eureka' moments might still be scribbled anywhere that can be found – John Lennon's original manuscript lyrics to *A Hard Day's Night* were scribbled in ballpoint pen on the back of an old birthday card[4] – annotated hard copy drafts of novels, poems, plays are increasingly rare in comparison to just a few decades ago. I, for example, have used the audio record function on my mobile phone to capture ideas that have come as I have been walking down the street and not had a pen to hand (and certainly I am not the only one to do so), but such recordings have a short life span. Of course one could argue that it is serendipitous that as much paper ephemera has survived as it has done over the centuries, but the sheer mass of digital information means it is much harder to predict what should be kept or what might be useful, and more time consuming to sift through what does remain. The historical record of the late twentieth and twenty-first century will be very different to the one with which historians are used to working and we need to consider the conceptual and methodological implications of this now in our work and teaching.

One could argue that living in the digital age, everyday actions of emailing, taking digital photographs, sending a text message, using the internet and so forth, have become so routine as to be taken for granted. Jim Mussell (4) makes the forceful but often overlooked point that digital technologies such as these 'are not just tools, but legitimate objects of historical enquiry in themselves'. Indeed, precisely because these actions are so ubiquitous in the digital age, it perhaps seems unnecessary to apply historical method *about* what we are doing. In other words, digital research methods appear so commonplace as to not warrant the same consideration as one would give to traditional research practices. This is especially pertinent in the case of students of history who do not have the rigorous professional methodology so deeply entrenched as more experienced practitioners, a point echoed by Riley's (8) analysis. It is our job as professional scholars to ensure that we educate the historians of tomorrow about information provenance in digital culture as much as we do about more traditional methodologies.

Education

Educating the historians of tomorrow is only part of the issue though. Professional historians themselves need to be open to the conceptual challenges and issues that the digital age is raising. As both Jim Mussell (4) and Crone and Halsey (5) argue, it is the responsibility of the user of any digital resource to educate themselves about what has gone on in its creation; in other words, as a historian, one would not passively engage with printed sources so the same should apply when using any kind of digital resource. If you use a digital database you should ensure you know the criteria for inclusion, what has been excluded, and exactly what you are searching. Should, as some already do, all digital collections come with disclaimers that note criteria for inclusion and exclusion? Since behind-the-scenes manipulation, filtering and editing is less visible than in traditional print sources we need to make sure we are more conscious of it when using the results from such resources in our own research.

This is an essential part of the process of contextualizing and interpretation. The historian who uses a digitized newspapers database, for example, should have a sense of which papers have been included, why they were selected, and what geographical and chronological period they might cover. In a hard copy search this process would be a fundamental part of research but in a digitized collection this 'behind-the-scenes' detail can have a tendency to be overlooked. These issues are not ones that require the historian to become fluent in computer code; they are essential and underlying tools of historical methodology but conceptualized in a different way. The students who use digital resources to access information for an assignment must be taught to apply the same rigorous historical methodology as they would be taught for a hard copy literature review. The two are not mutually exclusive; indeed, most professional historians would never consider abandoning the printed word, which for most is sacrosanct, but it has also become normalized to expect to do some kind of online research or email correspondence as part of any research process. Indeed, as Mark Sandle (7) notes, there are certain advantages to students being 'exposed at a far earlier stage of their intellectual development to sources and documents that they would never have been able to read and analyse twenty or thirty years ago'.

Most university students now have certain expectations that they should have access to a free university email account, that lectures and resources should be available online and that scholarly journal articles should be available to download in full via the library catalogue. Mark Sandle (7) and William J. Turkel, Kevin Kee and Spencer Roberts (3) demonstrate the mixed reactions of students when being presented with new methodologies or approaches which they do not deem to be traditional history. As discussed in the *Introduction*, digital information provenance is not routinely taught as part of historiography. Students tend to be over-exposed to the impact of new technologies without engaging in the conceptual implications this has for the discipline of history in the digital age. Likewise, if academics do not engage in these debates themselves, or even value them as necessary ones to have, then such issues will continue to be absent from university teaching – although perhaps this is changing as a new generation of digital-born teaching assistants and early career academics begin to filter into the system, as Charlotte Lydia Riley (8) argues. What is particularly significant about Riley's chapter is how it demonstrates the subtle but significant impact of scholarly experience in the way in which historians consider and use digital material. Professional academics are more likely to recognize the inherent quality of a resource than an undergraduate student, despite the students being more directly immersed in digital culture in their everyday lives, or indeed, digital-born themselves. This highlights not only the importance of including digital information provenance and the application of fundamental historical skills to the digital age within history courses, but also that it is too simplistic to make the claim that the 'us-and-them' culture is a generational issue. Being digital-born does not guarantee a rigorous consideration of digital sources, just as not all established scholars are digital Luddites. In some ways one could argue that we are looking at digital youth vs. analogue experience, and there needs to be a discourse between both in order to progress the conversation amongst historians.

The student responses in Turkel et al.'s (3) chapter focused on the practicalities, the usefulness of digital technologies in their research and study, but there were few comments that engaged with how such interaction had made them consider history and the historical record in a fundamentally different way. We must be careful though; in introducing such concepts to history students we must ensure that course assignments and discussion do not veer into anachronism or superficiality. Just because a digital source is there does not mean it is the only source or even the best source. Engaging our students, and each other, in a more meaningful dialogue about the conceptual and profound impact of history in the digital age seems a more powerful and consequential approach than simple exposure to new technologies.

Methodology

While the traditional skills and methods of the historian will continue to remain as potent as ever, there has already been much evidence to show how the digital age is introducing new types of research question and process. This does not mean teaching historians how to write computer code or how to create a database, although some may become proficient in both of these areas. Rather more powerfully, I believe, it means opening our minds to thinking about the past and the historical record in totally different ways. As Crone and Halsey (5) put it, this should be the '*raison d'être* of digitization, because what we lose from digitizing the original source we gain in terms of new methods of analysis'.

All of the chapters pick up on the idea that large digital collections allow one to stand back and perceive trends in ways that traditional archival research does not make possible. Databases have the advantage that they can deal with large volumes of information and can highlight patterns across bodies of material that may not be otherwise visible. Such collections require the skill of the historian in both their creation and their use. The *Reading Experience Database* (RED) discussed in Chapter 5 is an example of how seemingly insignificant details of an individual or group in the act of reading could be collected together to show patterns in behaviour across gender, class and time. One wonders whether a collection of evidence to demonstrate reading experiences will be possible in a digital age where such anecdotal examples are likely to have been in long deleted emails, texts or blogs. Of course, digital collections and digitized documents also come laden with inherent difficulties – most significantly the removal of context and an invisible process of selection and editing. It is down to the traditional skills of historical research, interpretation, questioning and contextualizing to balance such problems, and for the historian to consciously make the effort to treat digital sources with the same respect and consideration they would any other research material.

As noted by Thomas and Johnson (9), many digital collections thus far have been simply digital reproductions of an already existing set of source material – done more for issues of access and preservation than for conceptual challenge. What should be more conceptually exciting to the historian in the digital age is how material might be digitized for other reasons, in order to be able to explore it from a different perspective, alongside other traditional sources and perhaps to shed new light on established theories or sources. This is not an uncommon idea in history; there have long been watershed moments when contemporary events cause historians to reconsider the past in a new light. The 'information turn' in history is one recent example of this where scholars have engaged with a new historiography of information.[5] This seems to be more acceptable to traditional historians than anything tagged with 'digital', and one wonders how much of that is down to an inherent disdain and distrust within the historical establishment of anything deemed to place the computer before the book.

The increasing emphasis of the visual in the contemporary record is also shifting traditional historical methodologies, although Mark Sandle (7) notes the fact that this visual shift is currently more of a corrective than an erosion of the predominance of text. In terms of methodology though this is significant since the internet is a much more visual experience than reading a piece of prose – even the way in which our eyes 'read' a computer screen uses different parts of the brain to when we read a printed text.[6] Brian Maidment (6) recognizes that there is a delicate balance between the glut of historical images now available on the web which do not, in most cases, represent comprehensiveness or representativeness, while the same superfluity of images, more than any scholar can view or explain in their lifetime, is 'both exhilarating and daunting'.

The chapters by David J. Bodenhamer (1), Turkel et al. (3), Mussell (4), Rosalind Crone and Katie Halsey (5) and David Thomas and Valerie Johnson (9) all touch upon the idea of history that is concerned with notions of geographic space. As Bodenhamer (1) demonstrates, the spatial humanities as a field has its own literature, but the field has tended to be ignored by traditional historians because of its associations with geographic information technologies. I would argue here that to overlook spatial history because of this is to miss the potential it offers in new ways of understanding the past. Maps and migration records have long been used within historical research, but what is new is the ways in which digitized material is facilitating new types of research questions and new conceptual challenges. People, sources and evidence, in other words the historical record, move around over time. As Mussell (4) notes, historical relationships can be 'visualized over time and space'. However, spatial history is not without its own difficulties. As Crone and Halsey (5) demonstrate, in their experience of the RED, geographical comparisons could be difficult to make since names of countries change over time, as do geographical borders. The spatial turn, as discussed by David J. Bodenhamer (1), has asked 'new questions about human experience and gained new perspectives'. Digital technologies are allowing new methodological questions and processes to emerge, but history and historians in the digital age should not focus upon technology to the detriment of traditional historical skills. As Bodenhamer (1) points out, technology can 'tell us nothing about the meaning of what we see'.

Interpretation

Technology *is* changing the field of history but in more complex and interesting ways than through just the digitization of sources and documents. As I argued in the *Introduction*, the medium changes not only the message but, for the historian, it can also change the interpretation. While this is an idea long recognized implicitly – historians teach and practise the importance of different forms of original source material as *par de course* – it has, to a large extent, been overlooked with the onset of digital technologies. Such databases are either esteemed as a new way of preserving the original document from destruction, or they are derided as a less valuable form of historical source than hard copy. What has been less discussed is how the act of changing the format of a source from original hard copy to a digital version also changes the original experience and thus the interpretive process of the historian. We lose the physicality and tangibility of the original newspaper artefact that was smudged from so many fingers turning the pages, or the steps which are worn from thousands of feet walking on them. When data is upgraded from a VHS cassette to a DVD or to an MP3 file, the information content is kept, but the original experience is changed. The intimacy of the original experience is lost.

This original experience can also be filtered through reproduction or replacement. Brian Maidment (6) and Rosalind Crone and Katie Halsey (5) observe that by including a digitized source in a database you are automatically including an additional layer of 'reproduction', as Maidment terms it, between the viewer and the original item. The historical context as well as the interpretation requires more filtering. Luke Tredinnick (2) notes that many tourists now view the *Mona Lisa*, one of the most famous paintings in the world, not through considered personal observation but through a camera lens or a mobile phone picture amongst a busy horde of sightseers. As Tredinnick argues, the digital age is gradually changing the relationship between the record and history. Indeed, not only does the medium change the message, or interpretation, but the medium itself is reflective of the present. It is 'historically contingent'.[7]

In history we strive to gain the most accurate picture of the original experience as possible and historians have long taught their students that context is everything. Arguably, some historians are taking for granted some of these changes in source material – or not taking them seriously – without continuing to apply traditional historical methodologies to digital material. In addition, both because established scholars are not teaching it, and also because it is so commonplace, a new generation of historical scholars are growing up without considering the difference the medium can make to the interpretation. Indeed, as Crone and Halsey (5) note, in some digital collections, 'the way in which the material is presented discourages examination of the physical form of the source' – would, they ask, interpretation be different if the original material was consulted as well in its full context? Jim Mussell (4) argues that 'digital tools and techniques make apparent the changing condition of historical evidence' which is often assumed to be static. As he shows, 'an engagement with the object in the present ... necessarily changes what it means'. This point is also picked up by Mark Sandle (7); the form matters and the process of research is constantly changing, but we must not forget the bigger picture that *all* traces of the historical record are subject to incompleteness and impartiality. This is true of the written word, digitized or otherwise, but, as Brian Maidment (6) points out, it is also true of the visual image which is often reproduced out of context or with limited information regarding its provenance. University lecturers can be as guilty of this as students. We are all familiar with 'snapshot' images copied and pasted into PowerPoint slides to demonstrate a point. Academics often do this understanding the limitations of the images they use but students do not always consider these points unless they are explicitly discussed. Context is vital, and whatever arguments may be made about the democratization of history in the digital age, it is here that the role of the professional historian really comes to the fore.

Public history

During the nineteenth century, Thomas Carlyle suggested that 'in a certain sense all men are historians'.[8] The digital age has often been championed as a great democratizer of information and access and, while that may be true, it is rather more complex than that when we come to the historical record and the public sphere. As Luke Tredinnick (2) argues, new forms of technology 'have shifted the site of history's making, and have transformed the public from spectators of distant actions to participants in historical dramas' and in so doing have 'altered the nature of history'. Popular engagement with history through wikis, blogs, Twitter, television programmes and suchlike have created new interactions between scholarly history and history in mass culture. This has profound implications for the study of shared experience, collective historical consciousness and public memory. Events of today are commented on, observed, documented, shared and recorded in multifarious and almost instantaneous ways that potentially offer a wealth of information to the historian. The extreme end of this is 'lifelogging' where individuals track the minute detail of their everyday lives, down to the routine behaviours of eating and sleeping.[9] The question remains though: how much of this potential source material will actually be recoverable, accessible and meaningful in years to come?

One must not forget that despite the vast amount of resources available online there remains a huge amount of material that is still undigitized, a point raised by nearly all of the contributing chapters. Thomas and Johnson (9) ponder whether this 'silent mass' of paper sitting in archives will ultimately regain status as the preserve of the 'real' historian while the interested amateur uses only digital materials. Arguably many traditional historians already feel this way, although professional historians will not be able to ignore digital material since so much of the historical record of the future will be only in a digital format. What seems more likely is that there will be a maturity in the relationship between public audiences and professional historians in the digital age. Recent examples from the mainstream press show how entrenched history and the digital age are to the mainstream public, and how concepts of the past, present and historical record are often blurred. An article in the UK's *Sunday Times Magazine* featured a piece suggesting that a man who kept a diary of his time in a Nazi prison camp essentially 'tweeted' his experience since each entry was short and never exceeded the 140 characters used on Twitter.[10] The soldier's grandson republished the diary in individual instalments on Twitter,[11] providing a new perspective on the notion that 'the past is never dead; it's not even past'.[12] Seeing the diary brought to life through very contemporary Tweets was unexpectedly reflective and moving. Undoubtedly though, the remaking of the past in such a dynamic way raises a myriad of issues and debates about our own relationship with the historical record in the digital age.

There are, therefore, different ways for the public and the professional historian to engage with one another. Crowdsourcing (a popular, in the true sense of the word, form of outsourcing) is not unique to the digital age. In eighteenth-century England, for example, Parliament offered a prize of £20,000 (a phenomenal sum by the day's standards) to anyone who could solve the problem of how to calculate longitude at sea. The challenge was taken up and solved by the Yorkshire carpenter and clock maker John Harrison. This kind of crowdsourcing has witnessed a resurgence in the digital age. Some academics are turning to the public to help deal with the immense task of research, particularly so in a time of reduced research funding. There are numerous large-scale projects underway which are reliant on voluntary public assistance, albeit mostly for time-consuming but often tedious tasks such as transcribing and cataloguing. One such project is, *Old Weather*, which asks the public to transcribe Royal Navy logbooks from the nineteenth century. These are ultimately stored in an international archive in Colorado which feeds computer programs that help scientists predict weather patterns in the global climate. Over 500,000 pages had been transcribed by the end of 2011.[13] As Crone and Halsey (5) demonstrate, the *Reading Experience Database* was another such project where crowdsourcing was essential to the collection of data. As they note though, such techniques can also contribute to a variety of bias and unrepresentative samples within the end collection. All sources, digital or otherwise, have limits. As long as digital collections are considered as rigorously as traditional sources in historical research this in itself is not necessarily a problem. Unlike less scholarly public collections such as Wikipedia, both RED and *Old Weather* use an editorial overview to all submissions in order to weed out potential duplications or errors.

One danger of public history therefore, is that those who do not have any background in the discipline of history may approach digital collections rather differently and arguably with a false sense of confidence about their completeness or impartiality. As Crone and Halsey (5) note, while the skills of the historian – evaluation and interpretation – are crucial to understanding material of any kind found online, they are 'generally underdeployed in a culture that values fast information in the same way it values fast food'. Everyone feels they can have a valid opinion on history even if they have no experience in the discipline; the same could not be said of experimental physics. Brian Maidment (6) uses an example of a project at Cardiff University which sent copies of illustrations to non-academic respondents asking them to describe the detail of the image. As Maidment argues, 'the discrepancies in their responses bring home the instability of "information" offered to the historian by visual sources', but his point might also be applied to public involvement in history more generally.

Historians, then, surely have a role to play in public history in the digital age to ensure there is balanced opinion and interpretation. There is a role for the historian to be more active and advisory in policy issues.[14] Ultimately 'being' a historian or 'doing' history involves much more than simply collecting facts; the professional historian adds context and a discourse of understanding about how one source might relate to another and to existing narratives. There is a call for historians to become more, not less, involved in the digital age, to ensure that proper historical methodology and rigour continue to be applied.

A final thought

None of the chapters in this collection suggest that historians must go digital or die. Nor do they suggest that traditional historical methods will end or the printed word will disappear from the historical record. Digital History, as a field of enquiry, is an essential part of historical discourse in the twenty-first century but it is not for every historian, nor should it be for every historian. The printed copy, the traditional archive and analogue research remain key constitute parts for most historians, and for many will remain precious and esteemed over digital copies. However, there is a need for traditional historians and students of history to seriously consider some of the conceptual and methodological challenges facing the field of historical enquiry.

The remit for this book was ambitious; to attempt an introduction to some of the more fundamental and conceptual issues facing the historical field in the digital age, aimed at traditional historians rather than digital specialists, and written without a technological emphasis. A collection of this nature cannot possibly be entirely comprehensive nor cover every subject in depth, but it is hoped that the chapters here will offer some pause for thought and an introduction to the bigger discourses going on elsewhere.

Whether or not you welcome it, the digital age is having an impact on the way in which we engage with the past. The creation of new technologies should not obscure the multifaceted challenges they raise for the historical record and the role of the historian. These challenges are more profound than an emphasis on learning to use a new database or understand computer code, neither of which are the main remit of the traditional historian. Conceptual change happens gradually within academia, but that does not mean that we should be blind to it because we do not believe it affects us or our scholarship. As the ancient Greek philosopher Heraclitus believed, 'nothing endures but change'. As historians living and working in the digital age we would be wise to heed such wisdom.

Notes

1 J. H. Robinson, *The New History: Essays Illustrating the Modern Historical Outlook* (Michigan: Walden Press, 1912), p. 25.
2 For example, see E. Hampshire and V. Johnson, 'The digital world and the future of historical research', *Twentieth Century British History*, 20: 3 (2009), 396–414; D. Cohen and R. Rosenzweig, *Digital History: A Guide to Gathering, Preserving,*

and Presenting the Past on the Web (Philadelphia: University of Pennsylvania Press, 2006); R. Rosenzweig, 'Scarcity or abundance? Preserving the past in a digital era', *American Historical Review*, 108: 3 (June 2003), 735–62.

3 This detail was mentioned during a general conversation with the Newnham College, Cambridge, archivist, Anne Thompson in 2005.

4 The card in question is now held in the Sir John Ritblat Gallery: Treasures of the British Library collection at the British Library in London.

5 See, for example, T. Weller (ed.), *Information History in the Modern World: Histories of the Information Age* (Basingstoke: Palgrave Macmillan, 2010); T. Weller, 'An information history decade: a review of the literature and concepts, 2000–2009', *Library & Information History*, 26: 1 (2010), 83–97; E. Higgs, *The Information State in England: The Central Collection of Information on Citizens since 1500* (Basingstoke: Palgrave, 2004); D. Headrick, *When Information Came of Age: Technologies of Knowledge in the Age of Reason and Revolution 1700–1850* (Oxford: Oxford University Press, 2000).

6 M. Wolf, 'Our "deep reading" brain: its digital evolution poses questions', *Harvard Nieman Reports*, Summer (2010), http://www.nieman.harvard.edu/reports/article/102396/Our-Deep-Reading-Brain-Its-Digital-Evolution–Poses-Questions.aspx [accessed: 25 March 2012]; A. Mangen, 'Hypertext fiction reading: haptics and immersion', *Journal of Research in Reading*, 31: 4 (2008), 404–19.

7 R. Mayhew, 'Denaturalising print, historicising text: historical geography and the history of the book', in E. Gagen, H. Lorimer and A. Vasudevan, *Practicing the Archive: Reflections on Method and Practice in Historical Geography; Historical Geography Research Series 40* (London: Royal Geographic Society, 2007), pp. 23–36.

8 T. Carlyle in G. B. Tennyson (ed.), *A Carlyle Reader* (Cambridge: Cambridge University Press, 1984), p. 56.

9 See, for example, http://lifestreamblog.com/lifelogging/ [accessed: 25 March 2012]; S. Cox, 'Memories are made of this', *Sunday Times Magazine*, 11 September 2011, 46–51; K. Kleiner, 'Your entire life recorded – lifelogging goes mainstream', *Singularity Hub*, 20 July 2010, http://singularityhub.com/2010/07/20/your-entire-life-recorded-lifelogging-goes-mainstream/ [accessed: 25 March 2012].

10 C. Ayres, 'Tweets from the Stalag', *The Sunday Times Magazine*, 1 January 2012, 44–51.

11 See https://twitter.com/#!/driverross [accessed: 25 March 2012].

12 Quote by Gavin Stevens in W. Faulkner, *Requiem for a Nun* (London: Vintage, 1996), Act I, Scene III.

13 See http://www.oldweather.org/ [accessed: 25 March 2012].

14 In the UK, the *History & Policy* project has made this its explicit aim, and is proving to be very successful achieving new dynamics between historians and policy makers. See http://www.historyandpolicy.org/ [accessed: 25 March 2012].

Index